Vietnam, Korea and US foreign policy

Christine Bragg

Series Editors
Martin Collier
Rosemary Rees

HEINEMANN ADVANCED HISTORY

Heinemann Educational Publishers
Halley Court, Jordan Hill, Oxford OX2 8EJ
Part of Harcourt Education

Heinemann is the registered trademark of
Harcourt Education Limited

© Harcourt Education, 2005

First published 2005

10 09 08 07 06 05
10 9 8 7 6 5 4 3 2 1

British Library Cataloguing in Publication Data is available
from the British Library on request.

10-digit ISBN: 0 435327 08 9
13-digit ISBN: 978 0 435327 08 8

Edited by Penny Rogers   Commissioning Editor – Kate Lowe
Proof read by Sandra Stafford   Managing Editor – Simon Brand
Indexed by Eleanor Holme   Production Controller – Siobhan Snowden
Typeset by MacMillan India   Reader – Steve Philips

Original illustrations © Harcourt Education Limited, 2005

Illustrated by Saxon Graphics Ltd

Cover design by hicksdesign

Printed in Great Britain by The Bath Press, Bath

Cover photo: © Dang Van Phuoc/Associated Press

Picture research by Frances Topp

Acknowledgements
The author and publisher would like to thank the following for permission to reproduce:
Quotations – pp. 25–6 Extract from Zhdanov speech with permission from the Open
University; pp. 26–7 Extract from Navikov telegram translation provided by
www.cwihp.org; p. 42 NKIPC telegram to Stalin Translated by Kathryn Weathersby.
For the full text see first entry for K. Weathersby in bibliography. To download go to
www.cwihp.org; p. 114 Kennedy telegram courtesy US State Department; p. 148
Extract from Clifford Report courtesy US State Department

Photographs – pp. 12, 100, 105, 167 Corbis; pp. 67, 123, 162, 176 Popperfoto; pp. 69,
144 Sovfoto; pp. 78 AP; pp. 109, 170, 172 TRH Pictures; pp. 132, 152 Getty; p. 145
Getty Archive Photos

Every effort has been made to contact copyright holders of material reproduced in
this book. Any omissions will be rectified in subsequent printings if notice is given to
the publishers.

CONTENTS

HOW TO USE THIS BOOK

This book covers the development of US foreign policy towards communism from the end of the Second World War to 1950 and the later application of this policy to the situations that developed in Korea and Vietnam, leading to US involvement in these two major wars.

The book provides an analytical narrative and an explanation of events that happened during this important period of history. It contains interpretations of the key issues of this period and examines aspects of historiography central to the study of history at this level. In this way students will be able to develop their understanding of the key themes and concepts required at A2 level. The book can also be used by AS students to extend their understanding of this subject.

At the end of the book there is an assessment section which has been designed to provide guidance on how students can meet the requirements of the A2 specifications provided by the Edexcel examining board for its unit entitled *Containing Communism? The USA in Asia 1950–73*.

It is hoped that the book will also be useful to general readers who wish to find their way around what is a sometimes complex but fascinating period of history. It is also a period of history that raises many issues about the justification and morality of intervening in the affairs of other countries. These issues are as relevant today as they were in the 1950s and 1960s.

ACKNOWLEDGEMENT

I would like to acknowledge all the research undertaken by historians and its contribution to my understanding of the complexities of the Cold War and the Korean and Vietnam Wars. My thanks go to them and to my husband Robert for all his patience.

INTRODUCTION

The foreign policy of the United States of America in the period 1945 to 1991 was dominated by its fear of communism. This attitude was to play a large part in the hostility that existed between the two superpowers – the USA and the Soviet Union (USSR) – in what became known as the Cold War. The US became convinced that the Soviet Union was determined to take every opportunity it could to spread its ideology of communism and undermine the freedoms that the US saw as its guiding principles. In order to meet this threat the US developed a policy of containment. US involvement in Korea and Vietnam was the product of this worldview and the policy of containment. It was a stance that the successive administrations from Harry S Truman through to Richard Nixon accepted without serious question.

Since the end of the Cold War in 1991 the historiography of the US role in Korea and Vietnam has been dominated by the view that the containment policy worked in Europe, and, thereby, contributed significantly to the spread of the Cold War. However, Leffler, Logerall and Offner have argued that containment was misapplied in Korea and Vietnam. The emphasis on the US determination to block the advance of communism ignores factors within the countries of the Far East that would have sparked off conflicts without outside interference. Thus, it is important to examine not just the US policy of containment, but also the nature of the movements involved in the struggles for self-determination in Korea and Vietnam. Divisions in these movements were to make the conflicts in Asia susceptible to involvement by the US.

The costs of this US policy were high.

- In the Korean War, there were 33,600 US deaths. For the Koreans the price was even higher with the death of 600,000 North Korean troops and 70,000 South Korean troops. In addition, it was estimated that 3 million Korean civilians died in the war.
- In the Vietnam War, there were 58,000 US deaths in Vietnam. For the Vietnamese the price was higher with 130,000 deaths among the South Vietnamese forces, and 1.1 million among the North Vietnamese and the National Liberation Front (NLF). In total, it is estimated that some 5 million people lost their lives in and around Vietnam during the US war against the communists.

The aim of this book is to explain the development of US foreign policy in the period 1945–50 and US involvement in the Korea and Vietnam Wars. The chapters in the book outline the important events and issues relevant to US foreign policy. Each chapter is prefaced with a brief overview and, where appropriate, biographies of some of the important figures in question.

The first two chapters of the book explore the origins of the Cold War and its implications for US foreign policy.

Chapter 3 focuses on the origins of the Korean War, and explains the role of the US in the division of Korea and its implications. Chapters 4 and 5 focus on the outbreak of the Korean War, the role of the Soviet Union and China, and the debates that surround their involvement. These chapters also explain the significance of the change in the US foreign policy of containment and the implications of this change when China became involved in the War.

Chapter 6 is an exploration of the roots of the Vietnamese conflict and the reasons for US intervention in 1949 in what was essentially a colonial war between France and the New Democratic Republic of Vietnam. Chapter 7 follows the involvement of the USA through the actions of Presidents Dwight Eisenhower and John F Kennedy, and the implications of their support for the regime of Ngo Dinh Diem, whose overthrow committed the US to the defence of South Vietnam.

Chapter 8 explores the role of President Lyndon Johnson in the escalation to war and the impact of the Tet Offensive on the American public in 1968. Chapter 9 argues that by 1969 when Richard Nixon came into office there was war weariness throughout the nation. Opposition to the Vietnam War became more vociferous as anti-war demonstrators clashed with the police and the National Guard across the US. Opposition from Congress and the withholding of economic funds to continue the War convinced Nixon and his National Security Adviser that the time had come to withdraw from the War. In January 1973, the Peace Plans were signed, despite opposition to them from the South Vietnamese President Thieu. In April 1975, as a result of a military campaign by the North Vietnamese, the South finally fell to communist forces.

At the end of the book there is an assessment section with advice about how to perform well in Edexcel's Unit 4, *Containing Communism? The USA in Asia 1950–73*.

CHAPTER 1

The background to the Cold War

AN OVERVIEW

Throughout the period 1943 to 1945 the leaders of the wartime alliance of Britain, the Soviet Union and the United States of America worked together to bring about the defeat of Nazi Germany and a swift end to the Second World War, and began to plan for post-war reconstruction. Certain historical assumptions have been made about the aims and goals of each of the **Allied powers** based on the events as they unfolded before and after the surrender of the Germans in May 1945 and Japan in August 1945. One such assumption is that the post-war aim of the Soviet Union led by Joseph Stalin was territorial expansion in Europe and Asia, followed by the brutal repression of any opposition. On the other hand, the actions of the USA were perceived to be promoting peace and stability in the world. These assumptions hid a more complex reality as the US sought to establish itself as a global power in the period 1945 to 1950.

The collapse of Germany and Japan in 1945 and the severe weakening of Britain and France had created a global power vacuum that the US and the Soviet Union were eager to fill. Discussions on Europe and Asia during the wartime conferences show clearly how the US and the Soviet Union sought to exert their ideological beliefs, **communism** and **capitalism**, into post-war policies through different economic and strategic policies in Europe, thus creating major divisions within the wartime alliance after 1945. At the wartime conferences were sown the seeds of the **Cold War** as both the major allies – the US and the Soviet Union – sought to impose these ideological beliefs. To understand why the US engaged in the wars in Korea from 1950 and Vietnam from 1964 it is important to understand how US foreign policy developed in the period 1945–50. Events in post-war Europe contributed to the development of US foreign policy as a tool for containing the spread of communism. This period saw the introduction of the Truman Doctrine, with its outline of the policy of containment, and Marshall Aid, a series of economic measures that worked in tandem as key elements in the struggle against communism.

BIOGRAPHIES

Winston Churchill (1874–1965) Of all the leaders engaged in the struggle with Germany and Japan in the Second World War, Churchill had by far the greatest experience in dealing with European and Far Eastern issues. He was first elected into politics in 1900 and became prime minister of Britain in 1940 after the downfall of Neville Chamberlain's government. In June 1940, after the surrender of France to the Germans, Britain stood alone. For support he turned to his old friend Roosevelt (see below), who procured a Lend-Lease Programme of military aid in return for 99-year leases on naval and air bases. In August 1941, Roosevelt and Churchill met together at Newfoundland, Canada, and drew up the **Atlantic Charter** which outlined the common post-war aims of both countries. Throughout the war years Churchill and Roosevelt worked well together, but differences over colonialism and free trade did occur. In addition, Roosevelt wanted to work with Stalin (see below), but Churchill did not trust him. This led to frequent interventions on Stalin's side by Roosevelt. At the Allied conference at Potsdam, Churchill tried to establish a working relationship with Truman but, later in July 1945, Churchill lost the British general election and the post of prime minister went to Clement Attlee.

Franklin D Roosevelt (1882–1945) The longest serving president in the history of the US is credited with pulling the country out of the Depression and leading it through much of the Second World War. In 1941, Roosevelt led the USA in the war against Japan, and later Germany and Italy. Roosevelt and Churchill forged a strong alliance and, in 1943, at the meeting of the US, British and French in Casablanca demanded an unconditional surrender from the Axis powers, Germany, Italy and Japan. Roosevelt worked with Stalin and Churchill at the Tehran Conference in 1943. In 1944 he was elected for a fourth time, and met with Stalin and Churchill at Yalta in February 1945. He died suddenly on 12 April 1945.

Joseph Stalin (1879–1953) As unchallenged ruler of the Soviet Union from 1929 to 1953, he was viewed by the US government as a totalitarian leader who imposed fear and terror on the population of the Soviet Union. After the invasion of Russia by the Germans in June 1941, Stalin formed an uneasy alliance with Churchill and Roosevelt. The first face-to-face meeting of the 'Big Three' (as they were collectively known) occurred in Tehran in Persia in 1943; they met later at Yalta in the Crimea in 1945. Stalin's confrontational foreign policy led to tensions and disagreements with Truman at Potsdam that in some ways contributed to the origins of the Cold War.

Harry S Truman (1884–1972) Elected vice-president in 1944, a few months later he became president after the sudden death of Roosevelt. Virtually unbriefed in foreign affairs, he nevertheless continued Roosevelt's internationalist stance in foreign policy. Truman finalised the arrangements for the UN (United Nations) Charter. After the surrender of Germany to the Allies on 7 May 1945, Truman attended his only Allied conference at Potsdam in July 1945. While in Potsdam, he heard of the successful test of the atomic bomb and sanctioned its use against the Japanese in August 1945.

James Byrnes (1879–1972) Byrnes had acted as special adviser to Roosevelt at the Yalta Conference before becoming Secretary of State for

Truman in July 1945. He therefore provided some continuity in US diplomacy and was useful to Truman as someone who was at least partly aware of previous actions in relation to negotiations with Stalin. Byrnes was criticised for being too soft on the Soviet Union and adopted a firmer stance before resigning in 1947.

Vyacheslav Molotov (1890–1986) Soviet foreign minister from 1939 to 1949. He was a leading supporter of Stalin and made foreign minister in 1939 on Stalin's self appointment to the post of Prime Minister. A hardliner able to argue forcibly with western foreign ministers, he lived up to his name which meant 'hammer'. Inflexible and obstinate, he was, however, a skilful politician who often infuriated those in the West who had to deal with him. He regained the position of foreign minister in 1953 when Stalin died, but was dismissed in 1956.

THE WARTIME CONFERENCES, 1943–5

The start of Soviet–US competition emerged during the discussions between the major Allies, collectively known as the 'Big Three', at three important wartime conferences:

- Tehran, 28 November to 1 December 1943
- Yalta (Crimea), 4 to 12 February 1945
- Potsdam (Berlin), 17 July to 2 August 1945.

The main aims of the wartime conferences were to discuss the progress of the war in Europe against Germany and in the Pacific against Japan. Both the US and the Soviet Union were unused to diplomatic negotiations, as both had adopted policies of **isolationism** in the 1920s and 1930s. In addition, in the 1930s by staying out of other nations' troubles both the Soviet Union and the USA were able to keep foreign affairs costs low while they invested in their growing domestic economies and in the case of the Soviet Union a large rearmament programme in 1935.

Thus, during the Second World War, when the US and the Soviet Union were virtually thrown together to defend their nations' security from the German and Japanese threat, they had to relearn the art of diplomacy. During the wartime conferences, the different styles of diplomacy not only reflected the ideological stances, capitalist or communist, of each of the major Allies but also the political culture of the nations from which they came. For Churchill and later Clement Attlee, the democratic system of government in Britain required the skills of debate and discussion in cabinet and the Houses of Lords and Commons and, from these, agreements on domestic and foreign policies were made. For Roosevelt and later Truman, the democratic system of government required compromises and concessions to be made with Congress, comprising the president, the House of Representatives and the Senate, over domestic and foreign policies. For Stalin, the Soviet Union was ruled in an authoritarian way, and domestic and foreign policies were based on the party line as agreed by Stalin and the **Politburo**.

Unlike Churchill, Attlee, Roosevelt and Truman, Stalin found it most difficult to engage fully with his allies because of the Soviet political culture. Used to having his orders obeyed without question, he now found himself having to negotiate military war and post-war policies that were not always strictly in line with communist ideology. The negotiating and diplomatic styles of the Big Three during the wartime conferences of Tehran, Yalta and Potsdam over the key issues of the United Nations, Poland, the Far East and Germany clearly reflected their different political ideologies. This strange alliance of competing ideologies – the communist system of the Soviet Union was the antithesis of the capitalist system in the US – ensured that once the war was over it would prove difficult to maintain a working relationship committed to world peace.

THE TEHRAN CONFERENCE AND THE SECOND FRONT

The Tehran Conference of 28 November to 1 December 1943 was the first time the Big Three – Roosevelt, Stalin and Churchill – met together face to face. The aim of the conference was to discuss the progress of the Second World War and plan the Anglo–US 'Second Front', a landings of troops in France to defeat the Germans. Stalin was increasingly anxious that Britain and the USA should open a second front in Europe to reduce the pressure on the Red Army fighting the Germans in the Soviet Union. In addition, Roosevelt sought the military help of the Soviet Union in the war against Japan. Stalin agreed to this once the Germans had been defeated in Europe. Political issues took second place to military ones at Tehran, but the control and division of Germany and the Polish settlement were discussed. Final actions and decisions were deferred to the next conference in Yalta.

The United Nations

One of the major successes of the alliance of Britain, the Soviet Union and the US was the commitment to the creation of the United Nations (UN) and **collective security**. The idea for the United Nations, a world organisation for the preservation of peace under the protection of the four world 'policemen' – the Soviet Union, the USA, Britain and China – was first promoted by Roosevelt at the Tehran Conference.

The concept of the UN represented Roosevelt's commitment to **internationalism**. Roosevelt advocated an organisation dedicated to the social, economic and security interests between nations based on international law: a body that represented individual nations who would intervene collectively at times of threat, famine or national disaster. Roosevelt believed that the US had an important role to play in maintaining world peace once the war against Germany and Japan was over. Further, he recognised a shift in global political forces with the reduction of Japanese, German, British and French influence and the emergence of the Soviet Union and the US as superpowers.

Preliminary discussions were held on Roosevelt's idea for the UN between the Big Three plus China at the Dumbarton Oaks conference in Washington DC from 21 August to 7 October 1944. The representatives of the four main powers had a difficult task to perform and a short time in which to put together proposals that could then be considered by the future member states. Using the Covenant of the **League of Nations** and the lessons of its failures in the inter-war years, the delegates devised a plan that differed in a number of ways from the League. This time, the US and the Soviet Union were to be key members. A Security Council was to be formed from the 'Big Five' – France, Britain, China, the Soviet Union and the US – supported by six members elected from the General Assembly of all the nations.

The role of the Security Council would be to:

- investigate any situation threatening international peace
- recommend procedures for peaceful resolution of a dispute
- call on members to sever diplomatic and economic relations with belligerent powers
- enforce its decisions militarily, if necessary.

The employment of economic or military sanctions required the unanimous approval of the Big Five, even if any one of them was party to the dispute in question. Truman blatantly disregarded this principle when he sought support against the North Koreans in the early weeks of the war in 1950. The Soviets were not present in the Security Council for the vote because they had left the UN in protest at communist China's seat being given to the Chinese Nationalists. (See p. 53)

The principal function of the UN was to enforce peace and security and to prevent aggression by one member against another through collective security. Disputes would be settled through conciliation and arbitration by members of the UN together with the elected secretary-general. From 26 April to 26 June 1945, the Dumbarton Oaks plan was put before representatives of 50 nations at a conference in San Francisco, and the Charter for the UN took effect on 24 October 1945. According to **Eichelberger** (1961), Roosevelt had been very anxious that the foundations of the UN were laid before the war ended. Roosevelt's great fear was that once the fighting ended, the Big Three alliance would fall apart making it very difficult to gain the commitment of the principal allies to an organisation dedicated to collective security.

THE YALTA CONFERENCE

The Polish issue

The most troublesome issues confronting the Big Three at Yalta concerned Poland – its borders and the formation of a new Polish government. Stalin wanted the Lublin government, which included many communists and individuals sympathetic to the Soviet Union, to form the basis of a new government in Poland. The Lublin government had been formed after the destruction of the Warsaw government by the Germans in 1944. Stalin had stated after the end of the siege of Stalingrad on 6 February 1943: 'The Polish question is a matter of life and death for the Soviet Union.' He meant that never again would a hostile force use Poland to invade the Soviet Union. However, Churchill wanted the Free Polish government based in London to be included in the post-war administration. The British government, whose declaration of war in 1939 had been a response to the German invasion of Poland, now felt a primary obligation to ensure a free and independent Poland.

The debate that followed caused a rift in the relationship between Churchill and Roosevelt, whose primary concern at this time was to gain the support of the Soviets in ending the war with Japan. Ultimately, Churchill, endorsed by the views of Averell Harriman, US Ambassador to Moscow, wanted to challenge Stalin's aim to turn Eastern Europe into a Soviet sphere of influence. The final agreement outlined in the Yalta Papers called for: 'Free and unfettered elections in Poland to be organised on the basis of universal suffrage and a secret ballot. All democratic and anti-Nazi parties were to have the right to take part and put forward candidates.' However, while the settlement on Poland reflected the ideals of free and democratic elections for the liberated states outlined in the Declaration on Liberated Europe incorporated into the Yalta agreements, there were no mechanisms available for its enforcement.

The drawing of the Polish border along the Curzon Line was accepted at the conference despite Stalin's determination that the final border would follow the Oder–Neisse rivers, which incorporated the German states of Pomerania and Silesia within the new Polish state. At a time when Poland was occupied by the Red Army of the Soviet Union, Stalin was determined to demand for Poland a regime that would be friendly towards the Soviet Union and saw the annexation of German territory as a form of reparation for the Polish people. In an attempt to accommodate both sides, Roosevelt referred the problem to the Soviet foreign minister and the US and British ambassadors, who were authorised as a Commission to consult with members of the Polish provisional government and other democratic leaders from within and outside Poland on the composition of the new government. At this time, Roosevelt was willing to compromise with Stalin because he feared the Red Army would withdraw from the war against Germany once it reached the borders of Poland and Germany, and this would allow the Germans to use all their divisions against the Anglo–US forces now in Europe.

The post-war German settlement

At Yalta, the situation regarding Germany was initially less ambiguous than that of Poland. The three Allies, having called for the unconditional surrender of Germany at the Tehran Conference, now sought to develop a working definition of what this would mean for the German people. Churchill and Roosevelt were well aware of the discrimination against the Germans in the Treaty of Versailles and the implications of this for peace in Europe. Unconditional surrender was defined as the temporary control of Germany by the three major Allies and France as they saw fit. Churchill's single positive success at Yalta related to the inclusion of France as a member of the Allied Control Commission of Germany and, in addition, France was given a zone of occupation. Each of the Big Three plus France was to occupy and control a separate zone with a control council established in Berlin to coordinate their actions. The role of the Allied Control Commission, established by the Yalta agreements on Germany, was to ensure German military power was dismantled and Nazi war criminals brought to trial.

Churchill and Stalin had heated arguments about the amount of German **reparations**. Ultimately they agreed to create a Reparation Commission in Moscow. The Commission was to apply the principles under which Germany was obliged to pay reparations in kind: goods, plant and raw materials, principally coal. As a basis for discussion, the Soviets suggested that the total sum should be US$20 billion and that 50 per cent of this should go to the Soviet Union. Churchill argued that no figures should be used as the basis of debate because at that time no one fully knew what the financial situation was like in Germany. In addition, Churchill did not want to see the resurgence of German resentment and hostility as had happened after the First World War when reparations were set too high for the Germans to pay. But, in principle, Roosevelt supported Stalin and the figure he proposed in recognition of the immense losses experienced by the Soviets.

These compromises were dictated by the realities of the military situation and the damage inflicted on the Soviet Union by the Germans. **Leffler** (1999) pointed out that in the Soviet Union the Nazi armies had:

- destroyed 1700 cities and towns, and more than 70,000 villages and hamlets
- ransacked the countryside, destroying tens of thousands of collective farms and machine and tractor stations
- demolished 31,000 industrial enterprises, 1100 coal pits and 3000 oil wells
- slaughtered tens of thousands of livestock.

Twenty-seven million people perished within the Soviet Union during the war with Germany, many from Stalin's actions, but most as a result of Nazi atrocities and battlefield casualties.

On the other hand, the US had suffered little physical damage to its economic infrastructure and during the entirety of the Second World War, 425,000 US troops were killed. There was also considerable support for the Soviet Union among the American population. According to Secretary of

State Byrnes: 'In 1945 the attitude of the people of the US toward the Soviet Union in the days immediately following the German surrender was very favourable. In the US a deposit of goodwill towards the USSR was as great, if not greater, than that of any other country.' Clearly, US domestic opinion had some influence on the actions taken by Roosevelt at Yalta.

Roosevelt recognised that the Soviets had legitimate interests in Eastern Europe that had to be accommodated if there was to be genuine cooperation between the two countries in the post-war era. Of greater importance to Roosevelt was the belief that by accommodating Stalin's demands at Yalta it might enable him to safeguard at less cost more vital US and British interests elsewhere in the globe. Roosevelt's carefully developed compromises were not just prompted by the desire to recognise the Soviet's interests in Eastern Europe. At the same time they were intended to ensure continued US participation in world affairs with the support of Congress for the United Nations, the International Monetary Fund and the World Bank. By the time of the next wartime conference at Potsdam, Roosevelt was dead and his replacement, Harry S Truman, while maintaining an internationalist approach dealt with Stalin in a more forceful way.

Death of Franklin D Roosevelt

The US political system during the war years had become a more presidential one: Roosevelt, in the role of both president and Commander in Chief of the Armed Forces, took total control of the wartime planning as well as developing alliances with friendly powers engaged in the struggle against the Germans and the Japanese. When Roosevelt died suddenly on 12 April 1945, Truman had no experience in diplomatic relations with Britain or the Soviet Union, and no firsthand knowledge of Churchill or Stalin. He had no background in foreign policy and had no expert or experienced advisers of his own. Roosevelt had done nothing to keep him informed or provide the background on decisions and plans at the highest levels. This made it difficult for Truman to grasp fully why Roosevelt made so many concessions to the Soviet Union and Stalin. According to **McCullough** (1992), Roosevelt had never talked confidentially with Truman about the war, foreign affairs or what he had in mind for peace after the war. Truman eventually turned to James Byrnes, whom he appointed as his Secretary of State in July 1945, whose political judgement was recognised by Roosevelt. Roosevelt had relied heavily on Byrnes's support with Congress in the 1930s and 1940s, and wanted him to run as the vice-presidential candidate in the 1944 elections. In addition Byrnes was Roosevelt's special adviser during most of the wartime meetings between the Big Three, but even he had been unable to fully grasp what Roosevelt was trying to achieve.

Molotov–Truman talks, April 1945

The controversial Molotov–Truman talks of 22–23 April 1945 have been seen as the start of the significant deterioration in Soviet–US relations. In

April, Foreign Minister Vyacheslav Molotov went to the US to pay Stalin's respects on the death of Roosevelt, to attend the founding conference of the UN in San Francisco and to establish a personal contact with President Truman. The discussions between Molotov and Truman led to a clear difference of opinion about the new government and territorial borders of Poland. Truman resolved, probably more categorically than Roosevelt would have done, to hold the Russians to what they had agreed at Yalta. Truman's determination was recorded in his memoirs in 1955. At the end of the session, Truman had firmly and directly challenged the right of the Soviets to impose on Poland a government of their choosing. In response to this directness, Molotov stated: 'I have never been talked to like that in my life.' Truman replied: 'Carry out your agreements as we in the US are prepared to do and you won't get talked to like that.'

Truman's interpretations of the event played a central role in many historians' interpretations of the origins of the Cold War. **Gaddis** (1972) wrote of 'Truman's undiplomatic lecture' and concluded that 'there is little doubt that the Russians interpreted Truman's stormy interview with Molotov as evidence that the new administration had abandoned Roosevelt's policy of cooperation with the Soviet Union'. **Daniel Yergin** (1978), on the other hand, argued that while 'a stern lecture by the President of the US was hardly the cause of the Cold War, the exchange did symbolise the beginning of the post-war divergence that led to confrontation. It signalled to the ever-suspicious Russians that Roosevelt's policy might well be finished, and that, with the war in Europe ending, the Americans no longer needed the Russians.'

The problem with the reconstruction and interpretation of the Molotov–Truman encounter is that it corresponds with neither the US nor the recently opened Soviet records of the talks. **Charles Bohlen**, Truman's interpreter, recorded the Molotov–Truman talks in two memorandums published in *Foreign Relations of the US (FRUS), 1945,* in 1967. In the first memo, Bohlen commented that Truman greeted Molotov in a warm and friendly way and stated that 'he stood squarely behind all commitments and agreements taken by our late great President Roosevelt'. The only difference that emerged was when Truman said that a 'proper solution of the Polish question was of great importance because of its effect on US public opinion'. Molotov replied that 'it was even more important for the Soviet Union, because Poland bordered on the Soviet Union and it was therefore vital for them'.

In the second memo, Bohlen reported that the failure to come to an agreement on the Polish question with Foreign Minister Molotov and the British Foreign Secretary Anthony Eden and US Secretary of State Edward Stettinius when they met again in Washington on 23 April 1945 was what led Truman to take a firmer line with Molotov. Reiterating that the USA would 'carry out loyally all the agreements reached at [Yalta], Truman only asked that the Soviet government do the same'. It is evident from Bohlen's report that Truman spoke firmly, even bluntly, to Molotov about the Polish issue, but there was no sense of a 'dressing down'. From the Russian archives, the Soviet reports compiled by **V. N. Pavlov**, Molotov's and Stalin's interpreter, broadly correspond to Bohlen's reports and confirm that Truman did take a firm stand on Poland, particularly at the second meeting, but there was no evidence that the meeting had been stormy or even undiplomatic.

Truman's firm stand on Poland was a reflection of the strong pressures on him to adopt a more hard-line policy towards the Soviet Union. Ambassador to the Soviet Union Harriman warned Truman that senior officials within Stalin's government mistook Roosevelt's generosity and readiness to cooperate as a sign of 'softness', and this had led Stalin to think he could do what he wanted. On the one hand there was Averell Harriman arguing that now was the time to use US leverage and power in negotiations with the Soviets by reducing Lend-Lease: in April 1941, Roosevelt had gained the agreement of Congress to send Britain arms on credit; this was extended to the Soviet Union in October 1941. On the other, British Foreign Secretary Eden was pressing Truman to confront Molotov on Poland in the hope of extracting some concessions on the issue from the Soviet side. In May 1945, Truman sent Roosevelt's trusted aid Harry Hopkins to Moscow to broker a Polish solution and, in July, the dispute was resolved by the recognition of the Polish government, with a broader composition but one that continued to be dominated by pro-Soviet sympathisers. This outcome confirmed for Stalin and Molotov that the implicit spheres of influence arrived at with Roosevelt at Yalta would continue to form the basis of Soviet–US relations.

THE POTSDAM CONFERENCE

The central issues to be resolved at Potsdam were no different from those at Yalta: the political future of Eastern Europe, and Poland in particular, the occupation and dismantling of Germany's military and wartime industries, and a commitment from the Soviets to help defeat Japan. The tensions between the two superpowers were caused by a number of issues.

- There was discord among the Allies about the treatment of states like Bulgaria and Romania and the overt interference by the Soviets in their elections.

The 'Big Three' – Attlee, Truman and Stalin – at Potsdam

- The US had refused the Soviet request for a US$6 billion loan and Lend-Lease to the Soviets had virtually ended by May 1945.
- Truman, on the advice of Hopkins, his special envoy to the Soviet Union, ordered US military forces in Czechoslovakia and Eastern Germany to withdraw, leaving the Soviet Red Army to occupy pre-agreed areas of Eastern Europe. Hopkins had argued that any delay in the withdrawal of US troops from the Soviet zone was certain to be misunderstood by the Russians.
- Agreement on Poland's western frontier and the division of Germany among the Big Three was proving difficult. As a compromise Byrnes, now Secretary of State, offered a way of achieving an agreement by combining the Polish border issue with German reparations. The US would recognise the role of the Polish government to administer the German territories up to the western Neisse, pending the final determination of Poland's borders in the peace settlement. In return, the Soviets would accept the principle on German reparations put forward by Byrnes, that each of the occupying forces would take reparations from its own zone in the form of goods and industrial equipment. In recognition of the immense damage inflicted on the Soviet Union it would receive an additional percentage of industrial equipment, either from the Ruhr or from the three western zones taken together.

Far East agreements

The secret agreements made between Roosevelt and Stalin on political and economic influence in the Far East created a major problem for Truman at Potsdam. At Yalta, Roosevelt had sought to secure Soviet military support for the war against Japan. However, Stalin saw this as an opportunity to acquire further influence in the Far East once the war was over. In return for Soviet military support, Roosevelt secretly agreed to territorial concessions in the Far East, including parts of China and Japan. Neither Churchill nor the Chinese nationalist leader, Chaing Kai Shek, was consulted about the concessions made to the Soviet Union. Yet Churchill became one of the three signatories to the secret agreement because he wanted to ensure Britain preserved an active role in Far Eastern affairs because of its interests in India, Hong Kong, Malaya and Singapore.

The vague wording of the secret Far Eastern agreements entered into by Roosevelt and Stalin presented formidable diplomatic problems for Truman. In return for participation in the war against Japan, Stalin claimed Soviet rights of occupation on the South Sakhalin and Kurile Islands from Japan. In addition to this he requested lease rights to Port Arthur, access to the port of Dairen, and a joint Soviet–Sino commission to build the Chinese Eastern Railroad and the South Manchurian Railroad. The status of Outer Mongolia was to be 'preserved'. Roosevelt agreed to Stalin's demands but in return asked Stalin to enter a pact of friendship and alliance with the National Government of China led by Chiang Kai Shek.

Roosevelt hoped this alliance would reduce Soviet support for Mao Zedong and the Communists in the Chinese civil war against the Nationalists.

In early July, Truman, not wishing to be seen as either supporting or rejecting the provisions of the Yalta agreements, encouraged Chiang Kai Shek to delay the talks with the Soviets in an attempt to keep the Soviets out of the war with Japan. Further evidence to show that Truman was determined to keep the Soviets out of Japan is the Potsdam Declaration released on the 26 July 1945. Phrased as a joint statement by Truman, the new British Prime Minister Clement Attlee and Chiang Kai Shek called on the Japanese to surrender unconditionally or face the alternative, 'prompt and utter destruction'. Stalin was not a signatory to this declaration, probably because Truman and his administration sought to prevent the Soviets being part of the occupation force of Japan. However, Stalin was determined to expand his influence in the Far East, and on 8 August the Soviets declared war on Japan and moved troops into northern China and Manchuria, just two days after the use by the USA of the first atomic bomb on Hiroshima and one day before the atomic bomb on Nagasaki.

The atomic dimension

According to **Alperovitz** (1965), the sole reason for the US using the atomic bombs on Japan was to impress the Soviet Union. He argues that the war against Japan was already won in a military sense. Although few historians would go this far, **Gaddis** (1987) argued that the use of the atomic bombs against the Japanese in August 1945 was as much a deterrent to Soviet activities in Eastern Europe and the Far East as it was a weapon to force the unconditional surrender of Japan. At the Potsdam Conference, Truman casually mentioned to Stalin on 24 July that 'we had a new weapon of mass destruction. The Russian Premier showed no special interest. All he said was that he was glad to hear of it and hoped we would make good use of it against the Japanese.' Unknown to Truman, the Soviets were also working on a smaller bomb of their own.

The use of the atomic bombs on Hiroshima and Nagasaki brought angry protests from the Soviet Union. In his memoirs, **General Zhukov** stated: 'The Government of the United States of America intended to exploit the atomic weapon for the attainment of its imperialist aims from a position of strength in the Cold War.'

But not all the evidence supports the argument that the use of the atomic bombs was a critical factor in the start of the Cold War. The view that the US used the atomic bombs against Japan as a way of 'blackmailing' the Soviets into agreements in Europe and the Far East has limitations. At this time, the US possessed only the two atomic bombs it used against Japan. The Soviets were well aware of this because Klaus Fuchs, a Soviet spy and one of the atomic scientists working for the USA, had already informed

Stalin about the first successful trial on 16 July 1945. However, the global balance of power was now shifting more favourably towards the US and in effect contributed to the growing unease in the Soviet Union about international relations in the post-war years.

The Far East after Potsdam

On 14 August 1945, Japan unconditionally surrendered to the US, General Douglas MacArthur was appointed Supreme Allied Commander and received the formal surrender on 2/3 September. In a further attempt to limit Soviet influence in the Far East, the US directed Japanese troops to surrender to the Nationalists in all areas of China south of Manchuria and to the Russians in Manchuria and Korea north of the 38th Parallel. These surrender orders were intended to achieve two purposes: to preclude Japanese surrender to Communist Chinese troops and to minimise the Soviet occupation role in China and Japan. Stalin immediately protested that these surrender provisions violated the Yalta agreements and demanded that the Soviet surrender zone include the Kuriles and Hokkaido, the northern sector of Japan. Truman compromised by allowing the Soviets to occupy the Kuriles but not Hokkaido. In response

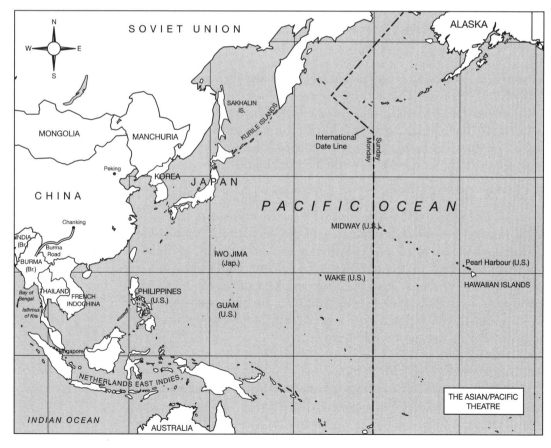

The Asian/Pacific Theatre

to Stalin's rejection of an air base on the Kuriles, Truman pointed out that the Kuriles were not Soviet territory. Although Yalta had permitted the Soviets to occupy the Kuriles, their final status would be determined at a future peace conference.

The occupation of the Kuriles by Soviet troops caused bitter protests against Truman's actions in the Far East by conservatives in Congress and the US press who charged that Soviet occupation of these islands directly threatened the security of the USA and its future role in Japan. Byrnes, eager to deflect attention away from the secret Yalta agreements, informed Congress that the decision leading up to the withdrawal of US troops from the Kuriles was in accord with 'discussions' conducted at Yalta. Patrick J Hurley, Ambassador to China, resigned his post over what he perceived to be US collusion with the Chinese Communists; he accused the State Department of being subverted by 'communists' and 'imperialists'. The publicity surrounding Hurley's allegations forced Byrnes to announce that the Kuriles and South Sakhalin had in fact been ceded to the Soviet Union under the secret Yalta agreements between Stalin and Roosevelt. The manner in which the war ended in the Pacific clearly reveals the tensions and mistrust emerging between Truman and Stalin; even Stalin had acknowledged that it was easier for them to cooperate when they were struggling against a common foe but in peace time it would be difficult.

In the case of **Indochina**, Truman and Churchill and their combined chiefs of staff had made a secret agreement concerning military operations. It was decided for operational purposes to divide Vietnam at the 16th Parallel with China in the north and British forces in the south, leaving little opportunity for the unification or independence of Vietnam and ample opportunity for the return of the French colonial power.

In Korea, the basis of US policy was the Cairo Declaration of 1943, in which the US, Britain and China promised that Korea would, in due course, become free and independent. This pledge was reaffirmed in the Potsdam Declaration to which the Soviets agreed as they entered the war with Japan. However, in preparation for the surrender of Japanese forces throughout the Far East it was agreed that the Japanese north of the 38th Parallel would surrender to the Soviet forces. At the time, and given the other decisions faced by Truman – both political and military – issues in the Far East came low on the US agenda.

The Council of Foreign Ministers

One solid achievement that emerged from the Potsdam Conference was the creation of the **Council of Foreign Ministers**, including those from Britain, France, China, the Soviet Union and the US. Their aim was to continue the discussions started at Potsdam on the various peace treaties, national borders and the issue of German reparations. The first meeting, held in London between 11 September and 2 October 1945, focused on the peace treaties for Italy, Finland, Bulgaria, Romania and Hungary. There is little doubt that Stalin attached great importance to this meeting because he was determined to bring governments sympathetic to the Soviets into power in Bulgaria, Romania and Hungary, collectively known as the Balkans. On the other hand, Secretary of State Byrnes wanted **self-determination** for the Balkans. Molotov, infuriated at Byrnes's blocking of the peace treaties for the Balkans, threatened to refuse to sign the peace treaty with Italy. Unable to find a way forward and with refusals to compromise on both sides the conference adjourned on 2 October, having accomplished little in the preparation of the peace treaties.

The Moscow conference of December 1945 saw agreement on several important points.

- The procedures for making peace treaties with the Balkans and Poland were agreed.
- A three-power commission was to be sent to Romania to prepare the country for free elections. The Soviets agreed to add two representatives of democratic groups to the Bulgarian cabinet.
- There was to be a Soviet–US conference on Korea.
- The troops of both powers were to be withdrawn from China.
- It was agreed to establish the UN Atomic Energy Commission.
- Discussions on reparations were deferred until the report from the Allied Commission was completed.

Byrne's diplomatic style took a compromising stance against Soviet influence in Bulgaria and Romania. In a letter he read to Byrnes in the White House in January 1946, Truman attacked the agreements made at Moscow. What is more important is that the text of this letter clearly shows how the relationship between Truman and the Soviets had changed. Truman was now fully convinced that the Soviet Union posed a major threat to the security of the US and its allies.

This fear was further reinforced by the Soviet refusal to leave Iran. This led to further protest from the Americans, who together with the British had a large stake in the Iranian oil fields. In May 1946, the Soviets withdrew from Iran having negotiated the formation of an Iranian–Soviet oil company subject to ratification by the Iranians. This was later refused but the incident further reinforced Truman's belief that the Soviets were intent on world conquest.

CONCLUSION

The year 1945 was one of key importance in international relations. From the ashes of the Second World War emerged a new world order dominated by two superpowers: the US and the USSR. The relationship between these two countries had deteriorated during 1945 and the change in US presidents played an important part in this. Roosevelt's conciliatory manner was replaced by Truman's more forceful approach. One of the key factors underlying this change was the personal experience of the individuals involved. Roosevelt's approach was in part a product of his confidence and experience that gave him the ability to establish a useful and in some respects rewarding relationship with Stalin. Truman, on the other hand, lacked confidence in international affairs and struggled to get to grips with what was a very complex brief. In response to this, he decided that there was greater safety in adopting a much firmer approach to the USSR in order to safeguard US interests. By the middle of 1946, US policy towards the Soviet Union was starting to reflect the belief of many in the US government, including Truman, that Stalin was intent on expanding communism throughout the world.

CHAPTER 2

The Truman Doctrine, Marshall Plan and deepening of the Cold War

AN OVERVIEW

By the middle of 1946 there were both political and economic pressures steering Truman's foreign policy towards a firmer and more forceful stand against the USSR. This was a move away from the direction taken by Roosevelt. Negotiation and compromise were no longer seen as productive methods of dealing with the USSR. Ignoring the USSR's security needs, Truman's actions were aimed at limiting Soviet power and influence. Key aspects of this new approach were the Truman Doctrine and the Marshall Plan. Both of these policies were provocative, increased mistrust and as a result helped to deepen the divide between the two superpowers.

George Kennan (1904–2005) Deputy Chief of Mission in the US Embassy in Moscow in 1946. Kennan's analysis of Soviet foreign policy was given in the *Long Telegram* of 1946. He saw the USSR as aggressive and suspicious, and recommended firm action by the US against what he viewed as Soviet expansion in Eastern Europe. The *Long Telegram* was to be highly influential on Truman's foreign policy and led to the policy of containment. These views were developed further in an article 'The Sources of Soviet Conduct' written in 1947 by Kennan under the pseudonym Mr X. Kennan later returned to the Soviet Union as US Ambassador 1952–53.

George Marshall (1880–1959) The mastermind of US military policy in the Second World War, Marshall was appointed Secretary of State by Truman in 1947. He launched the Marshall Aid programme to provide American financial support to war-torn Europe. All countries in Europe were eligible for Marshall aid but the conditions attached made it impossible for the communist states of Eastern Europe to apply. Over US$17 billion were provided to Europe and by 1952 Western Europe's economy was experiencing sustained growth.

Chiang Kai Shek (1887–1975) Leader of the Chinese Nationalists (Guomindang) from 1927 until overthrown by the Chinese communists in 1949. He had received US support in the civil war against the communists but his brutal and corrupt policies caused concern in the US government. In 1949 he was forced to flee to the island of Taiwan, which he ruled with US protection until his death.

DEVELOPMENT OF THE TRUMAN DOCTRINE

Breakdown of talks on reparations

The major issue facing the USA and the Soviet Union in 1946 and early 1947 was how to deal with post-war Germany and reparations. At the end of the Paris Conference of Foreign Ministers in April to July 1946, it became apparent to the major Allies that the agreements laid down at Potsdam, to divide Germany into zones of occupation with reparations drawn from within each of the Allied zones, was unworkable. The USSR wanted US$10 billion in reparations and at least US$2 billion from the Ruhr region, to which the British objected. James Byrnes, Secretary of State for Harry S Truman, suggested that each power should collect reparations from within its own zone. But the Soviets still insisted on 10 per cent of reparations coming from the western zones. Soviet intransigence on this point led to deep divisions between Byrnes and Foreign Minister Molotov. Since early 1946, US and British officials had doubted whether it was possible or desirable to work with the Soviet Union on a solution for Germany within a four-power framework. Other events in 1946 made any resolution of this problem even more unlikely.

Kennan's Long Telegram

What undoubtedly contributed to these feelings of apprehension in the US administration was the Long Telegram from George Kennan sent to the State Department in February 1946, as Kennan was the Deputy Chief of Mission in the US Embassy in Moscow. In his summary of the foreign policy goals of the Soviet Union, Kennan stated that:

> The Kremlin believed that everything must be done to advance the relative strength of the USSR as a factor in international society. Conversely no opportunity must be missed to reduce the strength and influence, collectively as well as individually, of capitalist power.

In addition, Kennan stated that the Soviet leadership:

> ... in the name of Marxism sacrificed every single ethical value ... today they cannot dispense with it. It is a fig leaf [cover] of their moral and intellectual respectability ... World communism is like a malignant parasite that feeds only on diseased tissue. One should therefore deny it opportunities by affording a more positive leadership to a war-torn Europe.

Kennan's analysis of Soviet foreign policy emphasised the role of communist ideology. He saw the Soviet leadership as suspicious and aggressive; insecurities that stemmed from their view of the outside world as virulently anti-communist. Given this outlook, there could be no compromise with the USSR. The Long Telegram formed the firm basis behind the belief that only a hard-line approach towards Stalin and the Soviet Union would work in containing communism and safeguarding US interests. The Long Telegram was so influential because it expressed clearly and cogently attitudes that Truman and many in his administration were beginning to adopt.

Churchill's 'Sinews of Peace' speech at Fulton, Missouri, March 1946

On 5 March 1946, Winston Churchill's speech to an assembly at Westminster College in Fulton, Missouri, reinforced the fears of Kennan,

Byrnes and Truman about Soviet expansionism in Europe and Asia. In May 1945, Churchill had already identified the Soviets as a 'menace' when he instructed Foreign Secretary Anthony Eden to make the US officials at the San Francisco UN conference aware of the implications of US troop withdrawals from Eastern Europe. According to Churchill, this would mean 'the tide of Russian domination sweeping forward 120 miles on a front of 300 to 400 miles. It would include all the great capitals of Middle Europe.' In his speech at Fulton, Churchill returned to this theme:

> *Beware I say; time is plenty short …*

> *A shadow has fallen upon the scenes so lately lightened by the Allied victory. Nobody knows what Soviet Russia and its communist international organisation intends to do in the immediate future, or what are the limits, if any, to their expansive and proselytising tendencies … From Stettin in the Baltic to Trieste in the Adriatic, an iron curtain has descended across Europe. Behind that line all the capitals of the ancient states of Central and Eastern Europe lie in what I must call the Soviet sphere, and all are subject in one form or another not only to Soviet influence, but to a very high and, in many cases, increasing measure of control from Moscow …*

> *From what I have seen of our Russian friends and allies in the war, I am convinced that there is nothing they admire so much as strength, and there is nothing for which they have less respect than weakness, especially military weakness …*

The development of the powerful **Iron Curtain** image certainly influenced the US and British media. In a study of Churchill's speech, **Ryan** (1979) argued that Truman downplayed his own role in the development and presentation of the ideas expressed by Churchill for two reasons. First, he did not want Stalin to think there was some kind of secret intrigue between Truman and Churchill. Second, he believed the speech would have a greater impact on the American public because of their respect for Churchill.

Frederik Logevall (2004) pointed out that Churchill, who hated communism, had worked hard in the Second World War to improve the West's bargaining position. Churchill saw the importance of continued cooperation and diplomatic links with Stalin in order to limit Soviet expansionism after the war. In his speech, Logevall argues, Churchill clearly identified the danger of breaking off contact with the Soviets:

> *I do not believe that Soviet Russia desires war. What they desire is the fruits of war and the indefinite expansion of their power and doctrines. … What is needed is a settlement, and the longer this is delayed the more difficult it will be and the greater our dangers will be.*

This speech highlighted the growing suspicions of the British and the USA that Stalin and the Soviet Union must be contained. When Truman made his famous announcement in March 1947, it was clear that US attitudes towards the Soviet Union had changed from one of compromise and concessions to one of containment of the perceived Soviet threat.

The Truman Doctrine

The Truman Doctrine, announced on 12 March 1947, was a decisive turning point in the origins of the Cold War. After this important speech, the foreign policy of the USA took a more militant tone in the **containment** of what was perceived as Soviet expansionism. The Truman Doctrine was mainly a response to the political and social upheaval taking place in Greece and Turkey. The document stated:

> *Turkey has been spared the disasters that have beset Greece. And, during the war, the United States and Britain furnished Turkey with material aid …*
> *I am fully aware of the broad implications involved if the United States extends assistance to Greece and Turkey, and shall discuss these implications …*
>
> *One of the primary objectives of the foreign policy of the United State is the creation of conditions in which we and other nations will be able to work out a way of life free from coercion. This was a fundamental issue in the war with Germany and Japan …*
>
> *At the present moment in world history nearly every nation must choose between alternative ways of life. The choice is often not a free one. One way of life is based upon the will of the majority, and is distinguished by free institutions, representative governments, free elections … The second way of life is based upon the will of the minority, forcibly imposed upon the majority. It relies upon terror and oppression …*
>
> *It must be the policy of the US to support free people who are resisting attempted subjugation by armed minorities or by outside pressure. Help should be given through economic and financial aid, which is essential to economic stability and orderly political processes.*

The timing of the announcement coincided with the Conference of Foreign Ministers meeting in Moscow in March 1947. This meeting was dedicated to drawing up a peace treaty for Germany and resolving the reparations issues. It is possible that Truman timed his announcement to put pressure on Stalin and Foreign Minister Molotov in the hope that the Soviets would move towards the US view put forward by Byrnes in September 1946 that a united Germany was vitally important to the future of European economic recovery.

Withdrawal of the British from Greece

An analysis of other events in the lead-up to the Truman Doctrine reveals why the US decided to change its diplomatic stance towards Stalin and the Soviets. In February 1947, Foreign Minister Ernest Bevin announced the termination of British military and financial support for both Greece and Turkey. In Greece at this time, the Greek communists were engaged in a bitter struggle against a reactionary regime. Truman feared if the communists were successful they might align Athens with Moscow and give Stalin access to the Mediterranean. Interestingly at this time, Marshall Tito of Yugoslavia was providing most support for the rebels and not the Soviets. Tito's refusal to withdraw his advisers from Greece was one of the reasons he was expelled from **Cominform** (the Communist Information Bureau) in July 1949.

Truman and American public opinion

Historians, including **Logevall** (2004) and **Small** (1996) have argued that the Truman Doctrine was an attempt to influence American public opinion in the period leading up to the 1948 presidential elections. In November 1946, the mid-term congressional elections were a resounding success for the Republicans as they gained control of the Senate and House of Representatives for the first time since 1928. After the elections, Truman and his Democratic advisers met and decided that he would have to take definite steps if he was to have any chance of winning the 1948 presidential election. One such step was to make it clear to the American people that Truman strongly opposed Soviet actions in Eastern Europe and the Far East.

It could therefore be argued that the Truman Doctrine was an attempt to talk up the threat from the Soviet Union. In the months leading up to the elections of 1948, the administration took additional steps to show its commitment to contain communist expansion both within the US and externally. In spring 1947, Truman created the Federal Employee Loyalty Programme, which gave government security officials authorisation to screen 2 million employees of the federal government for any hint of communist sympathies.

National Security Act 1947

In July 1947, the National Security Act created the National Security Council (NSC) with the US President as chair, and the Secretaries of State and Defence as its key members, to coordinate foreign and defence policy and to reconcile diplomatic and military commitments and requirements. Under this Act, a Secretary of Defence, the Central Intelligence Agency (CIA) and the National Security Resources Board were established. The role of the NSC was to provide the president with information on the internal and external security of the US. In December 1949, NSC 48/2 extended the Truman Doctrine to Asia (see p. 22) and in April 1950, the NSC presented paper NSC 68 to Truman, asking for additional funds of US$40 billion to be used to provide an effective military deterrence and containment of the Soviet Union (see p. 31).

Response to the policy of containment

In July 1947, Kennan, writing under the pseudonym 'Mr X', published the article 'Sources of Soviet Conduct' in the influential journal *Foreign Affairs*. Kennan developed his idea that the foreign policy of the Soviet government was driven by its ideology of communism and the way that the US should meet this was through a patient but firm and vigilant containment of Russian expansionist tendencies. This led to a remarkable series of articles by **Walter Lippmann,** an influential columnist for the *New York Herald Tribune* in September and October 1947. These articles were later incorporated in a slim book *The Cold War, A Study in US Foreign Policy* (1947). Its title gave the name the Cold War to the Soviet–US competition. Lippmann was gravely concerned by the direction of US foreign policy of containment as reflected in the Truman Doctrine and Kennan's article. The columnist had no illusions about the Soviets' intention to expand their influence, but he rejected the view that the Russians were devils incarnate. Stalin, he argued, had genuine fears for the security of the Soviet Union and was motivated primarily by a defensive concern to prevent the revival of German power; hence his determination to assert Soviet control over Eastern Europe. Lippmann claimed that a policy of containment would draw the US into defending any number of far-flung areas of the world. This would lead to heavy defence costs and would militarise American society, meaning a high number of individuals in the armed forces and a foreign policy dominated by military policy.

Lippmann argued that continued negotiations would achieve at least a partial resolution of Soviet–US differences. 'You did not have to like the Soviets,' Lippmann was saying, 'you just need to talk to them.' This was the critical issue in Kennan's article that Lippmann was attacking: the notion that built into containment was a refusal to engage in diplomatic discussions with the Soviets. In response to Lippmann's criticism, Kennan responded: 'Washington should be forthright in its dealings with Moscow and always be willing to negotiate while never appearing false or weak. Nothing is to be gained by purposeless concessions without receiving a demand in return.'

THE MARSHALL PLAN

The Truman Doctrine led to the Marshall Plan of June 1947. They were both aimed at containing communism to the extent that Truman, in an interview in 1960, claimed they could be seen as 'two halves of the same walnut'. Yet the State Department officials who were working on the plan were keen to differentiate the economic aid advocated in the Marshall Plan from the militaristic aims of the Truman Doctrine. In a speech at Harvard University on 5 June 1947, Secretary of State George Marshall outlined a plan for economic recovery in Europe. The plan identified in Europe the practical difficulties of getting the European economies working again.

- The damage inflicted by the war on industrial production and the inability of those industries that had survived to produce peacetime goods led to a serious decline in the amount of capital circulating in Europe.

- In addition, there was a serious shortage of dollars to buy in food because of a lack of export sales to the US and other countries.
- US aid that should have gone towards the reconstruction of the European economies was used to buy foodstuffs instead of the raw materials (for example, coal and iron ore) necessary for industry.

According to Marshall, only the US was in a position to help: 'Our policy is directed not against any country or doctrine but against hunger, poverty, desperation and chaos.' The remedy for the chaos was to break the 'vicious circle' of decline and 'restore the confidence of the European people in the economic future of their countries and of Europe as a whole'. The great fear of Marshall at this time was that the economic distress clearly evident in Britain, France and Italy would push these states towards communism. The revival of German economic power was essential to this recovery, but the talks between the Americans and the Soviets at the Moscow Conference in April 1947 on the reunification of Germany and reparations had collapsed. **Eisenberg** (1996) questions the commitment of the US at this point to the reunification of Germany. She shows that the plans of the US for the recovery of post-war capitalism depended on the revival of the German economy. The resources of the Ruhr and the Rhineland were essential to this recovery, and it was therefore in the interests of the US to block reunification in order to ensure that Germany and its resources did not fall under the control of the Soviet Union.

However, there are other interpretations about why the US was keen to enter into an economic alliance with Europe. **Jackson** (1979) shows that there was considerable evidence indicating that the USA was headed for a recession: first, because of inflationary pressures within the economy due to rising prices and wages; and second, because of the lack of dollars in circulation in Europe, US exports were declining and industrial output was slowing down. The reintegration of Germany into Europe and the revitalisation of coal production and German industry were essential for European recovery and ultimately the US economy.

Reactions of the Soviet Union to the Marshall Plan

According to **Leffler** (1999) and **Offner** (1999), Stalin viewed the Marshall Plan as a 'watershed' event, signalling a US effort to dominate Europe. This spurred the Soviets into a comprehensive shift in their own foreign policy from one of collective action to isolationism. The prominent Soviet politician A A Zhdanov's 'Two Camps' speech at the founding conference of Cominform in September 1947 revealed clearly the depth of division between the wartime Allies:

> *A new alignment of political forces has arisen. The more the war receded into the past, the more distinct becomes two trends in post-war*

international policy, corresponding to the division of the political forces into two major camps; the imperialist and anti-democratic camp on the one hand, and the anti-imperialist and democratic camp on the other. The principal driving force of the imperialist camp is the United States and with it are Britain and France ... The anti-fascist forces comprise the second camp. This is based on the Soviet Union and the new democracies ... The anti-imperialist camp is backed by the labour and the democratic movement and by the fraternal communist parties in all countries, by the fighters for national liberation in the colonies and dependencies.

The Marshall Plan furthered the political isolation of the Soviets and led to a turning point in Soviet foreign policy. It signified for the Soviets the final failure of the integrationist strategy in foreign policy – that is, working in collaboration with Europe and the US, and a return to separation, isolation and consolidation within their own zone of influence that had been gained as a result of the war. However, **Roberts** (1994) challenges this view of Stalin's reaction to the Marshall Plan. He argues that the initial response, as expressed in articles in the Soviet newspapers *Pravda* and *Soviet News*, was negative. But Stalin did agree to send Foreign Minister Molotov to meet with his British and French counterparts in Paris on 27 June 1947 to discuss the conditions for participation in the plan. Roberts argues that despite all the difficulties and conflicts in Soviet–US relations since 1945, Soviet foreign relations were still dominated by a commitment to a policy of **peaceful coexistence** and collaboration with the West.

In interviews in the period 1946 to1947, Stalin had reaffirmed his commitment to post-war international cooperation. In April 1947, he described the Council of Foreign Ministers debates as:

... something like combat reconnaissance. When the partners have exhausted one another, the moment for a possible compromise arrives. The result may be attained at the next session rather than the current one, but on all important issues, such as democratisation, political organisation, economic unity and reparations, compromise is within reach.

Initially, the Soviets viewed the Marshall Plan as part of the post-war international cooperation policy of the US. However, Soviet Ambassador Nikolai Novikov, based in Washington, sent a telegram on 24 June 1947 to Stalin expressing the following view:

A careful analysis of the Marshall Plan shows that in the end it amounts to the creation of a West European bloc as an instrument of United States policy ... The enormous relative weight of the USSR in international affairs in general and in European countries in particular, the independence of its foreign policy, and the economic and political assistance that it provides to neighbouring countries, both allies and former enemies, has led to the growth of Soviet political influence ... Such a situation in Eastern and South Eastern Europe cannot help but be regarded by the US imperialists as an obstacle in the path of the expansionist policy of the United States.

Another Soviet view of the Marshall Plan was put forward by Eugen Varga, economic adviser to Stalin, who stated in a memorandum dated 24 June 1947:

> *There can be no doubt that Mr Marshall's proposal is conditioned by the present position of the economy of the UNITED STATES OF AMERICA. It is almost universal opinion that the post-war boom is drawing to a close ... The Marshall Plan, it would appear, represents a programme for the solution of the US export problem, providing for the over-coming of the ever-sharpening dollar crisis in many European countries.*

Molotov arrived in Paris at the end of June with 100 advisers, which, according to **Roberts** (1994), was a definite sign of the seriousness of Moscow's approach to the plan. However, when the conditions attached to the assistance were made known – the creation of a centrally coordinated programme of US assistance and the directive that German economic resources could not be used as part of the reconstruction plan – Molotov rejected the plan. Roberts rejects the view that Stalin blocked the East European states' acceptance of Marshall Aid. On 5 July 1947, Moscow sent two messages to all ambassadors in Eastern Europe. The first was to give an explanation of the Soviet stance on the Marshall Plan. The second was to the leaders of the communist parties urging East European participation in the conference on Marshall Aid on 12 July. Participation by East European countries, it was assumed by Stalin, meant that individual states would have to meet certain political conditions, most notably loyalty to the Soviet Union, the occupying force.

Ultimately, Roberts argues, it was opposition from Yugoslavia, Romania and possibly Poland's communist leadership to Marshall Aid that led to the refusal of participating in the plan. Many of these states rejected the plan because they believed that capitalism had let them down in the inter-war years and was responsible for the outbreak of war in 1939. This rejection of Marshall Aid, together with Soviet fears that the main aim of the forthcoming conference was an attempt by the US to interfere in Eastern Europe, led to the creation of the Cominform in autumn 1947.

The aims of Cominform were to:

- respond to the Marshall Plan by uniting East European countries against it
- establish links and political cooperation between communist parties, not governments
- create an information exchange between members.

Cominform was not intended as an organisation whose principal aim was world revolution.

Comecon (the Council for Mutual Economic Aid), founded on 25 January 1949, was the Soviet alternative to the Marshall Plan. However, this was a trading agreement between those states that lay in the sphere of Soviet influence; it did not provide financial aid. The announcement of Comecon stated:

> *The governments of the United States, Britain and some other countries in Western Europe are to all intents and purposes boycotting trade relations with the countries of the people's democracies and the USSR. … In order to effect broader economic cooperation among the countries of people's democracy and the USSR the conference found it necessary to establish a Council for Mutual Economic Assistance.*

This action by the Soviet Union and the failure of the London Conference of Foreign Ministers in December 1947 to agree on a policy for Germany contributed to the division of Europe in 1949.

Congress and the Marshall Plan

After six months of planning by the State Department, the Marshall Plan was placed before Congress in January 1948. Proponents of the plan saw it as a bulwark against communism, an economic measure that would help to maintain the conditions of prosperity present in the USA in the late 1940s, a device to continue US export trade and as aid to others in the tradition of US generosity and kindness. The opposition to the plan denounced the cost (some US$17 billion), argued that it would not be effective in the battle against communism, saw it as another failure of the Democrats' foreign policy, and objected to it as a sign of US economic and political imperialism. According to **Hitchens** (1968), there was positive support for the plan from the American public, radio broadcasters and the press, in particular the *New York Times* and the *New York Herald Tribune*.

The legislation for the Marshall Plan, or European Recovery Programme as it was known in Congress, was finally passed on 31 March 1948. Congress adopted a bipartisan approach. In other words, both Democrats and Republicans supported the programme, first because of the communist coup and fall of the democratically elected government in Czechoslovakia, and the murder of Foreign Minister Jan Masaryk, the leading advocate of democracy, in February 1948. This event shocked Congress and the American public, and was certainly an important influence on the passing of the Marshall Plan. A second key influence was the Berlin Blockade, begun in June 1948. This action was seen as a provocative attempt by Stalin to widen Soviet influence in Berlin and Germany, and both the Republicans and Democrats called for direct action to support the population of Berlin.

The Berlin crisis, 1948–9

The introduction of the West German mark in the merged zones of France, Britain and the US in March 1948 and the London agreement to form a West German state in June were the immediate reasons for the Berlin Blockade. The most divisive issue that confronted the Big Three and France after 1945 was the peace settlement for Germany. The inability to reach any consensus on reparations in the Council of Foreign Ministers and the withdrawal of the Soviet Union and Eastern European states from the Marshall Plan conference in Paris in June 1947 forced the western Allies to proceed with currency reforms in West Germany and West Berlin in order to counter the inflation and difficulties in trade. In June, Stalin initiated the Berlin Blockade which led to the disruption of the flow of US supplies, electricity and overland communications through East Germany to the western Allies sector of Berlin. Truman recognised that to withdraw from Berlin would seriously undermine the influence of the US in Europe and the Economic Recovery Plan and destroy his presidential standing in an election year. Unsure of Soviet motives, Truman authorised a temporary airlift of essential supplies into Berlin; he was determined to avert a military confrontation. Secretary of State Marshall announced on 30 June the US intention to stay in Berlin also revealing the transfer of B-29 heavy bombers to Germany and Britain. By mid-July, the Americans faced a full-blown war scare when the Soviets rejected protests by the US and continued the blockade.

Eventually, Truman and the airlift succeeded against the blockade and Stalin gave in to a face-saving Conference of Foreign Ministers in May 1949 that ended the blockade but offered nothing new on the resolution of the German question. The ideological threat posed by the currency reforms in Germany in 1948 represented a very real threat to the Soviets. What they feared was a revived Germany coopted into a western alliance committed to the downfall of communism and, by implication, the Soviet Union. Therefore, the response of the Soviet Union to the failure of the Berlin Blockade was to isolate Eastern Europe from any western influence.

THE STRENGTHENING OF THE SOVIET HOLD OVER EASTERN EUROPE

Stalin decided to clamp down on Eastern Europe the only way the Soviets knew how: by consolidating their power through repression, oppression and totalitarian rule. This view is supported by **Gaddis** (1997), who argues that Stalin's murderous domestic rule was the key determinant of Soviet foreign policy and the Cold War. In a superb book on the Soviet occupation of East Germany, **Naimark** (1995) showed that the Soviets were driven by concrete events in their zone of occupation not by preconceived plans or ideological beliefs. They "bolshevised" the zone not because there was a plan to do so, but because that was the only way they knew how to organise society. They acted similarly wherever their troops occupied territories.

These views were challenged by **Roman** (1996) in his study of Hungary in the period 1945–50. Roman argues that there is no evidence to show that Stalin planned to 'sovietise' Hungary before 1949. **Leffler** (1999) pointed out that in Eastern Germany, Hungary, Bulgaria and Czechoslovakia, local communists intent on seizing power for themselves disliked the constraints imposed on them by Stalin. The Soviet leader continued to waver until 1949, assessing the chances for perpetuating the wartime alliance and gaining the advantages that would be derived from it. However, Stalin saw the correlation of forces turning against him as a result of the Truman Doctrine, the Marshall Plan and the Anglo-American initiatives in Germany, and so ended any form of collaborative action with the West. The Soviet turn to Cold War policies in autumn 1947 was, at one level, simply a response to perceived threats and conditions that called for a strengthening of the Soviet position, particularly in Eastern Europe. At the same time, Soviet policy took a militant and ideological form, the delineation of a world split into two camps and the demand that states and peoples decided which side they were on.

Establishment of NATO, 1949

Stalin's aggressive actions in Berlin accelerated the negotiations that led to the creation of the North Atlantic Treaty Organisation (**NATO**) in April 1949. In effect, the treaty pledged the US to the defence of Europe by providing mutual assistance to any member in case of aggression against any of the signatories. For the first time in its history the US had entered an entangling alliance in peacetime. It was now committed to:

- guarantee the maintenance of other social structures and governments
- close peacetime military collaboration with the armed services of other nations
- defend its allies with nuclear weapons.

Truman sought the opportunity to use the atomic bomb as a deterrent to a Soviet attack against Western Europe, and for this purpose US military bases were established in Germany and other European states. Truman was forced to confront opposition in Congress to the development of NATO by explaining that all the signatories would contribute to the costs. However, the explosion of the first Soviet atomic bomb on 29 August 1949 gave Truman the opportunity he needed to apply pressure on the Senate to pass the Mutual Defence Assistance Bill on 28 September 1949, granting an expansion of the US armed forces and development of the hydrogen bomb.

The fall of China to communism, 1949

Partly because of the Europe-first orientation of the Truman administration, but mainly because of the budget ceilings within which Congress forced Truman and his government to operate, the problems in Asia had reached crisis point. Wars of independence between the French colonial powers and their colonies in Laos, Cambodia and Vietnam erupted in 1946. The actions of the French in Indochina were supported by the British, fearful that nationalist unrest would spill over into areas of British control or influence, in particular Malaya and Burma. The US did not view the wars in Indochina as serious enough to become involved. However, the civil war being fought in China was perceived to be more serious and the US administration had supported Chiang Kai Shek's Guomindang Party. Between 1946 and 1949 hundreds of millions of dollars in aid and almost all Chiang's military equipment were from the USA. In early 1949, Truman insisted on a flexible policy towards China; however, when China fell to the Communists led by Mao Zedong in October 1949, his response was to close numerous consulates there and refuse to recognise the sovereignty of the People's Republic of China.

The Republicans used the loss of China to further discredit Truman and the Democrats by accusing them of being soft on communists, in particular the Soviet version. For many in Truman's administration the fall of China further highlighted the weaknesses of US military forces. The lessons drawn from the fall of China to communism and the loss of Eastern Europe to the Soviet Union were that the USA must: spend more on security; expand its armed forces; extend its military bases in the Pacific; and extend economic aid to those states struggling against what were perceived to be Soviet-sponsored forces. The outcome of the fall of China and the first test of an atomic weapon by the Soviets was the subject of NSC 68.

NSC DOCUMENT 68

NSC 68, a discussion document commissioned by Truman and produced in April 1950, represented the practical extension of the Truman Doctrine, which had been worldwide in its implications but limited to Europe in its application. The fundamental aim of the NSC 68 policy was containment of the Soviet threat by:

- an increase in defence expenditure in both nuclear and conventional weapons, and expansion of the armed forces to put them on a par with those of the Soviet Union
- exposing the falsities of Soviet pretensions
- inducing a reduction of the Kremlin's control and influence
- rolling back the Soviet drive for world domination
- fostering the seeds of destruction within the Soviet system in order to force the leaders of the Soviet Union to modify their behaviour and conform to generally accepted international standards
- resolving worldwide conflicts without resorting to war, the idea being to exert pressure in such a way that would avoid directly challenging Soviet prestige and leave open the possibility of diplomatic negotiations.

The NSC 68 document provided the justification for the US to assume the role of world police officer and came close to saying that all political change was directed by communists and should be resisted. The document clearly showed the US perceptions of Soviet intentions:

> *The fundamental design of those who control the Soviet Union and the international communist movement is to retain and solidify their absolute power, first in the Soviet Union and second in the areas now under their control. In the minds of the Soviet leaders, however, achievement of this design requires the dynamic extension of their authority and the ultimate elimination of any effective opposition to their authority.*

In other words, the foreign policy of the Soviet Union was no longer driven just by ideology; it stemmed simply from the inability of a totalitarian system to tolerate diversity. From this, Soviet expansion had gained strength from the victory of communism in China, the Soviet atomic bomb and the continued military build-up at a time when the US was running down its armed forces.

The intention of the document was not essentially defensive in nature, and the aggressive thrust of it was probably linked to concerns about restoring the power balance between the US and the Soviet Union through means other than all-out war. The authors of the document were concerned that the Soviet Union was spending far more on military expenditure than the US. However, the measure used as an indicator, gross national product (GNP), was flawed because the total gross national product of the US was four times that of the Soviet Union. Therefore, if the Soviet Union was spending twice its GNP on military expenditures it was still a great deal less than that of the US. According to **Gaddis** (1982), it is difficult to avoid the conclusion that a double standard was being applied here: potential Soviet military capabilities were being taken into account, but not those of the US.

In NSC 68, the Truman administration emphasised that containment required the US 'to possess superior overall military power in ourselves or dependable combination'. Without such military strength a policy of 'containment is no more than a policy of bluff'. Seeing itself challenged by growing Soviet military power, by a reckless regime in Beijing and by revolutionary nationalism in Indochina, the US adopted the principles of NSC 68 and incorporated them into its foreign policy in the period 1950–75.

CONCLUSION

- The end of the Second World War generated considerable inevitable Soviet–US conflict as two nations with entirely different ideological, political and economic systems confronted each other over Europe and Asia. Truman and his administration sought to fashion US foreign policy on a world-order friendly to the interests of the US and to achieve national security by preventing any nation from cutting US ties to its traditional allies and vital areas of trade and resources.

- Truman favoured a continuity of the internationalist ideals of Roosevelt and the creation of the UN, fostered foreign aid and reconstruction in the form of the Marshall Plan, and sought to avert entanglement in wars.
- However, from the Potsdam Conference through to NSC 68 in April 1950, Truman had contributed significantly to the growing Cold War and militarisation of the foreign policy of the US. Truman assumed that through its economic–military–moral superiority, the US could reorder the world on its own terms and he ascribed only dark motives to Stalin and the Soviet Union who appeared to resist his views.
- Monopoly control of the atomic bomb between 1945 and 1949 heightened this sense of power. The bomb added to the confidence of the Truman administration in its dealings with the Soviets over German reparations, despite Soviet claims to compensation for its wartime suffering.
- Truman's inexperience in diplomacy and foreign policy led him to seek active policies to counter what he perceived to be threats from the Soviet Union. He attributed every national conflict that emerged in the period 1945–50, in Germany, Iran, Turkey, Greece and Czechoslovakia, and finally Korea in June 1950, to Soviet plots and insisted that Stalin and the Soviets had broken every agreement and were bent on world conquest.

The fall of China to communism, the Korean War and the Vietnam War (discussed in the following chapters) were all viewed in the context of the Cold War. Truman remained convinced in his view that Stalin and the Soviets were untrustworthy, at the root of every problem from Europe to Asia and that the US had 'saved' the world from totalitarianism. Truman therefore promoted an ideology and politics of Cold War confrontation that became the system of working for successive administrations and presidents including Dwight D Eisenhower, John F Kennedy, Lyndon Johnson and Richard Nixon.

CHAPTER 3

The background to the Korean War

AN OVERVIEW

Following the defeat of the Japanese in August 1945, Korea was occupied by the armed forces of the US and the Soviet Union. The division of Korea at the 38th Parallel with the US occupation forces in the south and the Soviet forces in the north led to great disappointment among nationalist-minded Koreans. In 1948, this division became permanent as the Soviets and the USA established two separate states in Korea: the Republic of Korea in the south and the People's Democratic Republic of Korea in the north. This action of the occupying forces was not for the benefit of the Koreans but part of the Cold War struggle between the US and the Soviet Union as both sought to extend their influence in the Pacific region. However, the communist Kim Il Sung in the north and the right-wing nationalist Syngman Rhee in the south had never accepted the division of Korea as legitimate or permanent, and both sought ways to achieve a unified and independent Korea.

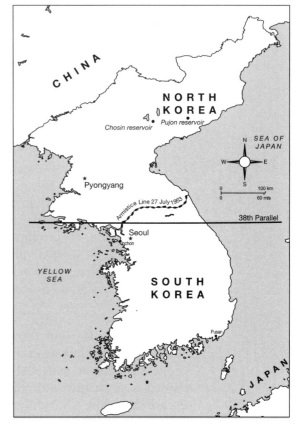

The Korean Peninsula

The Korean War was a significant turning point in the Cold War because it reflected the changing balance of power in the Pacific region. Having been blocked by the robust containment policies in Europe and the Middle East, Joseph Stalin viewed the fall of China to communism in 1949 as evidence of a lack of interest by the US in Asia. The Korean War also marked the rise of China as an international power and important player in the Cold War. The Chinese volunteer forces achieved many successes in the war and the US was forced to acknowledge communist China's power and influence in Asia. However, the success and resolve of the UN forces in Korea ultimately deterred the Soviets and China from extending the war.

BIOGRAPHIES

Kim Il Sung (1912–94) In early September 1945, Kim Il Sung returned to North Korea along with Soviet troops. Kim Il Sung was little known among the Korean people untill he was introduced by leader Cho Mansik at a mass rally in October 1945 as a national war hero. However, more important for Kim Il Sung was his patronage by Stalin who saw in him the potential to destroy left-wing factions in the north and his ability to unite the people under a communist leadership. The North Korean Workers' Party (NKWP), founded in July 1946, was the vehicle through which Kim Il Sung gained widespread support in the north. The establishment of the Soviet-sponsored Democratic Republic of Korea in 1948 gave him the premiership.

Syngman Rhee (1875–1965) In mid-October 1945, Rhee, aged 70, returned to South Korea from the US. Throughout his time in exile he had lobbied the US Congress against the Japanese domination of Korea and was viewed by the right-wing nationalists as a potential leader. His prestige as a patriot who had devoted his life to the goal of Korean independence together with US support ensured elimination of any opposition from the left. In January 1946, he led the opposition to the Moscow Accords in the guise of leader of the Representative Democratic Council and in 1948 was elected as the first president of the US-sponsored Republic of Korea.

HISTORICAL INTERPRETATIONS

Since the late 1950s there has been an ongoing debate about the origins and perpetuation of the Korean War. The traditional interpretations tended to agree with the views of the Americans who saw the invasion of South Korea as further evidence of Stalin's determination to extend communist influence in Asia. In an early account, entitled *Korea: the Limited War* (1964), **David Rees** saw the outbreak of the Korean War as the outcome of unprovoked aggression by the Soviet Union, which was intent on extending its influence in Asia. Similarly, in *Conflict: the History of the Korean War* (1962), **Robert Leckie** concluded that Stalin was responsible for the planning, preparation and initiation of the attack.

In contrast, in *The Origins of the Korean War: Liberation and the Emergence of Separate Regimes* (1981), **Bruce Cummings** challenged these interpretations for their downplaying of internal Korean factors and their overemphasis on Soviet and North Korean aggressiveness. He criticised the US military government for applying a policy of containment in 1946 as it sought ways to prevent the expansion of communist influence. When war eventually broke out in 1950 it was not, as the US declared, an example of the expansionist aims of the Soviet Union but a civil war. Yet **William Stueck**, in *Rethinking the Korean War* (2002), stated that the origins and causes of the Korean War were not shaped by the Koreans. The war was the result of the actions and ideologies of the US, the Soviet Union and China forged in the early years of the Cold War. Stueck's most significant contribution to the debate is to show how the civil war moved to an international war in the period 25–30 June 1950.

These interpretations were challenged by the works of **Kathryn Weathersby** in *Soviet Aims in Korea and the Origins of the Korean War, 1945–50: New Evidence from the Russian Archives* (1993) and *'Should we fear this?' Stalin and the Danger of War with America* (2002). In these studies, Weathersby argued that the Soviets played a direct role in the Korean War. The new evidence demonstrates conclusively that North Korea was a satellite of the Soviet Union. Stalin's control over Kim Il Sung was such that it prevented him from attacking the south in spring 1949. Kim had to wait until the Soviets gave their permission and provided weapons and military support in spring 1950.

In summarising the debate, there appear to be three clear views emerging from the evidence:

- the traditional view that the North Korean attack in June 1950 was the result of Stalin's desire to expand Soviet control over Asia
- the revisionist view that the decision for war was primarily Korean with the support of the Chinese
- the new evidence suggesting that Stalin was intent on creating a Soviet bloc in Asia similar to that in Europe, and that he controlled Kim's decision about when to go to war.

The interplay between factors internal and external to Korea was to produce a level of tension that made war likely. The division of Korea and the subsequent growth of tension were to develop quickly after the Second World War came to an end.

THE DIVISION OF KOREA, 1945

The Potsdam Declaration of July 1945 promised that Korea, once liberated from the occupying force of Japan, would in due course become free and independent. However, the rapidity of the Japanese collapse and the US desire to keep casualties to a minimum led to the military division of Korea in August 1945. On 8 August 1945, the Soviets declared war against Japan and proceeded to move into Manchuria and, on 10 August, into Korea. With the sudden collapse of the Japanese army in Asia on 15 August 1945 and with Soviet troops already in Korea, President Harry Truman feared that the Soviet Red Army would occupy Korea and – like Poland, Hungary and other states in Eastern Europe – it would ultimately fall under Soviet control. In an attempt to block this, Truman proposed dividing the Korean Peninsula at the 38th Parallel with Soviet forces in the north and US forces in the south. Their role was to accept the surrender of the Japanese troops. Stalin agreed to this proposal without any debate and instructed the Soviet forces to stop their advance into Korea at the 38th Parallel.

With the US troops still several hundred kilometres away from Korea and Soviet troops well positioned to occupy Korea, why did Stalin accept Truman's proposal? A number of reasons are suggested for Stalin's actions.

- The US had mobilised huge forces in the area in preparation for the invasion of Japan.
- The overall strength of the Soviet forces was no match for the US.
- Stalin feared that Truman would enter into a deal with the Japanese troops to continue to resist the Soviet advance in Korea.
- Stalin hoped that the US would grant the Soviet Union a share in the occupation of Japan.
- Stalin was willing to work with the Big Three in the hope of achieving an independent Korea that would establish friendly and close relations with the Soviet Union.
- Stalin feared the atomic bomb.

THE OCCUPATION OF KOREA

After the initial occupation of Korea in August–September 1945, the Soviets and the Americans quickly sought to extend their influence over their respective zones. Both of the superpowers made many mistakes. Both overlooked the fact that Korea was a recently liberated country not subject to the demilitarisation undertaken in former enemy states and its division into two occupation zones polarised the political divide between the communists in the north and the more conservative forces in the south. Further, Korea was a predominantly peasant country politicised by the occupation policies of the Japanese. After the fall of Japan, the Koreans organised themselves into **People's Committees** at a local government level, and proceeded to occupy Japanese industries and organise the distribution of land and food. In the north, the People's Committees formed the basis of the Soviet military government, whereas in the south the US military government viewed the People's Committees (PCs) with suspicion, seeing them as chaotic and led by communists.

South Korea and the US occupation

When Lieutenant-General John R Hodge and his staff arrived in Korea in September 1945, they were overwhelmed by the serious disorders throughout Seoul and the provinces as the Koreans seized the assets of the departing Japanese. The initial difficulty they faced was the fact that no Korean they met could speak English; they had one officer who was a Korean speaker, but insufficiently fluent to conduct negotiations. In an attempt to establish communications, Hodge turned to the Japanese officials who could speak both Korean and English.

The second difficulty was Hodge's refusal to work with the PCs. These predominantly peasant-controlled organisations with local leaders drawn from the resistance movement were now required to obtain legal permission from the military government or face closure. PC members were removed from government positions and, on occasion, arrested for opposition to the US-led military government. In November 1945, in Namwon, south of Seoul, five PC leaders were arrested, leading to a demonstration of some 15,000 people with three killed by police fire. While suppressing popular organisations such as the PCs, the military government kept the Japanese governmental framework and even restored government officials who had served under the Japanese. The Japanese economic agencies, the Oriental Development Company and Chosen Food Distribution Company, were revived as the New Korea Company (NKC) and the Korean Commodity Company (KCC). Korean peasants regarded the restoration of the colonial system and the reappointment of collaborators to key positions as unjust and illegitimate.

Hodge chose to work with Japanese administrators and police to restore order to the chaotic political situation existing in South Korea. Koreans therefore were affronted by the willingness of the Americans to work with the Japanese and the respect shown to them in contrast to the thinly veiled contempt offered to the Koreans. According to **Cummings** (1981): 'It did seem that from the beginning many Americans simply liked the Japanese better than the Koreans. The Japanese were viewed as more cooperative, orderly and docile, while the Koreans were seen as headstrong, unruly and obstreperous.' The ignorance about Korean politics and culture and the stubbornness of the military bureaucracy led by General Hodge resulted in a lack of cooperation by the South Koreans.

Unpopular policies

Unrest in Southern Korea was not just focused on the role of the Japanese. In addition, the military government ignored peasant demands for land reform and instead re-established the hated Japanese rice collection policy, supposedly to support the urban population. Police involvement in rice collection further exacerbated peasant discontent, as peasants complained that rice was taken in much the same way as under the Japanese. Many peasants turned on landlords, particularly those who had collaborated with the Japanese, and refused to yield their quotas of rice. To ease the problem with the peasants, in November 1945 Hodge introduced a free market in rice. This action unleashed a wave of speculation and hoarding, and forced the price of rice, which was the staple diet of the South Koreans, from 9.4 yen a bushel in September 1945 to 2800 yen a bushel a year later. Rationing had to be introduced in spring 1946, as many South Koreans struggled to obtain enough food.

Uprisings

In autumn 1946, peasant uprisings in the Kyongsang and Cholla provinces, the richest rice-producing provinces in the south, sought to reverse many of the policies implemented by the military government. The suppression of the riots and the destruction of the PCs represented a significant turning point in the fortunes of the right led by Syngman Rhee and the expansion of the national police in the south. General Hodge suspected the riots were coordinated by the North Koreans and immediately ordered a clamp down on all communist and left-wing activity in the south.

By early 1947, the US occupation government realised that it had made little progress towards creating an ordered and democratic society in Korea. The activities in the north of Korea by the Soviets only increased Korean respect for Soviet strength and diminished still further US popularity. The main problem for the Americans in South Korea was their arrogant belief that the Koreans were incapable of governing themselves and therefore it was their duty to impose on them a government sympathetic to US ideals of freedom and democracy. In many respects their actions were no different than those by the Soviets in the north.

North Korea and Soviet occupation

In North Korea in autumn 1945, the Soviets established their dominance by taking control of the economic activity between the north and south zones. Soviet troops halted mail deliveries and rail traffic across the 38th Parallel, stopped shipments of coal and obstructed the transmission of electricity to the south in order to supply their own zones in the Soviet Far East. The regular reports between the Soviet Foreign Ministry officials in Pyongyang and Moscow showed that the Soviets viewed the physical resources of coal, food and minerals as their own and were flabbergasted when the Americans requested the reconnection of 'Soviet' electricity to the south. In November 1945, as a result of shortages of raw materials to keep industries operating in the north and a shortage of rice that traditionally came from the south, demonstrations and riots broke out in Sinuiju and other provinces that had to be suppressed by Soviet troops.

While the Soviets imposed severe restrictions on the movement of physical resources to the south they did little to curb the flow of people from the north. Many of these individuals were returning to their original homes in the south from forced labour camps at industrial sites in Manchuria and North Korea. According to the *Foreign Relations of the United States* (*FRUS*) records in 1945, approximately 1,600,000 people moved to the southern zone during autumn 1945; about 500,000 from North Korea and the rest from Manchuria. In addition, the Soviets mounted a **united front policy**. This entailed the appointment of communists who had spent the war in the Soviet Union to important government positions and cooperation with one of the more popular non-communist groups led by the conservative Christian Cho Mansik. In this way, Stalin wanted to show the US a unified 'friendly' North Korea leaning towards the Soviet Union for support. In December 1945, Kim Il Sung became head of the Northern branch of the Korean Communist Party (NKCP). The NKCP was used to coordinate land reforms in the north and the reorganisation of heavy industrial enterprises such as steel, ship-building and chemicals.

WHY DID THE OCCUPATION POWERS FAIL TO ACHIEVE AGREEMENT ON UNIFICATION?

A weak political culture

One of the major problems faced by the Americans in South Korea in August 1945 was the deep political cleavages between the political parties within Korea and in exile in China and the US. Under the control of Japan since the 1890s, Koreans had been unable to develop political institutions, parties or a population experienced in self-government. Many Koreans who had gained administrative experience in governing prior to 1945 were long-serving collaborators with the Japanese and detested by their fellow citizens for their service to the colonial power and the support they gave to the suppression of opposition to Japanese rule. During the Second World War, Koreans living in exile were divided into factions and were unable to mobilise sufficient forces in Korea or to provide leadership in the struggle against the Japanese. In addition, thousands of Koreans in Manchuria fighting with partisans against the Japanese were opposed by strong anti-guerrilla forces made up of Koreans. The Big Three at the Yalta and Potsdam Conferences in 1945 (see pages 7 and 12) came to the conclusion that Korea lacked a viable leadership to take it forward to independence because of the deep social and political divisions within its society. With few exceptions, US analysts believed that the factionalism of the exile political groups and their shallow roots among Korea's population made them unlikely instruments for stable self-rule. Therefore the Americans and the Soviets agreed to occupy the country until the Koreans were capable or ready for self-government.

Trusteeship for Korea

At the Yalta Conference in 1945, it was decided that Korea would be placed under the UN international trusteeship scheme that would provide support for the development of self-government for those states formerly in the Japanese Empire. The UN Declaration on Trusteeship (1945) stated:

> *Members of the United Nations which have, or assume responsibilities for, the administration of territories whose peoples have not yet attained a full measure of self-government recognise the following principles. That the interests of the inhabitants of these territories are paramount, and accept as a sacred trust the obligation to promote to the utmost, within the system of international peace and security established by the present Charter, the well being of the inhabitants of these territories.*

The specific undertakings of trusteeship included the political, economic, social and educational advancement of the dependent peoples and protection from exploitation.

The pledge on Korea was reaffirmed by the Big Three at the Potsdam Conference in July 1945 and it was decided that the Council of Foreign Ministers would develop the final agreement on Korean trusteeship. The

Agreements reached at the Moscow Conference of Foreign Ministers in December 1945 stated:

> *[T]he Soviet–US Joint Commission would establish a provisional democratic government in Korea together with the Korean political parties.*

After a period of self-government under international trusteeship for four years Korea would achieve its freedom and independence. Paradoxically, in August 1945 both the Soviet and US leaderships wanted to see a united and independent Korea only as long as it favoured their strategic and economic interests in Korea. But at the same time they sought to keep Korea ideologically divided with the development of political parties in the north and south favourable to the occupying powers. Although ideological confrontation between authoritarian communism and liberal capitalism often appeared to be at the heart of the outbreak of the Korean War, it invariably was filtered through nationalist perspectives, domestic pressures and individual personalities.

Political parties in Korea, 1945

One of the reasons for the mixed reaction to the Moscow Agreements in December 1945 was the way in which the political parties had developed in Korea. In the north, the Communist Party (NKCP) supported the Moscow Accords. However, in the south a number of parties competed for support to block the trusteeship proposals put forward in the accords.

- Korean People's Republic (KPR) – formed in 1945, its principal spokesperson was Yo Un-Hyong. This group contained members of the PCs, peasants, nationalists, prominent members of the anti-Japanese resistance, and elements of the left and communists.
- Korean Democratic Party (KDP) – formed in September 1945, this group contained landowners, collaborators with the Japanese and right-wing elements. The nationalists initially refused to work with them.
- Korean Provisional Government (KPG) – based in China and established in 1919 in opposition to the Japanese occupation, Syngman Rhee claimed leadership of this party even though he was based in the USA and had little to do with Kim Ku, its president.
- The Korean Communist Party (KCP) – based in the south and led by Pak Hon-Yong.
- North Korean Communist Party (NKCP) – formed in October 1945, it comprised returning exiles from Yennan in China, the Soviet Union and Korean communists.

The initial reaction to the Moscow Accords was mixed because many Koreans viewed the notion of trusteeship as a betrayal of Korean independence. The reaction was so strong because in 1905 the Japanese had taken over Korea under what they called a 'trusteeship'. The KDP, the KPG, and the Central Council for the Rapid Realisation of Korean Independence together with numerous small political factions formed the anti-trusteeship **Representative Democratic Council (RDC)** led by Syngman Rhee in early February 1946.

At the first meeting of the RDC, there were 28 political leaders, 24 from right-wing parties, four from the left. The popular KPR leaders were not represented because, in the eyes of the US military government, at least half of them were identified as having socialist and communist sympathies. Further, it was believed they were funded and given direction by the Soviet Union. The essential task of the RDC was to present a united front of South Korean political groups that the US could offer to the Soviet-US Joint Commission as a basis for the provisional government of all Korea.

Although very popular in the south, it would be wrong to assume that the KPR with its strong alliance of peasants, workers and some intellectuals could have provided the leadership for a provisional government in Korea. US reports in early 1946 viewed the leftist KPR as an instrument of Soviet influence in the south. The KPR did, however, continue to support the notion of trusteeship in spite of strong opposition from the RDC and the US military government.

In the north, the NKCP continued to support the idea of trusteeship for Korea and Kim Il Sung sought to achieve a unified front though the North Korean Interim People's Committee (NKIPC). NKIPC developed in February 1946 as a reaction to the development of the RDC. Its role was to assist in the process that would lead to a government for the whole of Korea.

WHY DID THE SOVIET–US JOINT COMMISSION FAIL?

The opposition of the RDC led by Syngman Rhee in the south provided the Soviets with an opportunity to influence the unification of Korea in their favour. According to **Kathryn Weathersby** in *Soviet Aims in Korea and the Origins of the Korean War, 1945–50: New Evidence from Russian Archives* (1993), documents reveal Stalin's commitment to a unified Korea but one that leaned heavily towards the Soviet Union. In a statement of support for trusteeship sent in 1947 to Stalin, the NKIPC in Pyongyang asserted:

[A]t the present time the three great powers Britain, US, and the Soviet Union are continuing to carry the responsibility for the leadership of the world. Therefore the decision of the Moscow Conference is a further development and strengthening of democracy … The decision was engendered by the situation which exists in Korea itself, specifically the ruinous consequences of the long period of Japanese imperial rule and the lack of national unity … Despite this, several individuals are attempting openly and directly to oppose the decision of the Moscow conference.

They portray the friendly aid and cooperation of the three states as the establishment of an imperialistic protectorate, similar to the earliest rule of Japanese aggressive imperialism.

According to US Under-Secretary of State Dean Acheson, the 'emotional popularity of Rhee, with his sympathy toward conservative banking, landlords and merchants, his opposition to the Moscow Accords and his ability to exploit this in his campaign against trusteeship' contributed to the eventual shift in US policy from trusteeship towards a separate unified state in South Korea in 1947.

Throughout the lengthy negotiations of the Joint Commission based in Seoul in the period 1946–7, Stalin and the Soviet government held firmly to the principle outlined in the Moscow Accords. They argued that any group opposed to the notion of trusteeship should be excluded from consultation on the formation of a provisional government. The representatives from the US refused this limitation since it would mean only those groups on the left, the NKCP and the KPR, would participate in forming the provisional government. As a compromise, in May 1947 the Soviet Union and the US agreed to exclude any group that instigated active opposition to the Moscow Accords.

Negotiations of the Joint Commission broke down again in June 1947 because the US refused to disqualify the RDC led by Syngman Rhee. The RDC continued to campaign against trusteeship and should have been excluded then from the Joint Commission consultations. Rhee had calculated that once the Joint Commission presented the US with the establishment of a left-wing provisional government dominated by the NKCP the talks would be abandoned. After November 1947, the RDC was used by General Hodge as an advisory body and went on to form the basis of the interim legislature.

THE ROLE OF THE UN AND THE CREATION OF TWO KOREAS

In an attempt to avoid civil war and to contain the threat of communist expansion in the south, in August 1947 President Truman proposed secret elections based on universal suffrage for all Koreans. The Soviet Union rejected the terms of the proposal because the communists in the north would be defeated. North Korea had a population of 8 million, in the south it was closer to 20 million. A counter-proposal was put forward by the Soviet Union that all occupying troops were to be removed from Korea during 1948. However, President Truman was keen to defend the fragile democracy in South Korea and so took the problem of elections to the UN in September 1947.

In a speech to the General Assembly of the UN in September 1947, Secretary of State Marshall outlined the reasons why the Americans were referring the issue of Korean elections to the UN. He clearly blamed the

Soviets for the failure to achieve agreement, but omitted the responsibility of the anti-trusteeship alliance led by Syngman Rhee for the breakdown of talks. The resolution of 14 November 1947 created the UN Temporary Commission on Korea (**UNTCOK**):

> *The General Assembly*
>
> *2 ... Resolves that in order to facilitate and expedite participation by the indigenous population and to observe that the Korean representatives are in fact duly elected by the Korean people and not mere appointees by military authorities in Korea, there be forthwith established a United Nations Temporary Commission on Korea, to be present in Korea, with right to travel, observe and consult throughout Korea. Further recommends that elections be held no later than 31 March 1948.*

UNTCOK was to replace the Joint Commission in taking Korea forward to unification and independence. Interestingly, the UN did not recognise the right of the US or Soviet military governments established in Korea to appoint representatives for the consultative process.

Following the creation of UNTCOK, the Soviets refused to recognise or admit the representatives to the northern zone, arguing that it did not conform with the Moscow Accords. In February 1948, the UN decided that if national elections were impossible, then elections could be held in South Korea. Syngman Rhee and his supporters led the opposition to this resolution because it would perpetuate the division of Korea. The US Congress, on the other hand, was keen to reduce economic and military aid to Korea in order to reduce the fiscal burden on US tax-payers. In late 1947, the **Joint Chiefs of Staff** had to make difficult choices regarding the occupation of Germany, Austria, Japan and Korea. In the opinion of Army Chief of Staff Dwight Eisenhower, Korea had little strategic interest and should the Soviets attempt to extend their control over the whole country the USA could neutralise this threat by 'air action'.

The creation of the Republic of Korea

In May 1948, UNTCOK supervised free elections in South Korea and the elected National Assembly selected Syngman Rhee as President of the Republic of Korea (ROK). Of the 7.8 million eligible voters, 95 per cent participated in the elections and the UN Commissioners declared the vote represented a valid expression of the people. In October 1948, the new republic was recognised by the UN and thus ended the role of General Hodge and the US military government. In June 1949, US forces withdrew from South Korea, leaving a 580-strong US Military Advisory Group. Under the leadership of Syngman Rhee in the south, a ruthless dictatorship had emerged by 1949. A peaceful transition to democracy was undermined by Rhee's dependency on army and police officers, a large number of whom had been trained by the Japanese, and the repression of all left-wing political parties.

Rebellion

An illustration of the repression of the regime is how it dealt with the communist-inspired rebellion on Cheju-do Island. In summer 1948, a rebellion had broken out in response to the government's unfair policy on the redistribution of land formerly held by the Japanese. The 2000 police sent to deal with the incident in October 1948 mutinied at Yeosu because they sympathised with the demands of the rebels who opposed not only the government's land policy but also the way in which grain was collected by the government and the use of 'colonial' police, those who had been trained by the Japanese to suppress any form of dissent. This revolt spread quickly and in November more police revolted at Taegu, the third largest city in the south. Rhee responded to the unrest by declaring martial law and removing leftist elements in the ROK constabulary. The rebellion was finally defeated at a cost of more than 1000 lives.

The creation of the Democratic People's Republic of Korea

In North Korea after the breakdown of the Joint Commission, the Soviets proceeded with elections to the Supreme People's Assembly in August 1948. In September 1948, the Democratic People's Republic of Korea (DPRK) was formed with Kim Il Sung as Premier. Having established a firm grip over the north, Stalin ordered Soviet troops to withdraw in December 1948, six months before their US counterparts in the south. In the north, land reform and the expansion of trade with the Soviet Union proceeded and in comparison with the south the transition to independence was more peaceful. However, unlike his counterpart in the south, Kim Il Sung chose to work through the PCs drawing on them for local support and local government and the formation of a police force that was locally rooted.

CONCLUSION

By 1948, the hopes of a united independent Korea had been crushed. The USSR and the US had established separate states in their own zones of Korea: a communist system was to be applied in the north, a capitalist system in the south. This division was not put in place primarily for the Koreans' benefit but was a product of the Cold War divisions that had developed between the superpowers. By 1948 any chance for a unified Korea by peaceful means seemed lost. Korean politics had polarised as a result of the division of the country and it seemed that only military action would bring about unification. The withdrawal of Soviet and US troops from Korea by the middle of 1949 left the situation in Korea very unstable. It was in this context that the Korean War was to take place.

CHAPTER 4

The outbreak of the Korean War, 1950

AN OVERVIEW

The immediate cause of the Korean War was the invasion of the south by the North Korean People's Army (NKPA) on 25 June 1950 in an attempt to unify Korea under the leadership of Kim Il Sung. In order to understand the developments that followed this invasion an analysis of the origins of the war needs to be made. It could be argued that the Korean War was not the result of global conflict, but rather it was brought about by the desire of both the Republic of Korea and the Democratic People's Republic of Korea for the unification of Korea and an end to foreign domination of their country.

NORTH KOREA

After the creation of the Democratic People's Republic of North Korea in 1948, Kim Il Sung was determined to push for the unification of Korea under his leadership. The success of the communists in the north was the result of a determined attempt by Kim Il Sung (supported by Joseph Stalin) to achieve a united communist party that was ideologically in line with the Soviet Union. In addition, the North Korean People's Committees (PCs), which were made up mainly of industrial workers and peasants, played an important role in the consolidation of Kim Il Sung's leadership. The PCs appointed and allocated police within each province with the outcome being a popular and locally rooted police force, unlike the police in the south who were associated with Japanese rule.

North Korean propagandists asserted that Kim Il Sung was a 'faithful disciple of Stalin'; indeed, in his consolidation of power he does appear to have imitated Stalin in the way he divided the **Yenan group** and in 1947 purged the domestic communists. In late 1948, Kim Il Sung's final act in the establishment of his credibility as leader of the communist movement for the whole of Korea was the absorption of the South Korean Worker's Party, led by Pak Hon-Yon well known for his resistance to the Japanese, into the North Korean Communist Party (NKCP). This action gained Kim Il Sung a great deal of credibility with southern communist insurgents fighting against the Rhee regime.

After 1945, Kim Il Sung had been determined to conduct a revolutionary communist campaign to unify Korea under his leadership. In the propaganda war that followed the creation of the Democratic People's Republic of North Korea in 1948, Kim Il Sung frequently accused Syngman Rhee's government of the continuity of colonialist type repression. According to **Peter Lowe** in *The Origins of the Korean War* (1986), Kim Il Sung was as ruthless as his counterpart in the south and was a passionate nationalist determined to restore self-respect to Korea after the careless handling of his country by the superpowers after 1945. Kim Il Sung's stated aims were to 'liquidate feudalism and remove foreign dominance, US or Soviet from Korea'.

The desire to unify the whole of Korea under a communist regime was therefore a powerful motivating factor for war, but the northern regime was dependent on the Soviet Union for military and economic support. Nevertheless, Kim Il Sung was determined to retain these ties no longer than was necessary to unify Korea. In addition, the timing of the invasion was well planned with the return of two major Korean combat divisions who had been fighting in the civil war in China. These experienced fighters increased the size of the NKPA to 135,000 troops, a much larger army than that of the south with 98,000 – of whom 33,000 were non-combat troops. In 1949, US intelligence also reported the development of the North Korean air force with around 36 Yak-9 fighter planes (bought from the Soviet Union) and the construction of five new airfields, four of which were close to the 38th Parallel.

SOUTH KOREA

In the south, Syngman Rhee had similar intentions but needed the economic and military support of the US to achieve the unification of Korea. Rhee differed from Kim Il Sung in that he wanted continued support from the US following unification as a safeguard against communist China and the Soviet Union as both countries bordered Korea. Initially, Rhee found it difficult to convince the US of the need to supply his government with the necessary military resources to achieve unification primarily because in 1949 the US remained focused on a Europe-first strategy. The US government also became concerned about supporting the increasingly brutal and corrupt regime of Rhee.

US POLICY

It is evident that US foreign policy in post-war Korea was clumsy and ill-conceived. This was reflected in the lack of understanding of the deep divisions that split the Koreans: divisions between Japanese collaborators and underground dissenters, between landowners and peasants, between business owners and factory workers, and between police and civilians. These divisions had lain beneath the surface before 1945, as the Japanese used the strategy of divide and rule in order to subdue the Koreans. The US administration in the country had viewed Korea as nothing more than a bastion against communist expansion with limited strategic value.

In his speech to the National Press Club on 12 January 1950, US Secretary of State Dean Acheson excluded Korea from the defensive perimeter made up of the Aleutians, the Philippines, Japan and Okinawa established in the Pacific. Traditional historians, including **David Rees**, argued that this speech, together with the withdrawal of US troops in 1949 encouraged the North Koreans to invade the south. However, the purpose of Acheson's speech was to show the success of Truman's policy of containment, that it could achieve peace and stability not only in Korea but elsewhere in Asia. If the nations of Asia developed strong and democratic institutions and stable economies they could withstand communist subversion and penetration, and were unlikely to need a guarantee of military protection from the US.

However, the Truman administration had aligned itself with Syngman Rhee who could retain his position only with the aid of corruption, repressive measures and oppressive force. As the Cold War intensified in Europe and China in the period 1948–9 the Truman administration was determined not to allow Korea to assume an importance it did not deserve. The US was willing to provide South Korea with the means to defend itself against the mounting guerrilla activity and offered an aid package in 1948 of US$150 million, delayed until February 1950, for economic rehabilitation, education and government improvements. These measures would, it was hoped, placate the population and boost support for the South Korean government. However, it was unwilling to provide large quantities of weapons and aircraft to the South Korean army. General William L Roberts, head of the Korean Military Advisory Group (KMAG) established by the US in 1949, requested additional aircraft for the South Korean air force. In 1950, South Korea had fourteen planes, a large, poorly equipped army whose loyalty to Syngman Rhee was questionable, no navy and only 500 KMAG troops.

WAS GLOBAL RIVALRY A CAUSE OF THE KOREAN WAR?

It would be over-simplistic to suggest that the outbreak of the Korean War was the result of the northern and southern leaderships' desire for unification. The role of the US and the Soviet Union in bringing about the war must be considered. They both helped to create the preconditions for war, especially in instigating the divide along the 38th Parallel which was a result of their global rivalry. The two superpowers also provided the political and economic support for each side and ultimately supplied the military equipment with which the war would be fought.

In spring 1949, Kim Il Sung approached Stalin to support an attack by North Korea against the South, but Stalin refused. He could not afford to provoke the US at this time because of the growing combativeness of the US towards the Soviet Union after the Berlin Blockade in 1948–9 (see page 29) and the creation of the North Atlantic Treaty Organisation (NATO) in Europe in April 1949 (see page 30). In September 1949, Stalin and the Politburo began to reconsider the merits of an invasion of South Korea. The Soviet Union had just detonated its first atomic bomb and China was now an ally following the creation of the People's Republic of

China in October 1949. Furthermore, US policy towards South Korea by 1950 was sufficiently ambiguous to enable Kim Il Sung to persuade Stalin that an attack on the south would not trigger a major US response.

Korean responsibility

The historical debate led by **Kathryn Weathersby** in *Korea, 1949–50, To attack, or Not to Attack? Stalin, Kim Il Sung and the Prelude to War* (1995) rejects the traditional view that the Korean War was an example of Soviet-inspired external aggression. Weathersby built on the work of **Cummings** *The Origins of the Korean War, vol. 2: The Roaring of the Cataract* (1990), in which he argued that the actions of both North and South Korea were ultimately responsible for the outbreak of war in June 1950. Weathersby concludes that the war's origins lay primarily with the division of Korea in 1945 and the polarisation of Korean politics that resulted from the policies of the two occupying powers. The Soviet Union played a key role in the outbreak of the war, but it was as a facilitator, not originator.

Soviet support

Recent Soviet documents published in the *Cold War International History Project (CWIHP) Bulletin*, Issue 2 (Summer 1993) clearly show that the impetus for war came from Kim Il Sung and not from Moscow. In March 1949, Kim first requested Stalin's support for an attack against the south together with technical, industrial and military support. **Weathersby** (1995) concludes from archival evidence published in *CWIHP* (autumn 1993) that at this time North Korea was utterly dependent economically on the Soviet Union. Throughout 1949 and into spring 1950, Kim constantly lobbied Stalin for support. In the early months of 1950, Kim then sought the views of Mao Zedong, who agreed that only military action was capable of unifying Korea. The new documents reveal clearly how Kim Il Sung was able to play the Soviets off against the Chinese. For example, on 19 January 1950, General Terentii F Shtykov, the Soviet Ambassador to North Korea, reported a conversation he had overheard when Kim stated that 'if the Russians would not help him unify his country, Mao Zedong his friend will always help Korea'.

In April 1950, Kim Il Sung met Stalin again to seek support for an invasion into the south. Stalin finally agreed to support Kim on the understanding that a decisive victory would be achieved and that escalation of the war was impossible. Stalin and the Politburo were prepared to supply North Korea with military equipment, but there would be no direct Soviet intervention. On 13 May 1950, Mao, having met secretly with Kim Il Sung that day, wrote to Stalin seeking clarification of his position on the potential North Korean action to reunify the country. Stalin's response to Mao reveals a key turning point in the movement towards war by the north:

> *In a conversation with Korean comrades Filipov [Stalin] and his friends expressed the opinion, that in the light of the changed international*

situation, they agree with the proposal of the Koreans to move towards reunification. In this regard a qualification was made that the question should be decided finally by the Chinese and Korean comrades together, and in the case of disagreement by the Chinese comrades the decision on the question should be postponed until a new discussion.

This document reveals two important issues related to the war. First, Mao was clearly under pressure from Stalin to agree with the invasion of South Korea because, should the plans go wrong, he could argue that it was China that supported the decision to go to war, not the Soviet Union. Second, Stalin was suggesting that the Soviet leaders had altered their position after long resisting Kim's appeals due to the 'changed international situation'. The issue that interests historians is what had changed. As early as 30 January 1950 Stalin had indicated in correspondence with Shtykov, Soviet Ambassador in Pyongyang, that he was ready to approve Kim's request to attack the south, and to provide material assistance in the form of weapons and Soviet military advisers. Stalin's statement came less than three weeks after US Secretary of State Dean Acheson's famous National Press Club Speech (see pages 47–8) of 12 January 1950, in which he excluded Korea from the US's defensive perimeter in Asia. In addition, there was evidence from South Korea's elections to the National Assembly in May 1950 that Syngman Rhee's popularity was diminishing.

In an immediate sense, the signing of the Sino–Soviet Treaty in February 1950 increased Stalin's confidence in dealing with the US in north-east Asia. Stalin may have also been alluding to other more momentous developments in the international scene, especially the establishment of a revolutionary communist government in China and the Soviet's atomic bomb success in 1949, ending the four-year US nuclear monopoly.

US FOREIGN POLICY AND THE ORIGINS OF THE WAR

After the fall of China and the explosion of the Soviet atomic bomb, the US administration began to question its military capabilities in a world in which balance of power appeared to be shifting in favour of communism. The Truman Doctrine of containment was perceived to be too defensive and the US had come to rely too much on atomic weapons as a means of deterrence. The discussion document NSC 68 presented to Truman in April 1950 (see page 31) reaffirmed the Europe-first strategy and characterised the Cold War as an ideological struggle of global proportions. The authors of the report asserted that the Soviet Union was intent on expanding communism throughout Asia and Europe, and conventional forces were the most appropriate to block this.

However, at this time the Truman administration wanted a reduction in taxes, making the mobilisation of additional resources to fund an expansion of the armed forces very difficult. In May 1950, Truman even discussed a further reduction in defence spending. The outbreak of war in Korea validated the arguments for the additional defence resources put forward in NSC 68. On 27 June 1950, Truman justified the US's response to the North Korean attack on South Korea two days previously, on 25 June, by stating that, 'the attack upon South Korea makes it plain beyond all doubt that communism has passed beyond the use of subversion to conquer independent nations and will now use armed invasion and war'.

This reaction to events in Korea showed a clear change in policy when compared to the civil war in China. The White Paper on China produced by Secretary of State Acheson in autumn 1949 led to widespread criticism of Truman's Asia policies. The White Paper stated that it was impossible to continue to support the nationalist forces in China because Chiang Kai Shek lacked any cohesive support. In addition, Acheson refused to send in US military forces to prop up what was perceived by many in the US as a weak and corrupt regime. The idea took root in the US, fostered by the China lobby in Congress and the anti-communist campaign of Republican Senator Joseph McCarthy in Washington, that it was a lack of will and latent sympathy for communism in the administration that had led to the 'loss' of China. The explosion by the Soviet Union of its first atomic bomb five years before the date predicted by the National Security Council compounded the shock of the loss of mainland China.

The Red Scare and McCarthyism

The Red Scare that swept through the US in the early 1950s was further fuelled by the claims of Senator Joseph McCarthy in a speech in February 1950 that he knew of '57 cases of individuals who would appear to be either card-carrying members or certainly loyal to the Communist Party, but who nevertheless are still shaping our foreign policy'. This list of names was not a secret and had been published by the Secretary of State in 1947 after the initial screening of 3000 federal employees under the Federal Employee Loyalty Programme initiated by President Truman.

McCarthy's claim of a list of names was followed up in further speeches throughout 1950 and through his activities as chair of the Government Committee on Operations of the Senate. McCarthy found no real evidence of communist subversion; he probably had no list. Nevertheless, thousands of Americans were willing to believe him. In June 1951, the Supreme Court joined in the anti-communist crusade when it upheld the conviction of the US Communist Party under the Smith Act 1940, which outlawed teaching or advocating the overthrow of government. The anti-communist campaign also extended to the entertainment industry and universities, and underlined the strength of feeling among the American people.

In February 1950, Secretary of State Acheson, under pressure from the Republicans and some Democrats, publicly revised his view of Mao's victory in China by stating that 'evidence has shown that Moscow had trained the leadership in order to establish communist control over China'. Truman and his administration were now moving towards the so-called monolithic view of communism, whereby all communist activity throughout the world was inspired by Stalin and the Soviet Union. The perception was that the Soviets were exerting their influence in all the civil wars now taking place in Asia. It was no coincidence that Truman announced the decision to aid France in its struggle in Vietnam at this time (see page 79).

It is possible that Truman's actions in June 1950 after the invasion of South Korea were a response to the Republican allegations that he and the Democrats were soft on communism. The Republicans, who had been kept out of power for seventeen years, were hungry for political ammunition in order to discredit Truman. Having paid limited attention to the social and political unrest in South Korea, Truman now felt that 'losing' Korea would be a mistake he could ill afford to make. He felt compelled to hold the line in Asia and, after the fall of China to communism, he extended the Truman Doctrine to south and north-east Asia. US policymakers now came to the conclusion that Soviet expansion had reached a point beyond which it must not be permitted to go.

Truman and his administration viewed the North Korean attack as further evidence of Soviet aggression against an independent state that lay outside its sphere of control. The unanimous opinion within the Truman administration was this was a test of US resolve by the Soviet Union. If it did not act to counter this aggression, then the Soviet Union would move against other small states considered to be in the US sphere of influence – West Germany, Japan and Taiwan. The US, as co-founder and therefore guarantor of South Korea, was honour bound to defend South Korea.

JAPAN AND THE OUTBREAK OF THE KOREAN WAR
Japan played a crucial role in the chain of events leading to the Korean War. Complex issues involving the ending of the occupation of Japan by the US and the repercussions for powers in east Asia were closely linked. When Japan was first occupied by the US in 1945, the aim was to democratise Japanese society, end militarism and through tough reparations end Japan's economic competitiveness in the world markets. However, within the State Departments there was a fear that if the US imposed a punitive occupation on Japan it would push it into the Soviet sphere of influence.

In the period 1946–9, the US supported the Japanese with aid of US$500 million a year in an attempt to rebuild their shattered economy. A revived Japan, it was argued by George Kennan, would provide a bulwark against the Soviet Union and contribute to the economic revival of the newly independent states in south and north-east Asia. Japan, with its industrial *zaibatsu* (powerful companies such as Toyota, Honda, Sony) and a large concentration of skilled labour, was identified by Kennan in 1947 as one of the world's five most important military and industrial centres. Thus, in the period 1945–50 Japan's economy was reinforced with aid from the US while at the same time its political and military power was removed.

The success of the communists in China in 1949, together with the European crisis, accentuated concern over the vulnerability of Japan. The fall of China had also led to a power vacuum in Asia. The US was keen to build up Japan, rather than South Korea, as a major power and military ally to assist it in the Pacific region. NSC 48/1, discussed in December 1949, sought to establish a triangular trade system between the US, Japan and south-east Asia. It also called for a positive policy towards communist-held territory in east Asia; the goal was to 'contain and where feasible to reduce the power and influence of the Soviet Union in Asia'.

THE ROLE OF THE UNITED NATIONS

When Truman was informed that large numbers of the North Korean People's Army led by General Chai Ung Jun had crossed the 38th Parallel on 25 June 1950, his immediate thought was to block this act of aggression through appealing to the UN to use military force. Truman had witnessed events in the 1930s when failure to act by the democracies encouraged Italian, German and Japanese aggression against smaller nations and ultimately led to world war. He was aware that if the US and the UN failed to support the Republic of Korea, nations faced with similar threats would not have the courage to resist aggression by stronger communist neighbours in the future.

The attack by the NKPA was viewed by the UN as an act of aggression initiated without warning and without provocation. South Korea had been under the protection of the UN Security Council since 1947, when UNTCOK was formed to supervise elections in both North and South Korea and to assist in the eventual unification of Korea. On the same day as the attack, the US called on the UN for a resolution requiring the NKPA to cease hostilities immediately and withdraw its forces to the 38th Parallel. The UN Security Council passed this resolution by 9 votes to 0. The Soviet Union was absent from the meeting when the vote was taken, having withdrawn from the Security Council because the UN had given China's seat in the Security Council to Taiwan (an island off mainland China) rather than recognise the communist People's Republic of China.

The US response

Truman asked General Douglas MacArthur, the Far East Commander based in Japan, to survey the conditions in South Korea. In his report, MacArthur stated that the NKPA forces appeared to be overwhelming those of the Republic of Korea. After the Blair House meeting of 25 June 1950, the Joint Chiefs of Staff (JCS), Secretary of State Acheson and

Truman agreed on the immediate evacuation of the families of US military and diplomatic personnel. Naval and air power was to be used to defend Syngman Rhee's government, the South Korean troops and the 580 US military advisers against further attacks by the NKPA. The US Seventh Fleet was to be repositioned off the Taiwan coast to protect it from moves by the People's Republic of China. At this point, Truman was seriously concerned about the wider global implications of the communist threat against the Republic of Korea. Without consulting Rhee, Truman and the JCS initially defined the objective of US intervention as the restoration of the situation prior to the North Korean attack.

By 27 June 1950, it was apparent to the Truman administration that the aims of Kim Il Sung and the NKPA were nothing less than the complete take-over of the Korean Peninsula. By this date, Seoul, the capital of South Korea, had fallen and large areas of the country were now under the control of the NKPA despite desperate fighting by the South Korean troops. Broadcasting from Pyongyang in North Korea, Kim Il Sung now stated that the aims of the NKPA were to crush South Korea as swiftly as possible. President Truman and Secretary of State Acheson, convinced that the Soviet Union was providing the NKPA with military support, believed this attack showed that the communists had now passed from the use of subversion and guerrilla attacks to armed invasion in order to conquer independent nations.

The US then called on the UN for a second resolution to provide military support for the Republic of Korea (ROK). The second UN resolution, passed on 27 June, called for the creation of a UN Joint Command Force (UNC) that would fight alongside the South Korean troops to remove the NKPA from South Korea. However, the problems facing South Korea were desperate and the creation of the new US armed forces called for in NSC 68 was going to take time.

On 25 June 1950, Truman ordered US troops in occupied Japan, but not Europe, to be drafted to South Korea. Truman and Acheson were still apprehensive about the role of the Soviet Union in this new conflict. They believed the Korean conflict was a diversion created by Stalin to draw US troops away from the defence of

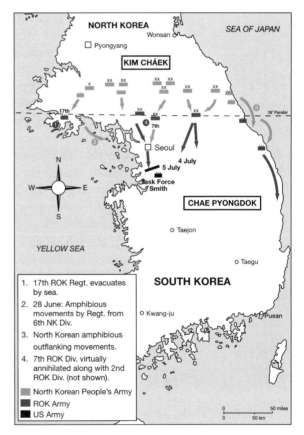

The North Korean Invasion, 25 June 1950

Europe, giving the Soviet Union an opportunity to extend its influence in Europe. If this should happen, they envisaged other European states entering into non-aggressive pacts with the Soviet Union and ultimately weakening their ties with the USA. For Truman, therefore, it was imperative that the conflict in Korea was brought to a quick end and for this reason he continued to put pressure on the UN to enforce the resolution passed on 27 June. Interestingly, before the resolution was passed by the UN, Truman had already sanctioned the use of US troops in South Korea. Furthermore, he had not referred the case of South Korea to Congress and had entered the war against the NKPA without seeking its permission.

Under pressure from the US for the first time since its founding the UN reacted to aggression with a decision to use armed force. Some 53 members responded to the Security Council's call for assistance, 29 of whom made specific offers of assistance of troops, military and medical equipment. The UN acknowledged the US as the major contributor of military assistance and appointed President Truman as the executive agent for the UN Security Council to execute its rules of engagement and General MacArthur as commander in the field, with a base in Japan. The US Joint Chiefs of Staff, the National Security Council, together with the Department of State, developed the military operations in Korea. By these actions the UN ensured that the US would be unable to withdraw from the conflict and would continue to support the war against the North Koreans.

CONCLUSION

The outbreak of the Korean War was provoked by events within Korea and by factors that were Korean in origin. The war was a civil war over the unification and future direction of Korea, but it became an issue of ideological conflict within the context of superpower rivalry engendered by the Cold War. The attitudes of the superpowers were to magnify the significance of the issues involved in this conflict. Pressures exerted by Stalin and Mao on Kim Il Sung played a part in determining the timing of the outbreak, as perhaps did Dean Acheson's statement in January 1949 that Korea was outside the US defensive perimeter in the Far East. Once the war had begun the superpowers were also important in determining the scale of the conflict. For Truman, under pressure at home from Republican critics and McCarthyite fanatics, the stakes were high. The American government by using the UN ensured that its Allies were also committed to the defence of freedom and against communism.

CHAPTER 5

The progress and outcome of the Korean War, 1950–53

AN OVERVIEW

The course of the Korean War was to involve a succession of rapid manoeuvres. First was the invasion by the North Korean army who were able to push the South Koreans to a small foothold around Pusan. Second, was the rapid counter offensive by UN forces led by General Douglas MacArthur which pushed north, over the 38th Parallel and towards the border with China. The success of this operation led the US government and its military to consider changing its policy from containing to rolling back communism. Finally there was an offensive by the Chinese and North Korean forces that was able to push south again to a line very close to the 38th Parallel where the war had started. There then existed a stalemate at the frontline.

The geographical make-up of Korea was such that the mountainous regions together with extremes of temperature, from 0° to 40° centigrade, were totally unsuitable for the operations of the UN forces. In addition, between Pyongyang and Wonsan the peninsula narrows to under 100 miles in an area that was to achive major significance as the UN forces struggled to achive a demarcation zone in North Korea.

To break the stalemate, MacArthur renewed his call for atomic bombs to be used against China. MacArthur's warmongering was beginning to cause tension between himself and President Truman. His demands and attitude amounted to insubordination. Truman sacked the general in April 1951 and replaced him with General Matthew Ridgway. Under Ridgway the stalemate continued and, in July 1951, both sides were ready to open peace talks at a teahouse at Kaesong.

The peace talks at Kaesong took place while heavy fighting continued and soon broke down. They were to resume later in the year at Panmunjon, although to little effect until early 1953.

In 1952 Dwight Eisenhower had won the presidential election in the US on the slogan 'I shall go to Korea'. This was widely interpreted by the American public as a desire to end the war. Thus, when taking office in January 1953 Eisenhower was ready to bring the peace talks to a conclusion. March 1953 saw another significant change of leadership when Joseph Stalin died. The new Soviet leadership was willing to see an end to the war and by this point the Koreans themselves were increasingly war-weary. On 27 July 1953 an armistice was finally agreed. China, North Korea and the US signed the cease-fire. South Korea refused to do so, but had little alternative other than to accept it.

BIOGRAPHIES

General Douglas MacArthur (1880–1964) On 15 August 1945, MacArthur was named Supreme Commander for the Allied Powers in the Pacific, and in that capacity he accepted the surrender of Japan aboard the USS *Missouri* on 2 September 1945. From his role as a military leader, MacArthur now became head of the Allied occupation of Japan. On 14 July 1950, he was named Commander in Chief of the UN forces (UNC) in South Korea. A controversial individual, he was, on the one hand, a brilliant strategist masterminding the Inchon landing and the counter-offensives against the NKPA and the CPV forces, but on the other, was an outspoken critic of Truman's plans in Korea. Fearful of MacArthur's plans to extend the war by bombing key targets in North Korea and China, Truman relieved him of his command on 11 April 1951.

Zhou Enlai (1898–1976) From 1927, he held a number of key positions in the Chinese Communist Party. He was the first premier of the People's Republic of China. He was an excellent negotiator and diplomat. He mediated disputes within the Party and in later years played an important role in handling the affairs of the PRC both with communist and non-communist countries.

Mao Zedong (1893–1976) In October 1949, Mao and the communists declared the People's Republic of China. During the Long March of 1934, Mao rose to command the Chinese Communist Party. In the period 1934–49 the struggle was initially against the Japanese and later the Guomindang, the Nationalist Chinese supported by the US. Once in power, Mao initiated ideologically driven policies including the destruction of the traditional elites and the elevation of the peasants in the countryside. Key sectors of the economy were rapidly brought under communist control.

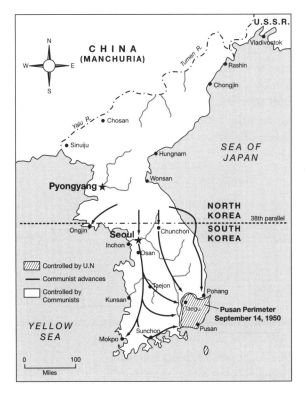

The North Korean advance, Summer 1950

General Matthew Bunker Ridgway (1895–1993) An experienced soldier in the Second World War, Ridgway led the US Eighth Army in the Korean War after the death of General Walton Walker in 1950, and replaced MacArthur as leader of the UN forces in Korea in 1951. Ridgway used a strategy of **attrition** involving a series of campaigns with limited objectives, which proved effective against the Chinese.

THE COMMUNIST ADVANCE

Throughout July 1950, the overwhelming power of the North Korean People's Army (NKPA) forced the combined UNC/ROK troops back to the south-east corner of Korea. In seventeen days of fighting the combined UNC/ROK force had been driven back more than 110 kilometres. On 29 July, General Walker, the commander of the US Eighth Army, issued a 'stand or die' order and created a defensive line known as the **Pusan Perimeter**. This defensive line ran north around the vital port of Pusan through which most of the US forces arrived from Japan with heavy military equipment. In addition, in this area Walker set about rebuilding the shattered divisions of the ROK and began to build the UN forward command line. The combined UNC/ROK forces at this time amounted to 100,000 men; they faced 150,000 NKPA troops, skilled fighters many of whom had fought as North Korean volunteers under Mao in the civil war in China. Walker's troops had limited military experience and equipment, and were no match for the hardened, experienced fighters of the north. In July, General MacArthur requested a further eight divisions to bring the troop strength up to a point whereby they could begin the counter offensive on the NKPA and force their way back to the 38th Parallel. By early August, the North Korean troops, far from being intimidated by the presence of US troops, continued to push southwards.

THE US RESPONSE

Truman was aware that the cuts in defence expenditure since the end of the Second World War had taken a heavy toll on the military capability of the troops defending South Korea. In June 1950, he returned to Congress in order to win support for an increase in military spending that would allow the US forces to counter the threat from communist North Korea. This required Congress to increase the military budget from US$13 billion in 1950 to US$48.2 billion by 1951, and expand the US armed forces from 630,000 in summer 1950 to 1,500,000 by 1955 to meet the global threat of the Soviet Union. The total mobilisation of the armed forces in the period 1920–52, including the army, navy, air force and the reserves, can be seen in Table 5.1.

Table 5.1 US troop numbers, 1920–52

Years	Active average	Wartime peak
1920–40	284,600	
1945		12,055,884
1946–50	1,826,900	
1952		3,636,912

Source: **Christopher Deering**, 'Congress, the President and Military Policy', *Annals of the US Academy of Political and Social Science*, 499 (September 1988) pp. 136–47.

Inchon landing

With Walker containing the threat from the NKPA in the Pusan area, General MacArthur started planning a more decisive action in the north, the Inchon landing (code named 'Operation Chromite'). This decisive action required the US forces to get behind the main NKPA forces and destroy their communication lines. By making a surprise amphibious landing on the western shore of Korea at the port of Inchon the newly formed X Command, made up of the US Tenth Corps consisting of 70,000 men together with the First Marine Division, could sever North Korean lines of communication and trap its army in the south. The project required the troops of X Command to disembark from assault craft when the tide was high and fight their way through to the city of Inchon and beyond to capture the airfield at Kimpo. As a result of this offensive, the ROK government in the capital of South Korea, Seoul, was restored. The success of the Inchon landing and the reestablishment of the South Korean government in Seoul on 15 September 1950 instilled a new confidence in the USA. Although the Inchon landing was full of risks because of the difficult geographical factors, it was an outstanding success for MacArthur and X Command. This attack, together with the breakout of Walker's troops in the south, trapped more than half the NKPA troops between the US Seventh Division in the north and the Eighth Division in the south. By 1 October, the combined UNC forces were back at the 38th Parallel.

TRUMAN AND THE CHANGE OF POLICY FROM CONTAINMENT TO 'ROLL BACK'

Truman and the Joint Chiefs of Staff now had to face the difficult decision of how to end the conflict in Korea. They could return Korea to its position before the invasion. However, a substantial part of the NKPA had retreated and this would continue to pose a threat to the existence of ROK. Complete victory and the reunification of Korea, a long-standing aim of the US and the UN, was also a possibility, but there was always the fear of intervention in the war by China who, as a long-term ally of North Korea, had proposed a Treaty of Friendship, Alliance and Mutual Assistance in May 1950.

Truman and the Joint Chiefs of Staff, confident that they had now won a major victory against the NKPA, contemplated changing their foreign policy from one of the containment of communism to that of the **roll back** of communism in the north. Truman and his administration, through a broad reading of the UN resolution of 27 June 1950, assumed that UNC forces needed to restore 'peace and security in the area' (Korea). This could not happen if the NKPA remained active in the north after a ceasefire. The only way to deter future aggression in South Korea was to unify Korea under a new government, preferably one ideologically closer to the US.

The UN Security Council was encouraged by the US to support entry into North Korea in order to bring about the reunification of Korea and the removal of communism. The tone of communications between Truman and the UN was that the UNC forces should be viewed as liberators rather than as seeking retaliation for the humiliation of the invasion of South Korea. President Truman continually described the US-led effort in Korea as a 'police action' determined to halt the aggression of the north. Truman was equally determined to avoid foreign-policy decisions that would force the Soviet Union and China to take action. Therefore, a case could be made for halting MacArthur at the 38th Parallel. Secretary of State Dean Acheson reiterated that the UN had intervened solely for the purpose of restoring the ROK to its status prior to the invasion; stopping would therefore be in line with the US policy of containment.

Problems for the USA

On the other hand, the major problem faced by the US at this time was that it could no longer work through the Security Council. The delegate from the Soviet Union had returned to his seat in August 1950 and would use the veto against any attempts by the USA to resolve the Korean problem. In order to avoid this complication, the US delegation moved the Korean question to the General Assembly of the UN where the Soviet Union had no veto power and where the US influence greatly outweighed that of the Soviet Union. On 7 October its resolution demanded that:

> *All appropriate steps be taken to ensure conditions of stability throughout Korea; and, all constituent acts be taken including the holding of elections, under the auspices of the United Nations, for the establishment of a unified independent and democratic government in the sovereign State of Korea.*

The resolution also established the UN Committee for the Reunification and Rehabilitation of Korea, which replaced UNTCOK. The resolution was used by the Truman administration to justify the change of policy in Korea and allowed UNC forces to cross the 38th Parallel in order to destroy the NKPA.

CHINESE INTERVENTION

The Inchon attack was a major turning point in the war because, more than any other factor (as has been argued by **Weathersby** (1993)), it was the reason for the entry of communist China into the Korean War on 14 October 1950. China, already concerned by the war in Korea, had despatched four armies to the North Korean border and had sent messages to the USA via KM Panikkar, the Indian Ambassador in Beijing, saying it would not tolerate US troops on its border. After the fall of China to communism in 1949, all US embassies in China were closed because the Chinese Communist leadership believed that the Nationalist forces of Chiang Kai Shek had been funded by the USA in the civil war in an attempt to block the victory of communism. Far East officials in the State Department warned Truman that a 'combination of expansionism, Soviet pressure and inducements, strategic anxieties, ideological zeal, domestic pressures and anti-Americanism might lead China to intervene in the war'.

Secretary of State Acheson, on the other hand, felt that China would not intervene in Korea for two main reasons.

- It would lose the opportunity to claim its seat on the UN Security Council.
- It would be dependent on the Soviet Union for military support to be able to wage war.

Therefore, the Joint Chiefs of Staff and Truman convinced themselves that US policies in the Far East presented no threat to China. However, the problem for the Truman administration was that Washington had no direct links with Beijing and therefore no way of knowing how Mao and the Chinese leadership viewed events in Korea. General MacArthur had made confident assurances to Truman at the Wake Island Conference on 15 October 1950 that the war in Korea would be over by Christmas and that there was very little chance of Chinese or Soviet intervention. Little did he know that the Chinese had already decided to enter the war on 14 October.

Reasons for China's entry into the Korean War

The question is why did Mao choose to enter the war at this point? Was it because of Soviet pressure to intervene or to help the North Koreans resist defeat?

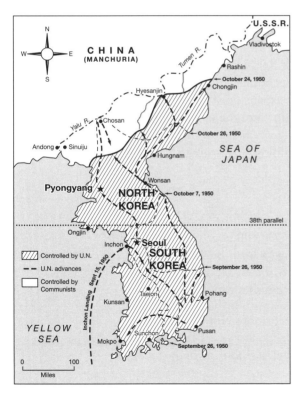

The UN Offensive, Autumn 1950

As the situation in the south deteriorated for the NKPA after the Inchon landing, Stalin urged Kim Il Sung to halt the offensive along the Pusan Perimeter and to redeploy his troops around Seoul and the north-east. However, even though the military situation in South Korea had become critical with the loss of contact with the front-line command in the south, Kim refused to redeploy his troops. At the beginning of October, Kim Il Sung wrote to Stalin pleading for direct military assistance to block the advance of the UNC forces across the 38th Parallel. Stalin was reluctant to engage in direct combat with the US and sent a request to Mao to despatch five or six divisions towards the 38th Parallel to support the NKPA. In addition, Stalin offered Mao shared command over the Chinese 'volunteer' troops and the NKPA if he entered the war. In the period between 27 September and 5 October 1950, the Soviet Politbuo adopted a major policy shift towards Korea. The leadership decided to limit Soviet military and political exposure in Korea while at the same time permitting greater involvement by China.

Traditional interpretations of the involvement of the Chinese in the Korean War assume that Mao had entered the war in response to the crossing of the 38th Parallel. A number of warnings had been sent via the Indian Ambassador in Beijing to the UN Command stating that should UN troops cross the 38th Parallel, China would enter the war. However, recent archival evidence has shown that Mao was reluctant to send troops into North Korea. A number of reasons are given.

- The Politburo of the Chinese Communist Party (CCP) was reluctant to engage in a war with the USA.
- The Chinese army was poorly armed and ill-prepared.
- China had little confidence it could defeat the modern military might of the USA.

Despite placing pressure on Chinese Prime Minister and Foreign Minister Zhou Enlai, Stalin found it difficult to convince the Chinese leadership of the need to send troops into North Korea. Was Mao's reluctance a carefully devised strategy to get additional military aid and equipment out of the Soviet Union or was he genuinely afraid of becoming entangled in a major conflict with the US? Certainly Stalin had decided by 6 October that he would rather abandon North Korea than engage in direct military confrontation with the US. On 14 October, Mao telegraphed Stalin to state that the CCP Politburo had finally decided after an emergency meeting to intervene in the Korean War before it ended in a victory for the US. The reason given was that the People's Republic of China (PRC) could not countenance having US troops on its border. Interestingly, the new evidence reveals that rather than form an expansionist cohesive force, the Soviet Union, the People's Republic of China and the North Koreans pursued policies during the war that were more amenable to their own domestic politics and used intra-alliance bargaining to get what they wanted.

China enters the Korean War
On 14 October 1950, Mao announced the formation of the Communist Party Volunteers Army Corps (CPV), a force of 300,000 poorly equipped but experienced fighters under the command of Peng Dehuai. By 28 October, the two armies had engaged in their first major battle which the UN forces won. The CPV were then involved in further skirmishes with the enemy.

- On 1 October 1950, the Republic of Korea's troops crossed the 38th Parallel.
- The US Eighth Army followed on 7 October and took Pyongyang on 20 October.
- The X Command seized Wonsan, an important port on the east coast on 26 October.

These first engagements were a carefully calculated strategy by the CPV; it wanted the UNC forces to view the Chinese as a weak force, thereby encouraging MacArthur and Walker to continue with their advance into North Korea. By late October, the UNC forces had penetrated deep into North Korea. However, the confidence of the UN commanders led to an overextension of their supply lines thus making it easier for the Chinese forces to encircle the UNC troops. In late October, the two armies engaged in fierce fighting with the CPV defeating the ROK Second Corps, and cutting off the US First and Ninth Marine Corps and US Second Infantry Division. By 25 November, the combined UNC forces were cut off in North Korea and the PRC's involvement in the war clearly established.

US REASONS FOR A LIMITED WAR IN KOREA

Truman was unwilling to engage in full-scale war with China but, on the other hand, he was not prepared to abandon Korea. In a press conference on 30 November he pointed out:

> *We may suffer reverses as we have suffered them before. But the forces of the United Nations have no intention of abandoning their mission in Korea … We shall continue to work in the United Nations for concerted action to halt this aggression in Korea. We shall intensify our efforts to help other free nations strengthen their defences in order to meet the threat of aggression elsewhere. We shall rapidly increase our military strength.*

In the same press conference, when pressed by reporters about the use of the atomic bomb, Truman replied: 'There has always been active consideration of its use. It is a terrible weapon.' When pressed further about the role of the UN and the bomb, he responded: 'The action against Communist China depends on the action of the UN. The military commander in the field will have charge of the use of weapons, as he always has.'

However, Truman was unwilling to move the war to mainland China.

- The Sino–Soviet Mutual Alliance would require the Soviets to enter the war on the side of their ally, China.
- The European allies of the US were deeply concerned at the thought of an expanded war, and Truman could ill afford to alienate any of his NATO allies because if the war should expand the US needed to be able to launch counter-attacks against the Soviets from Britain and Germany.
- Truman's greatest fear was that the US would become embroiled in a very expensive war in Asia. The more resources it expended in Asia, the fewer there would be for a potential conflict in Europe. Truman, the NSC and the Joint Chiefs of Staff were convinced that Stalin and the Soviet Union were behind the events in Korea, and Stalin's intention was to draw resources away from Europe so that he could extend his sphere of influence in Germany.
- Truman understood the US armed forces were poorly prepared for all-out war. In December 1950, he declared a national emergency and the

creation of the Office of Defence Mobilisation with sweeping powers to build up US military capacity.

THE UN SEEKS A RESOLUTION OF THE CONFLICT

At the end of November 1950, the US came under intensified allied pressure to end fighting in Korea. Unable to use the Security Council now the Soviet Union had returned, the US was forced to use the General Assembly. On 14 December, a resolution was passed in the General Assembly that called for the creation of a three-person group 'to determine the basis on which a satisfactory cease-fire in Korea can be arranged'. In response, the Chinese:

- condemned the resolution as illegal
- demanded the withdrawal of all foreign troops from Korea
- viewed the cease-fire as a means to secure time for UN forces in Korea to regroup for another offensive.

Nevertheless, on 13 January 1951 the UN Three-Person Armistice Committee presented to the UN General Assembly its five principles for ending the war. These included:

- a cease-fire
- foreign troop withdrawals from Korea
- UN supervision of Korea prior to unification
- a national Korean government
- a General Assembly to seek the peaceful resolution of issues in the East.

On 17 January, the Chinese rejected the principles. The US now moved to present a resolution in the UN condemning China as the aggressor in Korea and called for additional measures to be deployed to meet this aggression. There was no support from the UN for any further measures against the Chinese other than the possibility of an economic embargo.

UN SPRING AND SUMMER OFFENSIVES, 1951

The delays by the Chinese allowed the UN ground forces now led by General Ridgway who replaced General Walker (died December 1950) the opportunity to rebuild the morale of the UN forces after the winter and spring offensives of 1951.

Disregarding reports from the front about the intervention by the CPV army, Generals MacArthur and Walker would not allow any UNC forces to retreat before 28 November from positions in the north. By then most of the escape routes south had been blocked by the Chinese forces, trapping elements of the US Second Division and the US First Marine Corps at the Choisin Reservoir. The retreat of the majority of the UNC forces was, in the words of Captain Charles Bussey, a humiliating defeat:

We'd been humiliated, debased, overwhelmed – routed – Intelligence said they hit us with one-third of a million men. They turned our army into a leaderless horde, running headlong for Pusan. Our soldiers had lost every bit of confidence in all of their leaders, from the commander in chief to platoon leaders.

In the months following the disastrous rout from the North, General Ridgway instituted attrition as the new operational doctrine of the US Eighth Army. This meant a gradual wearing-down of the enemy by the use of heavy artillery and close air support. A second aspect of attrition was the limited objective attack, which concentrated on killing as many of the enemy as possible. Throughout the spring and summer offensives of 1951, Ridgway launched a series of limited objective attacks named Operations 'Killer', 'Ripper' and 'Rugged'. The communists in turn generally avoided a serious battle and in this way the UNC forces were able to extend their territorial control above the 38th Parallel.

Despite the success of Ridgway's strategy of attrition, General MacArthur never accepted it. The strategic objective of the UNC forces had now changed from one of the unification of Korea to a negotiated armistice. MacArthur instead called for a further escalation of the war with the bombing of strategic sites in China. After some discussion, Truman and the Joint Chiefs of Staff agreed that MacArthur would have to be removed.

THE DISMISSAL OF GENERAL MACARTHUR

MacArthur had been an outspoken critic of the lack of will by Truman and his administration to take a more aggressive stance against the North Koreans and then the Chinese. These criticisms revolved around the administration's failure to share his view that Asia and not Europe had become the decisive theatre of global struggle against communist expansion in the Cold War. MacArthur complained in December 1950 that the 'Europe Firsters', including Secretary of State Acheson and President Truman, did not recognise that Asia had been selected for the first test of communist power. The loss of Nationalist China and the problems in Korea revealed the extent of communist influence in Asia. Should the expansion of communist influence in Asia continue, MacArthur argued in a letter to Truman in March 1951, Europe would not have a chance with or without US assistance.

Despite Truman's order of December 1950 to restrict public comments to the press, MacArthur continued to make comments indicating discontent with the restrictions imposed by the Truman administration on military action. He argued that the blockading and bombing of industrial and military targets on mainland China would bring the war to a speedy conclusion. This continual criticism of the way in which Truman was handling the war came to a head in April 1951 when the Joint Chiefs of Staff and Secretary of State Acheson requested the recall, but not the sacking, of MacArthur. The great fear of Truman was that MacArthur would use his authority as Field Commander to expand the air war into China.

Far from being an example of presidential power, the removal of MacArthur from his position as Field Commander during the Korean War was, in fact, a confession of weakness. Truman had failed to influence the events as he chose in Korea. MacArthur wanted air attacks against China and Manchuria, but Truman did not want to risk starting a Third World War. The removal of MacArthur, a popular figure in the US, only confirmed what many had begun to suspect – that Truman was unsure of the way forward with the war, whereas MacArthur was very clear. The only way to create peace and stability in Korea was by destroying the North Korean army and possibly the CPV army. In this way, the US could guarantee the security of Korea's border with China and the Soviet Union.

NEGOTIATIONS FOR THE END OF THE WAR

After the recall of MacArthur in April 1951, Truman first needed to convey to the Chinese that there would be no US weakening over the unification of Korea. Second, Truman needed to show the American public that there was a plan to end the conflict other than the risk of expanded military operations. In early May, US officials made secret contact with the Soviet Union and China, indicating the USA was willing to end the fighting in Korea in the general area in which it had begun in 1950 along the 38th Parallel. The reason for the secrecy was because Syngman Rhee was committed to blocking a cease-fire and the US administration feared that he would order South Korean troops to keep fighting regardless of the UN commander's orders.

The Soviets took this opportunity to publicly announce in a UN radio broadcast *The Price of Peace* by Jacob Malik (the Soviet Ambassador to the UN), that they were willing to work on a cease-fire. Two days later, the Beijing *People's Daily* endorsed Malik's proposal. Having clarified with the Soviets that the aim of the peace talks was the restoration of the 38th Parallel, Truman instructed General Ridgway on 29 June to begin the discussions for an armistice. The points for the negotiations which began in Kaesong on 26 July included:

- the adoption of an agenda
- the establishment of a cease-fire line along the 38th Parallel
- arrangements for the realisation of a cease-fire and armistice in Korea
- the composition, authority and functions of a supervisory organisation for carrying out the terms of a cease-fire and armistice
- arrangements relating to prisoners of war.

As part of their ongoing discussions, the UNC delegation had managed to prevent the communists from including the mutual withdrawal of foreign troops from Korea as a principle. In this way the weaker South Korean army would be protected by the UN forces against the larger and well-trained forces of the north.

Why were the Chinese and Soviet Union willing to enter into negotiations at this point?

More than any other single factor, the changing military conditions and their personal and economic costs had led Stalin and Mao to reassess their views on the reunification of Korea and begin to move towards armistice talks. The spring and summer offensives of 1951 had led to a great loss of life, some 85,000 Chinese casualties plus 17,000 prisoners, many of whom were from the most experienced Chinese combat units. This, together with major shortages of ammunition and food, led to a loss of motivation by the CPV. In May 1951, the UN under pressure from the USA had imposed a stringent economic embargo on the sale of goods to and from China. The scale of defeat led the Chinese to realise that the UNC forces could not be decisively defeated. Rather, Mao decided that cease-fire negotiations were now acceptable; the Soviets had indicated a willingness to discuss a cease-fire; and the UN was keen to see an end to the fighting. The negotiations began on 10 July 1951 at Kaesong, located in 'no man's land'. But this did not mean the war was over; in fact it was to continue for a further two years.

Cease-fire negotiations at Kaesong

Prior to the negotiations, the CPV forces seized the Kaesong area. This action left the communists in control of movements in and out of the negotiating area, and the communists used the situation to depict themselves in the world's press as the victors and the UNC forces as the defeated. In many respects, this was the start of the psychological war between the global powers. The Chinese were keen to take every opportunity on and off the battlefield to show their strength and to undermine the confidence of the US and its allies. The first point under discussion was the military demarcation line and a demilitarised zone. The communists wanted the 38th Parallel to be the cease-fire line. The UNC, on the other hand, wanted the current front line – the line of contact, known as the Kansas Line – to be the cease-fire line. After many weeks of acrimonious talks with both sides alleging violations of the conference area and the neutral zone, the negotiations broke down on 23 August 1951.

Napalm strike against a train yard in North Korea, c. 1952

The air war

The two months following the breakdown of the talks saw some of the most ferocious fighting with heavy casualties on both sides. The policy of **interdiction** led to the increased use of air power. 'Operation Strangle' had begun in May 1951. Intended to disrupt supplies to the communist forces moving south it was extended to include air fields, rail tracks, bridges and trains in August 1951. Partly in response to 'Operation Strangle', the communists engaged in the first major fighter offensive with planes supplied by the Soviets. Initially there was a high loss of US aircraft, but a change of tactics led to eventual victory in the air war and the communists finally abandoned their air offensive after December 1951.

The UNC air war was extended in June 1952 to cover North Korean hydroelectric plants at Kojo, Fusen, Kyosen and Suiho. The UNC forces continued to use air strikes in order to weaken the communists' military capability. On 29 August 1952, the largest air raid of the war was made against the North Korean capital, Pyongyang. Although the strikes were aimed against military targets tremendous damage was inflicted on the civilian population, particularly when napalm was used. Kim Il Sung announced that 6000 civilians had been killed. International outrage accompanied the attack. After this the focus of air attacks turned to the remnants of North Korean industry.

Why did the negotiations take so long to reach an armistice?
The peace talks resumed in late October 1951 at a new site, Panmunjom, with both sides accepting responsibility for its security.

The key factors that slowed the negotiations were as follows.

- **The intense distrust each of the combatants felt for each other.**
  Both sides used the lull in the fighting to modernise their armed forces. The US took the opportunity to rebuild and remodernise the South Korean army. The new divisions were given proper levels of equipment, and a staff school and military academy were established in South Korea. The CPV also underwent major reforms in 1952. It was re-equipped, and new reinforcements were used to strengthen the front line. A new strategy was introduced: the **active positional defence** meant any UNC advance would be immediately counter-attacked by CPV and NKPA troops.
- **The issue of the prisoners of war**. The Geneva Convention of 1949, which the US had signed and which the UNC and the communists announced they would honour, stated that 'prisoners of war shall be released and repatriated without delay after the cessation of hostilities'. Mao wanted an all-for-all exchange, but the Americans felt this would provide the communists with a large resource of manpower. The UNC negotiators adhered to the principle of no forced repatriation: only those prisoners who chose to be repatriated would be allowed to leave. In April 1952, of the 132,000 POWs held in UN camps only around half wished to be repatriated. Many of those held and believed to belong to the NKPA were actually South Koreans forced into fighting

Anti-US posters in a North Korean village, January 1951

when the south was first occupied in 1950. More serious for the outcome of negotiations, of the 21,000 Chinese prisoners held, 16,000 said they did not want to go back to China. The talks went into recess in October 1952, as both the Chinese and US negotiators failed to come to an agreement.

Breaking the deadlock

Throughout 1952, the opinion polls for the US presidential elections indicated that General Eisenhower would be elected as the new president of the US. The popularity of Truman and the Democrats had crumbled as the Korean War dragged on with the high loss of US lives and an escalation in costs. On the other hand, Eisenhower had made it clear both in a visit to the battlefield in Korea and in his speeches that he was prepared to escalate the war in order to end it more quickly and that he was not afraid to use whatever weapons were available to him to bring about a cease-fire.

Two weeks after his inauguration, President Eisenhower announced that the US Seventh Fleet would no longer prevent attacks against mainland China by the Chinese Nationalists based in Taiwan. On 27 May 1953, Eisenhower authorised a letter from General Mark W Clark, the chief UNC negotiator, to the commanders of the communist forces in Korea, General Kim Il Sung and General Peng Dehuai, that the talks were at their last stage. The letter said:

> *I believe you are aware that it is not our purpose to engage in prolonged and fruitless repetition of arguments. It is our earnest hope that you will give urgent and most serious consideration to our delegations alternative proposals.*

These proposals included:

- the creation of a Neutral Nations Repatriation Commission to temporarily supervise the POWs after the armistice
- a period of 90 days during which each side would be allowed to send representatives to convince its POWs to return home
- the fate of those prisoners unwilling to be repatriated to be decided at a conference 30 days after the signing of the armistice.

Agreements for an armistice were concluded on 16 June 1953, but unfortunately this was not the end of the fighting. Syngman Rhee opposed many of the compromises made at Panmunjom and this led to fierce attacks against ROK divisions in the south by the CPV–NKPA forces. By this point, the US was not so concerned about the ground war and instead chose to intensify the air war. During the months of May, June and July 1953 more than 150 MiG-15s, Soviet-designed fighters, were destroyed. Additionally, General Clark targeted 20 dams in North Korea for destruction. One of the major targets was the Toksan Dam near Pyongyang, which flooded rice fields when destroyed and submerged 70 villages.

Conventional views suggest that the war was brought to an end by the US threat to escalate the war and its consideration of the use of nuclear weapons against targets in North Korea and China. There is little evidence to support this claim. The Chinese certainly recognised a change of mood among the new administration and they realised that an expanded war was possible. General Clark's letter of 27 May and the ultimatum it contained reinforced this view.

ALTERNATIVE EXPLANATIONS FOR THE WAR'S CONCLUSION

- Mao's government had particular domestic reasons for wanting to conclude the war. In December 1952, Zhou Enlai announced that the country was to begin its first Five Year Plan in 1953. It was necessary therefore to redirect resources away from military spending, which in 1951 had absorbed 48 per cent of the total budget, towards consumer and export industries.
- North Korean morale was at breaking point by the summer of 1953. National income had been diminished by a third, inflation was destroying people's livelihoods and food hoarding had forced Kim's government to introduce harsh confiscatory policies. Ultimately, the cumulative loss of manpower, destruction of industry and military expenditure were a heavy burden for the communist forces.
- In March 1953, Stalin died. At his funeral Georgy Malenkov (a member of the triumvirate who succeeded Stalin) placed an emphasis on peaceful coexistence with the USA. Significantly, on 30 March 1953, Zhou Enlai (who had attended Stalin's funeral in Moscow) put forward new concessions on the question of the POWs to the UN negotiators.
- In addition, George Kennan noted in the Policy Planning Staff Records that in April 1953 Soviet editorials on Eisenhower's 'Chance for Peace' speech revealed 'clearly that the present Soviet leaders are definitely interested in pursuing with us the effort to solve some of the international problems'. Kennan argued that the message the Soviets were trying to convey to the US was that progress towards an armistice could not be made while Washington persisted 'in acting as though the Chinese were Moscow's helpless puppets'.
- The final reason for the agreement to a cease-fire was, without doubt, the impact of the bombing of North Korea undertaken by the UN air forces from May 1953 onwards. The savage assaults undertaken from

June 1953 onwards had caused major communication problems. But the attacks against the dams created havoc in the countryside and led to the widespread destruction of crops and livestock. This would have caused famine and political unrest in the countryside, a burden the Democratic Republic of Korea was unable to bear alone.

CONCLUSION

It is now clear that the Korean War was a far more complex phenomenon than previously assumed. The debate over who was responsible for the start of the war continues as new evidence is released from the Russian and US archives. We now know that Stalin's motivations for the expansion of Soviet influence in Asia were driven by a 'changed international situation'. In effect, given the apparent reluctance of the US to prevent the fall of China to communism the Soviets believed they would face little opposition to the creation of a communist bloc in the Pacific region. The 'Defence Perimeter' speech by Secretary of State Acheson in January 1950 further indicated that the Truman administration had concluded that South Korea was not of sufficient strategic importance to the US to justify military intervention to prevent a North Korean take-over.

However, when the north attacked the south the issue for Truman was that the Soviets had supported aggression against an independent state lying outside its sphere of influence. Given that the state of South Korea was perceived to be closely linked to the US, Truman viewed the actions of the Soviet-sponsored north as a challenge to US resolve to contain communism and this had to be blocked.

The one issue that has been frequently overlooked by Cold War historians is how the Korean people felt about the division of their country. There is no doubt that the leaders in both the north and the south were determined to unite Korea as an independent state under their control. Both sides acknowledged that they could do this only with the support of the superpowers, which had created the division in the first place. Therefore, to gain an understanding of the complexity of the Korean War it is important to consider the strength of nationalist feeling prevalent in both North and South Korea in 1950 and its links to the outbreak of war in 1950.

Finally, the notion of limited war developed during the Korean War had important implications for the actions of the US in Vietnam in the period 1954–75.

CHAPTER 6

The first Vietnam War and the origins of US involvement, 1946–54

AN OVERVIEW

The area that became known as Vietnam fell under the control of France in the mid-nineteenth century. The French strengthened their presence in the region through a series of treaties including the Treaty of Saigon of 1862 and, more importantly, the Treaties of Hué of 1883 and 1884. The region remained a mainstay of the French Empire until the Second World War. In 1940, the Japanese occupied the region at the same moment that the German armed forces crushed French forces in Europe. Following the defeat of the Japanese in August 1945, Vietnam was for a brief period governed by the Democratic Republic of Vietnam under the leadership of Ho Chi Minh. In mid-September, the US Allied command divided Vietnam, at the 16th Parallel with the British in the south and the Chinese in the north, in preparation for the surrender of the Japanese troops. It soon became clear to Ho Chi Minh and the nationalist Vietminh that the British intended to hand the south back to France. Therefore, the Vietminh sought to establish a power base in Hanoi from which it could organise resistance to the French occupation of Vietnam.

Late in 1945, the French attempted to reassert colonial rule. They quickly seized control of Saigon and the south of the country. However, the north was dominated by the nationalist Vietminh. As part of the process of re-establishing themselves as the masters of the whole country, the French agreed to negotiate with the Vietminh. In September 1946, negotiations between the French and the Vietminh over the independence of Vietnam broke down. Ho Chi Minh returned to North Vietnam and continued to seek support for the peaceful move to independence. However, the French were determined to reoccupy what they perceived to be the richest of their colonies in **Indochina**. In December 1946, following the fighting in Haiphong between the Vietminh militias and the French troops, Ho and his supporters left Hanoi and began what was to become a war of national liberation for the Vietnamese.

The war did not go well for the French and so they turned to the US for military and economic aid. The years of defeat and German occupation had left the French economically weak. Initially, the Truman administration adopted a neutral stance to the conflict. However, by 1949 the French and British were able to convince the US that France was supporting the establishment of a free and independent nation in Vietnam. In particular, they were able to paint Ho as a communist.

In 1949, Dean Acheson suggested that Ho was 'as much nationalist as commie' and that 'all Stalinists in colonial areas are nationalists'. From this point, US aid flowed in to support the French in their struggle with the Vietminh.

The turning point for French involvement in Indochina was the defeat of its army at Dien Bien Phu at the hands of the Vietminh. In May 1954, a series of meetings was held in Geneva to discuss the future of Indochina. The outcome of the meetings, the Geneva Accords, was a military truce but no political solution, President Eisenhower failing to recognise the right of Vietnam to become an independent state. Eisenhower believed that a free and democratic Vietnam was vital in blocking communist expansion in south-east Asia. As a result, economic and military aid started to be provided by the US.

BIOGRAPHIES

Ho Chi Minh (1890–1969) Originally named Nguyen Sinh Cung, Ho became leader of the Indochinese Communist Party in 1930. In 1941, the Communist Party joined a broad range of groups to form the Vietminh, which was led by Ho. The Vietminh established a clear focus on gaining national independence from France. In 1945, Ho Chi Minh became the first leader of the Democratic Republic of Vietnam. He remained president of the Democratic Republic of Vietnam until his death in 1969.

Nikita Khrushchev (1894–1971) Head of the Communist Party bureaucracy in 1953 and premier of the Soviet Union after 1955, in 1956 he launched a major attack on Stalin which contributed to the Sino–Soviet split of 1958. In 1958, he attempted to improve East-West relations with the USA, which ultimately led to a period of détente in the 1960s. In a major speech in January 1961, he committed the Soviet Union to supporting national liberation struggles in the developing world. However, in this period the Soviet Union played a small role in the Vietnamese conflict.

Vo Nguyen Giap (born 1912) A key figure in the Vietminh and close associate of Ho Chi Minh, in 1946 he created the People's Army of Vietnam that defeated the French and withstood the military might of the USA. He was the chief strategist of the Democratic Republic of Vietnam from 1946 to 1975.

THE ORIGINS OF THE FIRST VIETNAM WAR, 1946–54

Communism in Vietnam: the 1930s

On 3 February 1930, the Vietnamese Communist Party was formed under the chairmanship of Ho Chi Minh. In October, following a Comintern directive, the name was changed to the Indochinese Communist Party

(ICP); it played a leading role in the anti-colonial struggle throughout Indochina. In its first year the movement coordinated strikes among the workers for higher wages, better working conditions and widespread peasant demonstrations against taxes in Vietnam. However, from 1931 onwards the French colonial regime sought to destroy the ICP by arresting all the leaders and by September 1931 the activities of the ICP were reduced.

A second period of Vietnamese communism emerged in 1936 when the Popular Front was in office in France and there was a relaxation of colonial policies on political debate. In Vietnam during the period 1936–9 a cultural front was opened with socialist and communist magazines and books published that promoted the ideas of Marx and communist theory. Once again the ICP encouraged strikes, demonstrations and public political debates – this time throughout Indochina. There were demands for political reforms, the abolition of the government monopoly of alcohol and salt, equal rights for women, enlargement of the education system and freedom of the press. The collapse of the Popular Front in France in September 1939 led to the resumption of colonial repression in Vietnam. The ICP networks were destroyed and some of its most experienced leaders were executed by the French.

The emergence of the Vietminh Front

Vietnamese communism now entered a new stage, one that led directly to the August Revolution of 1945. Since 1931, communist activities in Vietnam had emphasised the mobilisation of the workers and peasants in opposition to the French colonial power and land-owning classes. In 1941, the Eighth Congress of the ICP set forth a radical redefinition of the nature of the Vietnamese revolution and called for the establishment of a national liberation movement, the Vietminh. Ho Chi Minh, the first leader of the Vietminh, stated in a speech to the Congress:

> The Indochinese revolution during this period is a revolution of national liberation. Such a revolution can only succeed when there is a unity of all revolutionary forces throughout Indochina, not discriminating between workers, peasants, rich peasants, landlords or national capitalists. Whoever loves our country and race will together form a united front gathering all the forces to do everything possible to fight for independence, destroying the French and Japanese bandits who have occupied our country.

The Vietminh was not a political party as such but an organisation committed to Vietnamese independence. In many respects the appeal of the Vietminh throughout the two Vietnam Wars – the Franco–Vietminh War 1946–54 and the US–Vietnam War 1964–73 – can best be explained by the powerful nationalist belief that cut across all classes in Vietnam, that all Vietnamese had the right to live in a free and independent state.

The August Revolution, 1945 and the creation of the Democratic Republic of Vietnam

During the Second World War, the Vietminh remained a small but influential group, receiving no outside help despite advances to the US Office of Strategic Studies (OSS) and the Allied forces. However, on 9 March 1945 the Japanese, in response to the declaration of war against Japan by the **Free French**, ordered a *coup d'état* against the French colonial government based in Saigon. This action created a political vacuum with French power destroyed and Japanese power not fully consolidated. The coup provided the Vietminh with new opportunities: it was able to recruit 3000 experienced fighters from the formerly French employed militia, and acquire weapons and ammunition from the fleeing French forces. The new recruits joined the Vietnam People's Army, formed in December 1944 under the leadership of Vo Nguyen Giap. The newly acquired weapons were used to harass the Japanese troops and seize rice from Japanese depots for the local population.

The People's Revolutionary Committees

However, far more attention was paid to political tasks in this period as the Vietminh encouraged the creation of the **People's Revolutionary Committees** (PRCs), very similar to those that emerged in Korea in 1945. By the beginning of June, the Vietminh had declared a 'Liberated Zone' in North Vietnam and worked alongside PRCs throughout Vietnam to ensure that the people were fed and protected from the Japanese troops. This latter task was considered to have a huge propaganda effect in spreading the prestige of the Vietminh and provided the basis for the eventual overthrow of the Japanese in August 1945. In the first weeks of August, the Vietminh effectively took over the activities of local government. The fall of Japan on the 15 August 1945 was followed by the creation of a Committee for National Liberation, which acted as the Provisional Government of Vietnam (PRV) headed by Ho Chi Minh.

In mid-August, the major provincial cities of Vietnam came under the control of the PRV: Hanoi on 19 August, Hué on 23 August and Saigon on 27 August. On 30 August, Emperor Bao Dai, the last monarch of the Nguyen dynasty, formally abdicated. On 2 September, Ho Chi Minh proclaimed the Democratic Republic of Vietnam (DRV) and a challenge to the French:

> *Vietnam has the right to enjoy freedom and independence and in fact has become a free and independent country. The entire Vietnamese people are determined to mobilise all their physical and mental strength, to sacrifice their lives and property in order to safeguard their freedom and independence.*

The Provisional Government of Vietnam (PRV)

In September 1945, the arrival of the occupation forces of China and Britain in Vietnam signalled to the Vietminh that it was now a matter of urgency to establish the foundations of an effective government. The first decree of the DRV on 8 September called for national elections for a National Assembly to be held within two months, with all Vietnamese aged eighteen and over eligible to vote. On 20 September, a committee was established to draft a constitution for the DRV that included members of the socialist, communist and nationalist political parties.

- PRCs were established throughout Vietnam to cut across political and religious divides with leadership drawn from the local communities.
- Government offices were created, which included the Ministry of the Interior led by Vo Nguyen Giap.
- One of Giap's first decrees was the establishment of the Mass Education Service. In 1945, 90 per cent of the peasants were illiterate, a damning indictment of French educational policies. For Ho Chi Minh it was essential that all Vietnamese could read so that they could participate in political debates and elections.

Ho Chi Minh also made Vo Nguyen Giap responsible for establishing an army, but the government was desperate for money owing to the dislocation of the Vietnamese economy during the period of the Japanese occupation. A Central Fund was established and, on 17 September 1945, Ho Chi Minh inaugurated the famous Gold Week, during which people were invited to donate gold to the government. This gold was then converted into currency, which the Vietminh used to purchase weapons from the Chinese Nationalist (KMT) forces entering Vietnam. In return for the weapons, the DRV allowed the Chinese to use the port of Haiphong as an embarkation point for KMT troops moving into northern China to fight the Chinese communists.

The newly formed DRV was also faced with the threat of famine in the winter of 1945–6. In an attempt to reduce the impact of the shortage of rice, the DRV distributed hundreds of tonnes of rice seed, but the flooding and neglect of the paddy fields meant that it would be a long time before the crops could be harvested. Instead, the government called on the peasants to increase the growth of potatoes, maize and beans, which required a shorter growing period. These crops would provide an alternative food source and avert the threat of famine. In addition, the Vietminh suspended the agricultural tax and redistributed lands in the fertile central areas of Vietnam in an attempt to encourage the peasants to increase rice production. The initial record of the DRV and the success of some of its early programmes makes it easy to understand its popularity with many of the Vietnamese, particularly the peasants, after 1945.

France and the recolonisation of Vietnam, 1945

Unbeknown to Ho Chi Minh, French forces were to be returned to Vietnam under a secret agreement concluded at the Potsdam Conference of July 1945. The agreement to divide Vietnam at the 16th Parallel between the British in the south and the Chinese forces in the north paved the way for France to return to Vietnam. The Americans saw no major reason why they should involve themselves in Vietnam other than the observation of the disarming of Japanese troops and the repatriation of Allied prisoners. On 8 September 1945, the Chinese occupied the north and, on 12 September, the British occupied the south in readiness to receive the surrender of the Japanese troops after their defeat by the Allied forces.

Major-General Douglas Gracey, the commander of the British occupation troops sent to South Vietnam to accept the surrender of Japanese, aided France by suppressing Vietnamese agitation in Saigon and sponsored a *coup* against the DRV administrative institutions set up in the city. Discussions between the DRV representatives in Saigon, the French representative Jean Cedile and Lieutenant-Colonel Peter Dewey, the US representative from the Office of Special Operations (OSS), broke down in late September over the recognition of French authority in Vietnam by the DRV. On 17 September, strikes and demonstrations broke out in Saigon against the British and French occupation forces. On 22 September, Cedile ordered French troops to take over the key installations in the city and evict the DRV administration from the City Hall in Saigon. In the struggle, several Vietnamese troops were killed but France was once again in control in Saigon. It is no exaggeration to say that the British government, concerned with reestablishing its own colonial rule, aided the French in reinstalling their rule over Vietnam by mid-1946. This in turn made it possible for the French to wage war against the Vietminh.

With the Chinese commanders supporting the nationalists in the north and the British working with the French in the south, Ho turned to the USA for support. OSS Commander Archimedes Patti argued in correspondence to the State Department that the USA should support the Vietminh, but the Truman administration wanted to remain neutral. At this time, the US had no clear policy on how to deal with Indochina, and in

Vietnam and south-east Asia

particular Vietnam. The reasons for this were the divisions within the State Department between the pro-European and pro-Asian factions.

- The pro-European faction argued that France had an important role to play in the reconstruction of Europe after the Second World War and Truman was unwilling to be seen as acting against the French.
- The pro-Asian faction, on the other hand, wanted Truman to fulfil the Yalta Accord (see pages 7–10), which called for some form of trusteeship to be established in the former colonies of south-east Asia. Trusteeships were intended to support the colonies with the establishment of free and independent governments. This debate, together with the fear that any form of commission established on Vietnam would provide the Soviets with a foothold in south-east Asia, led the US to stay with its policy of neutrality in Indochina.

The Fontainebleau Agreement, 1946

French authorities, determined to restore colonial mastery over Vietnam, encountered fierce resistance from the Vietnamese nationalists led by Ho Chi Minh. In March 1946, negotiations were held between Major Jean Sainteny, head of the French Military Mission, whose role was to prepare Vietnam for the resumption of French authority, and the Vietminh. Ho was desperate to avert a war that he knew the Vietminh could not win, so he agreed to affiliate Vietnam with the **French Union** (the new name for the French Empire). In addition, the Vietminh agreed to allow 15,000 French troops to replace the Chinese occupation force in the north. In return, Sainteny pledged that there would be a referendum to determine whether Cochin China would rejoin Annam and Tonkin in a reunited Vietnam. The agreement recognised the DRV as a free state, with its own government, parliament, army and finances within the French Union.

Ho Chi Minh, 1946

In June 1946, the Vietnamese delegates met with French officials for a further series of talks on the future of Vietnam at Fontainebleau, near Paris. Throughout the summer months, Ho and the Vietnamese delegates sought to gain recognition for the DRV and Vietnamese independence. On 10 September 1946, the Vietnamese delegation broke off talks as it realised the French were not going to move over the issue of independence. Ho Chi Minh stayed in Paris and attempted to persuade the US through its Ambassador Jefferson Caffery to support the Vietnamese in their struggle. But the Truman administration took no action because it was unwilling to antagonise France whom it needed as an ally in the growing conflict between the USA and the Soviet Union. On 16 September, Ho Chi Minh signed a *modus vivendi* with the French, which recognised Vietnam's position within the French Union. Ho was aware that he had failed in his efforts to secure an agreement on Vietnamese independence and that, in the long term, the only resolution to the current position was armed struggle.

The Franco–Vietminh War

On his return to Hanoi, Ho defended the *modus vivendi* to the National Assembly, but, on 30 October, the DRV government resigned. The new government was dominated by the Vietminh and over the following days it discussed the new constitution for the DRV. But French observers could not ignore the fact that the new constitution declared the total independence of Vietnam and made no reference to the French Union. On 14 November, the National Assembly adjourned for the last time because of the growing unrest in Hanoi and the increasingly threatening French response.

Following the adjournment, there was considerable unrest in the north – particularly around Haiphong, which was an entry point for weapons and resources for the Vietnam army. In November, the French military forces took control of the port, which led to fighting between the French and Vietnamese militia. On 23 November, French troops were ordered to take over Haiphong. The subsequent shelling resulted in the deaths of thousands of innocent citizens. The French quickly attempted to gain military control of the north and established their own administration in Hanoi. On 19 December, in response to the attacks by the French, General Vo Nguyen Giap ordered a national resistance and the establishment of the People's Liberation Army.

The outbreak of the fighting provoked by the French authorities shattered international complacency and brought the problems in Vietnam to the attention of the US. The State Department sent Abbot Low Moffat, chief of the Division of South-East Asian Affairs, on a fact-finding mission. Moffat's report concluded that for the time being some sort of French presence was inevitable, not only as a means of limiting Soviet influence in the area, but also to protect Vietnam from attack by the Chinese. Following the outbreak of war in December 1946 between the French and the Vietminh, Moffat requested the State Department to put pressure on the French to end the war in order to save 'countless lives, protect US economic interests in the region and advance the spread of democracy'.

THE US AND VIETNAM, 1945–9

From the outbreak of the Franco–Vietminh War in December 1946, US policy was influenced by the actions of the French and British who were united in their determination to retain control of their colonies in Asia. The lack of clear policymaking with regards to Vietnam reflected the inability of the US, British and French governments to agree over what course to follow. **Mark Lawrence**, in *Transnational Coalition-Building and the Making of the Cold War in Indochina, 1947–9* (2002), argue that the fundamental differences between the three governments were outlined by policymakers who were determined to:

- rebuild French economic and political power and viewed the Vietminh as a serious challenge to western interests, advocating a military effort to destroy it
- recast the western relationship with the colonial world, and asserted that the war must be brought to an end and negotiations on independence reopened with the Vietminh (the political movement that represented the majority of the Vietnamese people).

In the US, policymakers were further divided over the best course of action over Vietnam. The 'Europeanists', who included President Truman and Under-Secretary of State Acheson, argued that they needed to back France as an important ally. Meanwhile, the 'Asianists' argued that the US should remain neutral.

On the one hand, the Europeanists stressed the growing Cold War tensions in Europe (see Chapter 1) and the need to show solidarity with France in a neo-colonial war with Vietnam. In a statement made shortly after the outbreak of fighting in Vietnam, Secretary of State James Byrnes stated that:

> *a friendly and militarily powerful France remained the cardinal tenet of US foreign policy; US aims were under threat from a powerful and disciplined Communist Party in France. The communists in France were growing stronger everyday and were well positioned to capitalise on any political turmoil created by US obstruction of French policy in south-east Asia.*

On the other hand, the Asianists believed the worsening situation in south-east Asia required that the US should avoid close association with France and try instead to mediate a settlement that would raise US standing in Asia. In the USA, the debate contributed to the lack of a clear policy on Indochina. In this context, Truman steadfastly refused to meet requests from the French for badly needed military resources and opted instead for a policy of **neutrality.**

THE VIEWS OF THE INTERNATIONAL COMMUNITY

In January 1947, the State Department offered the French government its 'good offices' to act as mediators in order to ease the tensions in Vietnam. Not unsurprisingly, the offer was rejected and the French Ambassador in Washington was instructed to tell the US that the French could handle the matter. But hostility to French repression in Vietnam culminated in a serious threat to France's military ability to continue the war in spring 1947. In Ceylon (Sri Lanka), Malaya, Singapore, Burma and India, dock-workers refused to service French ships carrying war materials to Vietnam. In addition, India and Burma limited the number of French aircraft that could fuel at their airports or pass through their skies. These actions seriously affected the maintenance of supplies to the French forces in Vietnam and forced the French to seek support from the international community in order to continue the war. There was considerable pressure in France to avoid humiliation in Vietnam. From the French communists to the new political party of the right, the Rally of French People (supported by General Charles de Gaulle), there was a consensus that the pride lost in the defeat by the Germans in 1940 had to be regained. So, by mid-1947, the French were far more willing to seek US support in order to continue what they saw as their *mission civilisatrice* (civilising mission) in Indochina.

FRANCE AND US SUPPORT

The Bao Dai experiment

One of the first strategies undertaken by the French to gain US support for their war on the Vietminh was the formation of a new government in Vietnam led by the ex-Emperor Bao Dai. On the one hand, the policy was designed to establish an alternative nationalist leadership, in opposition to Ho Chi Minh, with which the French could negotiate a settlement of the war and at the same time preserve significant French control in Vietnam. On the other, it was intended to project an image of French liberalism in their colonies and, thereby, influence the US in their favour. In December 1947, Bao Dai signed a protocol accepting negotiations to end the war, and in June 1948 signed a second agreement that recognised the 'independence' of Vietnam subject to the terms of membership in the French Union.

This action was not intended to provide any recognition of Vietnamese independence; if anything it was a ploy by the French to gain US backing for their activities in Vietnam. By the end of 1948, the French sought to involve the US Embassy in Paris in helping to persuade Bao Dai to return to Saigon and formally take up his new role. According to **Lawrence** (2002), in France's view, 'implicating the US in the Bao Dai policy would not only increase the chance of getting US support, but also demonstrate to the Vietminh the need to accede to French power because of international recognition of its actions'.

France and the containment of communism in Vietnam

The second strategy of the French to gain US support was to portray their role in the war with the Vietminh as a defence against communism in Indochina. Throughout 1948, nationalist unrest often with radical and communist undertones, emerged throughout much of south-east Asia. This unrest not only threatened French interests but also British interests in Malaya, Singapore and Burma. The unrest threatened the economic recovery of both France and Britain because both depended on the exports of rubber and tin from south-east Asia in the reconstruction of their economies. Faced with widespread hostility the French, with the support of the British, now sought ways to draw the US into making a major commitment in Indochina. Both countries chose to show that their struggle in south-east Asia was not about reimposing colonial power but to contain the communist threat.

The Elysee Accords, 1949

The third strategy the French implemented was the Elysee Accords, signed in Paris by the French government. This strategy was intended to convince Bao Dai and the US administration that France was preparing Vietnam for full independence. In many ways, the new agreements reflected the original Fontainebleau Agreement. Vietnam would be able to:

- conduct its own foreign affairs
- control its finances
- create a Vietnamese National Army.

Furthermore, Cochin China would now be included in the new state of Vietnam.

These Accords were influential in changing US foreign policy towards Vietnam from one of neutralism to support for the French in their struggle with the Vietminh. The agreement, while falling far short of the recognition of genuine Vietnamese autonomy that the US administration called for, did allow the 'Europeanists' within the Truman administration to argue for support for French policy in Indochina. On 22 June 1949, the US State Department publicly declared that the formation of the Bao Dai government and promises by the French of a new Vietnamese Constitution were 'welcome developments that would allow Vietnam to assume its rightful place in the family of nations. The Elysee Accords would form the basis for the realisation of the legitimate aspirations of the Vietnamese people.' Yet the US government stopped short of formal recognition of Bao Dai, to the dismay of the French.

THE VIETMINH, CHINA AND THE SOVIET UNION

Since the end of the Second World War in 1945, the Vietminh had had limited contact with its communist counterparts in China and the Soviet Union. However, when the war against the French broke out in November 1946, Mao and the Chinese Communist Party offered refuge to the Vietminh military units in southern China. The victory of the Chinese communists in October 1949 was welcomed by the Vietminh and it formally recognised the People's Republic of China (PRC) in December 1949. Following this declaration, the Chinese leadership invited Ho Chi Minh and a formal delegation to Beijing and offered them a limited amount of weapons, munitions and medical supplies for the struggle against the French.

The Border Campaign, 1950

On 18 January 1950, the PRC granted diplomatic recognition to the DRV and recognised it as the sole legal government in Vietnam. In the same year, Mao and Stalin signed the Sino-Soviet Treaty of Mutual Defence and Cooperation. The formal alliance between the Soviet Union and the PRC was to have important implications for the Vietminh as Stalin now directed Mao to play an important role in supporting revolution in south-east Asia. According to **MacDonald** in *Communist Bloc Expansion in the Early Cold War: Challenging Realism, Refuting Revisionism* (1995–6):

> *In their new role as communist bloc leader in the region, China began a large-scale effort in Indochina to support the Vietminh under the leadership of Ho Chi Minh. This was done for a mixture of security and ideological purposes. The new evidence shows that direct Chinese aid to the Vietnamese was critical to their military victory over the French.*

In an interview in 1968, Ho Chi Minh acknowledged that his strategic situation was difficult prior to gaining support from the Chinese in 1950. The Border Campaign of 1950 was an attempt to remove all French fortified outposts from the area of Vietnam that bordered China. During this campaign, the Chinese provided the Vietminh with:

- 60,000 small weapons
- 1700 machine guns
- 150 artillery pieces of different sizes
- large amounts of ammunition, medicine and uniforms
- communications equipment.

According to **Qiang Zhai** in *Transplanting the Chinese Model: Chinese Military Advisers and the First Vietnam War, 1950–45* (1993), the aid provided by the Chinese had a decisive impact on the success of the Border Campaign of 1950. But the most important influence on the Vietminh military activity was the work of the Chinese Military Advice Group (CMAG). General Chen Geng, a senior military officer, worked closely with the Vietminh troops and their leaders by explaining the importance of fighting a 'people's war'. Chen discovered that the Vietminh had neglected the mobilisation of women in the struggle with the French and pointed out to the Vietminh leaders that because they constituted 50 per cent of the population women were a valuable source of fighters. Chen's role was also critical in the re-education of the Vietminh army on strategic and battle plans.

In September 1950, Vietminh forces under the leadership of Giap captured Dongkhe and forced a French withdrawal from the important border posts of Langson, Laokay and Thai Nguyen. The success of the Border Campaign had great significance for the Vietminh. By the end of 1950, it had cleared the Chinese border of all French outposts and there were no longer any obstacles to the movement of men and supplies between China and the Vietminh. Over 6000 French troops had been killed or captured. The French writer **Bernard Fall** reflected that the fall of these outposts represented 'France's greatest colonial defeat since the fall of Quebec to the British in 1759'. The Vietminh was now confident that with the support of the Chinese it could ultimately remove French influence from Vietnam.

Despite the fact that the Korean War of 1950–3 coincided with the anti-French war in Vietnam, China continued to supply the Vietminh with support. According to **MacDonald** (1995–6), from 1950 to 1954 the CMAG drew up most of the strategic and tactical plans for the major campaigns against the French, and sent military advisers to command Vietnamese troops. In terms of military aid, the Chinese army armed and trained a total of 116,000 Vietminh troops, five infantry divisions, one engineering and artillery division, and one guard regiment. This constituted a significant effort to expand the communist bloc in south-east Asia.

US SUPPORT FOR FRANCE, 1949–54

US support for the French government steadily grew from June 1949. In February 1950, the US formally recognised the government of Bao Dai and granted US$15 million in US military aid in May 1950. The shift in US policy on Vietnam was the result of a number of factors, including:

- the fall of China to Mao's communist forces in October 1949
- the recognition for the DRV by Mao and Stalin in January 1950, and promises of aid to the Vietminh by the communist leaders for the military struggle against the French
- the ending of the stalemate on policymaking for Indochina in the US brought about by the divisions between the 'Asianists' and the 'Europeanists' as a result of the diplomatic recognition by the US of the Bao Dai government in February 1950
- the ability of the British and French to convince the US that the nationalist struggles in Asia were the result of a growing communist influence promoted and supported by the Soviet Union
- US concern to keep French support for NATO, an anti-Soviet military alliance created in 1949
- the outbreak of the Korean War in June 1950. The key shift in policy had been taken before the war but it seemed to validate the decision.

This period can therefore be seen as involving, but not committing, the US to Vietnam.

The extent of US involvement in Vietnam, 1950–4

To strengthen the Bao Dai government and increase its popular appeal between 1950 and 1952, the US spent more than US$50 million on economic and technical assistance. In an attempt to win over the peasants, US experts provided seeds and fertiliser to increase agricultural production. They also introduced health programmes aimed at reducing malaria and distributed health care to refugees coming to the south from the north. The US administration insisted that all the aid should go directly to the local government in an attempt to show the local population in South Vietnam the benefits of US support. Largely as a result of French obstructionism, the aid programme touched only a small number of the people.

In terms of the war the French were unable to win any major battles against the Vietminh. Reluctantly they put aside their prejudices and took steps to create a Vietnamese National Army (VNA). Understandably, the Vietnamese were reluctant to fight for the French and, by the end of 1951, the VNA numbered only 38,000 soldiers, far short of its projected 115,000. A small US Military Assistance and Advisory Group (MAAG) had been sent to Vietnam to assist in the training of the VNA as well as providing bombers, cargo planes, tanks, naval craft, automatic weapons, arms and ammunition, hospitals and engineering equipment. It is estimated that between 1950 and 1954, US investment in the war in Vietnam reached approximately US$3 billion. However, despite US aid and military support to contain the war in Vietnam, by 1952 the conflict had spilled over into Laos and Thailand. This represented an even greater threat to stability in Indochina and the possibility that the communists would use the unrest to achieve further gains in the region.

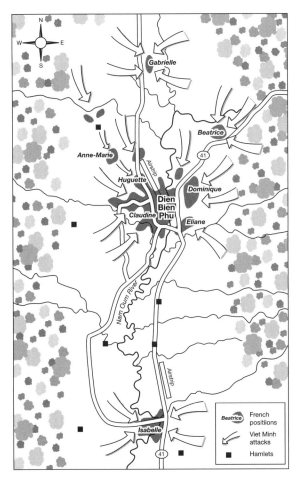

Battle of Dien Bein Phu, March – May 1954

DIEN BIEN PHU

By 1953, it was becoming obvious to the US administration from reports by the MAAG that the French were close to military defeat in Vietnam. The key event that led to the increased involvement of the US in Vietnam was the battle for Dien Bien Phu. In late 1953, the French army won support for an ambitious military plan by General Henri Navarre. The Navarre Plan called for ten additional French battalions in Indochina and an increase in the Vietnamese section of the armed forces. The plan was to establish a defensive position at a remote outpost in North Vietnam to prevent the Vietminh invading Laos and establishing bases there from which to attack the French. In response, General Giap surrounded the 13,000 French troops with 50,000 well armed Vietminh. The assault began on 13 March 1954. Despite French appeals for air attacks, President Dwight Eisenhower was reluctant to engage in another war, having just ended fighting in Korea.

United Action

Between 24 March and 1 April 1954, President Eisenhower and Secretary of State John Foster Dulles began to formulate a response. Dulles labelled their plan the **United Action**. This plan envisaged the creation of a coalition comprising, the US, Britain, France, Australia, New Zealand, Thailand, the Philippines and the associated states of the French Union, Vietnam, Laos and Cambodia. United Action was designed to ensure that any US intervention in Vietnam would be part of a collective effort. The regional forces would conduct the fighting and the US would provide military training and supplies. This attempt by the US to gain support for collective action coincided with preparations for the Geneva Conference of 8 May 1954, set up by the Foreign Ministers' Conference in February 1954 to discuss the Korean and Indochina conflicts.

Defeat for the French

It is in this context of growing international concern that the battle for Dien Bien Phu has to be set. The campaign now became an urgent matter for the Chinese as they sought to put pressure on the Vietminh to achieve a victory at Dien Bien Phu. In this way the Chinese leadership hoped to put pressure on the negotiators at Geneva in order to win greater concessions for the Vietminh. The French, on the other hand, now put further pressure on the US to initiate air strikes against the Vietminh troops engaged in the siege of Dien Bien Phu. Secretary of State Dulles could not authorise this extension of the war without support from the US Congress or the US's main ally, Britain. Events unfolded as follows.

- On 25 April 1954, the British Foreign Secretary Anthony Eden stated that in the view of the British government an air strike might not be decisive and that it would be a 'grave mistake' in terms of world opinion.
- On 29 April after a long and heated discussion, the US National Security Council agreed against immediate intervention. It was decided to hold up for the time being any military action in Indochina pending developments at Geneva.
- On 7 May, the French at Dien Bien Phu surrendered after 55 days of heroic but futile resistance. This battle was to be the last major campaign

fought by the French in Vietnam; their only hope for a role in the establishment of an independent Vietnam was the Geneva Conference.

The crucial point about Dien Bien Phu from the point of view of the Americans is that the US avoided involvement in the battle. Eisenhower had been elected on the basis of ending the Korean War in 1953. Starting a new conflict in Indochina a year later was unlikely to win him support. It would certainly adversely affect his chances of gaining a second term in office. At this point, the US was unwilling to commit to Vietnam without the support and help from its allies; therefore, its commitment remained limited to financial aid. Nevertheless, because of the political pressure used by the French, the US had become more heavily involved in the region, even overcoming its anti-colonial beliefs in order to contain communism.

THE GENEVA CONFERENCE, 1954
On 8 May 1954, nine delegations met in the old League of Nations building in Geneva with the supposed aim of coming to an agreement about the future of Indochina. Such were the entrenched positions of all concerned – including the Chinese, Vietminh and Americans – it is little surprise that no substantial agreement was reached. The Geneva Conference struggled to appease the interests of the delegates of the major powers and the different interests in Vietnam. Those interests were as follows.

- The French wished to retain control of Vietnam.
- The Vietminh wanted independence for the whole of Vietnam.
- The Chinese preferred French control to that of the Americans but, in reality, wanted no colonial involvement.
- The Americans wanted to contain any further communist gains.

At the Geneva Conference, the Vietminh was in a dominant position having defeated the French at Dien Bien Phu, and it dominated most of Vietnam politically and militarily. The participants acted as follows.

- Throughout the first weeks of the conference, Secretary of State Dulles continued to promote United Action, hoping that communist opposition to the role of France in Vietnam would persuade the French to accept the support of the US on its terms.
- The Chinese, aware of the attempts by the US to undermine the peace talks on Vietnam, sought to ally themselves with delegates from Britain, France, Laos and Cambodia in order to isolate the USA at the peace talks.
- After the victory of Dien Bien Phu, the Vietminh insisted that France withdraw from Indochina or face further defeat by the troops of the DRV. The Chinese Premier Zhou Enlai asserted that if the Vietminh continued the war, the governments of Cambodia and Laos would come under US protection. Its belligerence, he argued, would also ensure the success of the United Action plan proposed by the USA and

US involvement in Indochina. As a way forward, Zhou Enlai suggested a cease-fire agreement involving division of the country into two parts and then reunification through elections.

- France was reluctant to see US military intervention in Vietnam because it wanted to retain some influence in Indochina.
- The Soviet Union wanted to reduce French commitment to the US-sponsored European Defence Community and at the same time demonstrate its commitment to Khrushchev's foreign policy based on peaceful co-existence.
- Most importantly, the PRC supported an agreement and pressured the Vietnam delegation led by Le Duan and Pham Van Dong to accept the terms.

The underlying issue for all the powers was to keep the US out of Vietnam. However, the final Geneva Accords did not reflect this situation with Ho Chi Minh and the Vietminh acquiring only half the country.

- Vietnam was to be divided at the 17th Parallel with a 10-kilometre **Demilitarised Zone (DMZ)**.
- National elections were to be held in July 1956, following a year of consultation between representatives of the two zones, the French in the south and the Vietminh in the north.
- There were to be no troop reinforcements, no rearming and no foreign military alliances.

It would appear that only the wishes of the French and Chinese had been fully considered. For the Vietminh, the signing of the Accords would forestall US intervention and give it time to rebuild its influence in the south and eventually move towards unification through the 1956 elections outlined in the Accords.

The settlement, however flawed, did give Vietnam a chance for independence although, as the head of the conference remarked, 'everything now depended on the spirit in which Geneva is followed', but few documents were signed. If the outcome of Geneva was open to interpretation, the policy enacted by the US after August 1954 highlighted its position on it. It was concerned by the fact that the DRV had come out of the negotiations in a stronger position. South Vietnam was perceived to be weak with a leader, Bao Dai, who had very little popular support. On the other hand, the DRV in the north had gained in prestige by its defeat of the French and had achieved international recognition. Should the elections be held in 1956 it was certain that the communists led by Ho Chi Minh would win control of the country.

THE CREATION OF SEATO
Eisenhower and his administration worked throughout the summer of 1954 to build on its attempt to form a United Action alliance in the belief

that the loss by the French to the Vietminh had led to a loss of credibility for the US. In September 1954, NSC 5429/2 outlined the aims of Eisenhower.

> *The United States must protect its position and restore its prestige in the Far East by a new initiative in South East Asia where the situation must be stabilised to prevent further losses to communism through creeping expansion and subversion or overt aggression.*

Secretary of State Dulles was eager to build on the United Action initiative began during the Dien Bien Phu crisis. In summer 1954, he sought to establish a collective security alliance in south-east Asia. The **SEATO** Protocol was signed by Britain, France, the US, Australia, New Zealand, Pakistan, the Philippines and Thailand. In defiance of the Geneva Accords, which stipulated that Laos and Cambodia should remain neutral, the SEATO Protocol openly treated South Vietnam, Laos and Cambodia as its 'protected areas'. The US could now support South Vietnam against any perceived communist threat.

CONCLUSION

In *Intervention: How America Became Involved in Vietnam* (1986), **George McT Kahin** argued that US political and military involvement in Vietnam reflected a genuine fear of Chinese expansionism, a belief that communists in Vietnam were little more than a political tool of China. What really mattered to US policymakers about Vietnam, or Indochina as a whole, was not its economic importance, or its supposed position as the first in a row of dominoes, but the plain fact that it was the most likely place for a further communist advance in south-east Asia. The defeat of the French at Dien Bien Phu and the establishment of the Vietminh in North Vietnam had seriously worried President Eisenhower. In a debate in the National Security Council, Secretary of Defence Charles E Wilson argued that 'we [the USA] should not trap ourselves into going to war in south-east Asia to save South Vietnam'. Eisenhower responded that: 'Some time we must face up to it; we cannot go on losing areas of the free world forever.' In 1954 and after, the Eisenhower administration firmly committed itself to South Vietnam and its fragile government. US policy had now changed from one of no military intervention before 1954 to a pledge to provide military support, training and equipment for a South Vietnamese army.

CHAPTER 7

Increasing tension, 1954–63

AN OVERVIEW

The period from the Geneva Agreement of 1954 (see pages 87–89) to the assassination of the US President John F Kennedy in 1963 saw a gradual increase in the involvement of the US in the Vietnam conflict. The American government faced the dilemma of offering support to the regime of Ngo Dinh Diem that had been established in South Vietnam. Diem's government was corrupt, brutal and intolerant of all opposition. It was hardly the beacon of freedom and democracy against communism that the US would have preferred it to be.

The situation in South Vietnam was to worsen in the early 1960s as the insurgency activities of the Vietcong, aided by the People's Army of North Vietnam, increased. When Kennedy became president in 1961 he was faced with the decision of whether to expand US support for South Vietnam, under a regime the US was finding increasingly repellent, or to withdraw from Vietnam and risk the spread of communism in south-east Asia. Armed with conflicting evidence from a series of reports from advisers, Kennedy considered withdrawal as an option but decided to support South Vietnam. Failure to do so would seriously undermine the reputation of the US as the world's policeman against communist revolution. Yet, with the regime in South Vietnam becoming increasingly fragile, this decision seemed likely to entail greater US involvement.

BIOGRAPHIES

Senator Mike Mansfield (1903–2001) In November 1962, the US Senate Committee on Foreign Relations sanctioned Kennedy's request to send a fact-finding mission to Vietnam. This mission was led by Senator Mansfield, an expert on Asian affairs. In February 1963, extracts from his report were published in the *New York Times*. The publication of the findings stimulated a major debate in Congress about the future role of the US in Vietnam.

President John F Kennedy (1917–63) President of the USA between 1961 and 1963, Kennedy was committed to the containment of communism. His international stature was raised by the resolution of the **Cuban Missile Crisis** and in achieving the **Nuclear Test Ban Treaty** with Nikita Khrushchev in June 1963. However, his actions in Vietnam fundamentally committed the US to support the South Vietnam regime of Ngo Dinh Diem. In November 1963, Kennedy was assassinated in Dallas, Texas.

Ngo Dinh Diem (1901–63) An anti-communist nationalist who was appointed by Bao Dai as his prime minister in 1954, in 1955, following a national referendum, he became the first president of the Republic of Vietnam and governed South Vietnam with the support of the US administration until his overthrow in November 1963. He was fiercely anti-communist but lacked popular support because he was reclusive and was distrustful of the advice of anyone outside of his family.

HISTORICAL INTERPRETATIONS

Since the end of US involvement in Vietnam in 1975 there has been ongoing debate about the role of the US in the origins of the Second Vietnam War between the US and Vietnam in the period 1964–73. Early studies tended to focus on four main issues:

- the role of successive US administrations and decision making
- military tactics
- the debate as to why the US lost the war
- the moral arguments about US intervention in Indochina

David L Anderson's *Trapped by Success: The Eisenhower Administration and Vietnam, 1953–61* (1993) is one of the first comprehensive studies of Eisenhower's role in the origins of the Vietnam War. Anderson argued that the dominant characteristic of the Eisenhower administration's role in Vietnam was involvement and commitment to the Diem regime. He argued that Vietnam was a client state from 1954 with the USA providing economic aid in order to support the regime of Diem. In addition, the reason Eisenhower was prepared to invest so much in South Vietnam related to the **domino theory**. That is, Vietnam was the place in which the US would make a stand against the expansion of communism in south-east Asia.

One of the earliest accounts to explore the role of the Kennedy administration and its involvement in Vietnam was **David Halberstam**'s *Best and the Brightest* (1969, reprinted 1992). Halberstam's study argued that in its eagerness to succeed in the Cold War the Kennedy administration made many mistakes, the biggest being to pay insufficient attention to events in South Vietnam under the Diem regime. The second mistake was to believe that the Vietnamese wanted a democratic system based on that of the US. This point was further developed by **Frances Fitzgerald** in *Fire in the Lake* (1972), which explored the differences between the traditional world of the Vietnamese peasant and the US values of freedom, democracy and capitalism which underlay the decision to intervene in the Vietnamese conflict.

Later studies, including the work of **Leslie Gelb and Richard Bett**, *The Irony of Vietnam: The System Worked* (1979), argued that the Kennedy years are the key to understanding US policy in Vietnam. By using **Daniel Ellsberg**'s *Pentagon Papers* (1971) and other studies, they were able to analyse Kennedy's motives and policies in the period 1961–3. They argued that Kennedy did as little as possible to avoid defeat in order to protect his own position. Thus, any responsibility for mistakes was Kennedy's rather than government advisers. As Gelb and Bett were themselves government advisers, their argument was to some extent moving any blame for mistakes to the president rather than advisers. **Guenter Lewy**, in *America in Vietnam* (1978), while justifying US involvement in Vietnam because of the communist threat, nevertheless also criticised the military tactics adopted by the Kennedy regime as inappropriate and insufficient in responding to insurgent activity.

In contrast, historians in the mid-1980s started to explore the international aspects of the Vietnam War. In *An International History of the Vietnam War: The Kennedy Strategy* (1985), **R B Smith** placed the Vietnam insurgency into a global context. Smith contended that to comprehend the Vietnam problem during the Kennedy administration one must first visualise that Vietnam was just one aspect of a larger global world power struggle. This view was challenged by **George McT Kahin**'s *Intervention: How America Became Involved in Vietnam* (1986). Kahin analysed in depth the major US decisions between 1945 and 1965 and how they underestimated the role of the North Vietnamese in the origins of the US Vietnamese War. His basic argument is that the insurgency in South Vietnam was directed by the National Liberation Front in an attempt to reunify Vietnam. In other words, Kahin argued that if the US had been more sensitive to the demands of the Vietnamese it would have realised that the conflict that emerged in 1946 was primarily an anti-colonial struggle to remove the French. After 1959 it became a civil war as both the northern and the southern insurgents fought to reunify Vietnam.

Kahin challenged the view that Vietnam was important to the security of the US, a view supported by **Gabriel Kolko** in *Anatomy of a War: Vietnam, the United States, and the Modern Historical Experience* (1985). In this study, Kolko argued that US involvement in Vietnam was a natural outcome of its role in the modern world: the 'major inheritor of the mantle of imperialism in modern history'. The USA, he argued, acted not to defend a threat to its welfare but because it sought a controllable, responsive regime in Vietnam, one that was beneficial to the global role of the US. Maintaining US credibility in Vietnam was essential to that role.

In the late 1990s, Kolko's views on the Vietnam War were further developed by **Robert D Schulinzger** in *A Time for War: The United States and Vietnam, 1941–1975* (1997), who argued that there was always a sense among US officials that time was running out. This urgency exaggerated the strategic importance of Vietnam in the US's global conflict with the Soviet Union and China. Schulinzger concluded that the Kennedy administration's involvement in Vietnam was flawed: 'The position of the US in the world was not so precarious, and that of the

Soviet Union and other revolutionary movements not so dominant that an earlier communist victory in Vietnam would have changed the outcome of the Cold War.' In conclusion, Schulinzger argued that Kennedy defined a gain for the North Vietnamese as a gain for the Soviet Union and China, a sentiment that agreed with Eisenhower's view that. 'Some time we must face up to it; we cannot go on losing areas of the free world forever.'

The majority of studies on the origins of the Vietnam War have tended to focus on the origins of the Vietnam War from a US perspective, in particular exploring the war in the context of the US's struggle against the advance of communism in Indochina. **Yang Kuisong**, a professor in History at Beijing University, has argued in *Changes in Mao Zedong's Attitude Toward the Indochina War, 1949–1973* (2002) that the intervention of China in the Vietnam conflict was influenced by Mao's concern for China's security. In the Franco–Vietnam War, 1946–54, China had been a major provider of weapons and economic aid to the Vietminh in its struggle against French colonial power. According to Kuisong, the ideological conflict that emerged in 1958 between China and the Soviet Union initially led Mao to resume support for the Vietminh struggle for the reunification of Vietnam in 1960. But in 1963, when the US started to expand its military intervention in South Vietnam, China expanded its support in the interests of its own national security.

In support of Kuisong, **Ang Cheng Guan**, in *The Vietnam War, 1962–64: The Vietnamese Communist Perspective* (2000), has argued that the North Vietnamese sought an international conference on the neutralisation of Vietnam. In 1962, they looked to Mao for support but the growth of insurgency in South Vietnam led by the National Liberation Front had blocked any progress on this idea. Instead the Vietminh in the north decided to support the southern insurgents in the struggle against the US military advisers and Diem's regime with the help of economic and military aid from China. Again the emphasis in this study is that the war in Vietnam was a civil war.

In summarising the debates on the Vietnam War, there appear to be four clear views emerging from the evidence.

- The traditional view criticised US intervention as unnecessary and even immoral, and accused US leaders of deceiving the nation.
- The later views defended US policy and the war as a struggle against the aggressive expansion of communism in south-east Asia.
- The revisionist view argued the Vietnam War was, first, an anti-colonial war against the French, then the US; second, it was a civil war between the communists in the north and the pro-capitalist regime led by Diem in the south.
- The new evidence suggests that Mao Zedong, leader of the People's Republic of China, was intent on extending communist influence and control in south-east Asia through the support of wars of national

liberation and that the USA's actions were a response to this change in China's policy.

THE APPOINTMENT OF NGO DINH DIEM AS PRIME MINISTER OF SOUTH VIETNAM

In June 1954, in an attempt to win US support for South Vietnam, Emperor Bao Dai appointed Ngo Dinh Diem as prime minister. The US hoped that the staunch anti-communist Diem would construct a non-communist state in the south that was not only acceptable to the US but also popular with the majority of the South Vietnamese population. One of the major US criticisms of the French during the war had been that France never lent support to popular anti-communist nationalists who would have posed a real challenge to the leadership of Ho Chi Minh. To British eyes, Diem was unsuitable because of his reluctance to engage in the preparations for the 1956 elections. His history of opposition to the French meant that they were none too keen about his appointment. However, neither the British nor the French could find an alternative to Diem. Eisenhower and Dulles argued that his anti-colonialism and single-mindedness might prove useful in taking a stand against the communists.

Diem and the Sects Crisis, 1955

The exodus of almost one million Catholics to the south from the north after the Geneva Conference proved extremely embarrassing to Ho Chi Minh and the Vietminh. However, this 'forced' migration of the Catholics was more of a propaganda campaign organised by Diem, a staunch Catholic, and the US adviser Colonel Edward Lansdale than a flight from a repressive regime in the north. It was also possible that many of the migrants headed south because of the offer by Lansdale of five acres of land and a buffalo rather than his assurance that 'the Virgin Mary is going south'.

The most serious threat to Diem in the early months of his premiership was the **Sects Crisis** in spring 1955. The religious groups the Cao Dai and Hoa Hao represented the most potent political forces in South Vietnam. The Cao Dai claimed to have two million followers and an army of 20,000. Its power base was the Mekong Delta where it exercised local political control. The Hoa Hao also lived in the Delta region; it had as many as one million followers and an army of 15,000. Equally powerful was the Binh Xuyen, a mafia-like organisation with an army of 40,000. This group earned money from prostitution and gambling in Saigon, and virtually ran the city's police force. The French, unable to incorporate the sects into South Vietnam society, had virtually given them autonomy. When Diem was appointed they refused to surrender their power or fortunes to the new national government.

To win over their support Diem offered them posts in the national government but they refused and instead demanded autonomy in their own territories. In spring 1955, the army of the Binh Xuyen, together with the armies of the sects, joined forces and launched a mortar attack at the presidential palace. In response, Diem ordered the army to attack and the sects were defeated. This successful counter-attack demonstrated the loyalty of the army to Diem, his strength as a leader and US commitment to his leadership. The scale of the US commitment can be measured by the fact that Lansdale was prepared to spend over US$3 million in bribes to the leadership of the Cao Dai and Hoa Hao to buy their loyalty to Diem.

French withdrawal from Vietnam

The US commitment to Diem provoked the final crisis with France. In October 1954, Eisenhower made the decision to channel aid directly to Diem and bypass the French. The French government argued that Diem had handled the Sects Crisis badly and this demonstrated his inability to act as prime minister. The French now withdrew from Vietnam because they were no longer prepared to support the US decision to keep Diem in his post. Faced with rebellion in their North African colonies, the French began a phased withdrawal from what had been the most affluent colony in the French Union. The US took on the responsibility for the survival of South Vietnam.

DIEM AND THE ESTABLISHMENT OF THE REPUBLIC OF VIETNAM

From 1954, Diem, with the support of the US, ruled in a dictatorial fashion in South Vietnam. This was brought into focus when, on 26 April, eighteen of Saigon's most prominent anti-communists issued a public statement, the **Carvelle Manifesto**, named after the hotel in which they met. Their criticisms focused on Diem's 'anti-democratic elections, the continuous arrests that filled the jails to the rafters, and charged that effective power had been concentrated in the hands of an irresponsible "family", Ngo Dinh Nhu, from whom emanate all orders'.

The basis of Diem's support was the rich Catholic elite who exploited the Buddhist peasant majority; he offered no land reforms, rents were high and food was scarce.

- The Diem executive branch of the South Vietnamese government was dominated by his brothers who in turn were supported by wealthy Catholic landlords who used their positions to repress the peasants and Buddhists who represented the majority of the population of South Vietnam.
- All political parties were outlawed and press freedoms restricted.
- The bulk of Diem's government programmes were focused on how to secure further aid from the US to support the expansion of the Army of the Republic of Vietnam (ARVN). Perhaps the worst aspect of the US aid programme was the commercial import programme. As late as 1957, two-thirds of the imports consisted of consumer goods and very little financial aid went into industry or agriculture. This programme created artificially higher standards of living while contributing very

limited resources to development. In other words, Diem's regime was trying to buy the support of the South Vietnamese.

Having established his power base, Diem called for an election in 1955 to determine whether the South Vietnamese wanted to be ruled by a monarch, Bao Dai, or as a Republic under his leadership. Of the 6 million eligible to vote, 98.2 per cent supported Diem. In Saigon, he won 605,000 votes – 200,000 more than were registered. This blatant election rigging concerned the US administration but it continued to support him with economic aid and recognition of the Republic of Vietnam (RVN). With firm backing from the US, Diem also blocked the elections called for in the Geneva Accords. In August 1955, Diem made a statement supporting the principle of free elections but refused to enter into consultations with the North Vietnamese. Thus began the division of Vietnam into two separate states. Recognising that elections would not take place, the Soviet Union suggested the partition of the country along the 17th Parallel be made permanent. The Soviet Union and the US now vied for influence and sought to demonstrate the superiority of their respective lifestyles and ideologies in the region.

THE DEMOCRATIC REPUBLIC OF VIETNAM

Following the Geneva Conference, Ho Chi Minh and the Vietminh sought to establish support from China and the Soviet Union for the elections promised in the Geneva Accords. However, after the Korean War and the French–Indochina War both countries were focusing on improving relations with the US. Soviet leader Khrushchev was actively promoting the new Soviet line of *peaceful co-existence* to stabilise the situation in Europe and ease Cold War tensions. At the same time, Mao Zedong was promoting his five principles of peaceful co-existence:

- non-interference in the internal affairs of other nations
- internal disputes in a country to be dealt with by that country alone
- other countries should neither intervene nor exploit these disputes
- a government chosen by its own people should be recognised by other countries
- China would not export revolution.

China and the Soviet Union did take up the issue of South Vietnam's non-compliance over the national elections with the US, but it was only done in a half-hearted way. However, both leaders did promise to provide substantial financial support to the DRV – US$200 million from China and US$100 million from the Soviet Union – for post-war reconstruction and the advancement to a socialist society. On his return to Hanoi in October 1954 after eight years fighting in the jungle, Ho Chi Minh publicly thanked China and the Soviet Union for their economic assistance. The Vietminh now chose to achieve unification by peaceful means through a socialist programme of land reform and industrialisation, while at the same time supporting its counterparts in the south. The new slogan of the Vietnam was 'Build the north, look to the south'.

DIEM'S ATTACKS ON THE VIETMINH SUPPORTERS IN THE SOUTH, 1956–9

In the south at this time, Diem had stepped up his 'Denounce the communists' campaign and by May 1956 it was estimated that 94,000 former Vietminh supporters had 'rallied' to the government. Full figures were never released, but Diem's Secretary of State for Information claimed that between 15,000 and 20,000 ex-Vietminh had been detained in re-education camps. In the January 1957 edition of *Foreign Affairs,* **William Henderson** wrote:

> *In South Vietnam today is a quasi-police state characterised by arbitrary arrests and imprisonment, strict censorship of the press and the absence of an effective political opposition … All the techniques of political and psychological warfare as well as pacification campaigns involving extensive military operations, have been brought to bear against the underground.*

Thousands of communists and non-communist supporters of the Vietminh were killed or thrown into prison/concentration camps at least two years before the start of the communist-led insurgency. The high tide in the campaign of repression was the introduction of Law 10/59 on 6 May 1959. This went further than the earlier campaigns with the establishment of military tribunals which dealt with anyone perceived to have committed a crime against the new Republic. These charges included crimes of sabotage, belonging to the communists or Vietminh, or proclaiming or spreading unauthorised news about the economic situation in the Republic. This broad extension of crimes against the state allowed the regime to remove any form of opposition. Those charged had no right of appeal and were sentenced to death by guillotining. Together, Diem and Nhu tightened their control on the country through a range of laws that prohibited gatherings of any kind (including weddings) without permission from the government. They also imposed a rigorous censorship on both the Vietnamese and US press.

REASONS FOR INSURGENCY IN SOUTH VIETNAM, 1957–60

In 1959, the communist government in Hanoi authorised armed struggle against Diem's regime. Between 1959 and 1961, more than 4000 of Diem's officials were assassinated each year. There was increasingly little sympathy for Diem's regime in the countryside which made such a high level of political violence possible. In *Vietnam* (1983), **Stanley Karnow** pointed out that: 'The villages, open to Diem's troops by day, were run by the Vietcong at night.' Within his first two years in office, Diem replaced the local village councils with government-appointed officials, many of whom were northern Catholic. By 1959, Diem's government programme and the suppression of any opposition created a favourable climate in

South Vietnam for revolutionary activity. The peasantry was alienated from Diem's government by the programme of limited land reform and its pro-landlord stance. The sense of alienation was made worse by the introduction of the unpopular Khu Tru Mat, known as **agrovilles**. These were fortified villages protected by the army. Theoretically designed to provide a range of services – schools, medical facilities and electricity – many peasants deeply resented them because of their forced removal from their homes and lands, which contained the sacred tombs of their ancestors. The agroville programme was eventually abandoned, but only after it had provoked enormous rural discontent.

Diem also managed to antagonise many of the ethnically non-Vietnamese tribal groups that occupied over half of South Vietnam. The Montagnards under French rule had been allowed to retain their identity. However, in 1957 Diem undertook to impose Vietnamese culture on them and to integrate them into South Vietnam. He followed this with a policy of population transfer, whereby some 210,000 ethnic Vietnamese from the coast and Catholics from the north were resettled in fortified villages onto Montagnard-owned lands. The Montagnards played a key role in supporting the insurgency when it started in 1959. This attempt by Diem to artificially engineer changes in the social structure in South Vietnam fed into the discontent in South Vietnam and provoked an increase in revolutionary activity. Diem appeared unable to comprehend the needs of the peasants, who made up more than 80 per cent of the population of South Vietnam. Much of the economic aid supplied to the regime was being absorbed by the cities and towns, and not the rural areas, yet the corruption and dictatorial methods of Diem's regime led to the disaffection of the educated, professional and commercial classes in urban areas. US Ambassador Elbright Durbrow warned the Eisenhower administration that unless Diem reformed his government and mobilised popular support, the insurgency would overwhelm South Vietnam.

However, throughout much of 1960 the attention of the Eisenhower administration was focused on Europe. Cold War tensions rose in this period due to the disagreements over Berlin and the Soviet shooting down of an US U2 spy plane over the Soviet Union. This, together with the Cuban revolution in 1959, meant that problems in Vietnam, and in fact in the whole of Indochina, were not dealt with.

THE NATIONAL LIBERATION FRONT

At the Third National Congress of the Vietnam Workers' Party, convened in September 1960, much of the focus was on the success of the first Five Year Plans in North Vietnam. However, there was no consensus on how to proceed in the south and bring about the downfall of the Diem regime. What concerned many of the Vietminh was the fear that widespread armed resistance to Diem might precipitate direct US military intervention on his behalf. At the end of the conference, Ton Duc Thang called for a national liberation front that not only reflected the different social strata within South Vietnam, but also the various religious and ethnic minorities. The aim was to be the creation of a peaceful and unified Vietnam.

The National Liberation Front for the Liberation of South Vietnam (NLF) was formally established on 20 December 1960. Its task was to 'liberate the south from the rule of the US imperialists and their henchmen, and achieve national reunification and complete independence and freedom throughout the country'. In order to coordinate the military aspects of the insurgency in the South, the People's Liberation Armed Forces (PLAF) formed in February 1961. These insurgents came to be known as the **Vietcong**, a derogatory term applied by the Diem regime, meaning Vietnam Communist. Units from the DRV were sent to the south to perform a number of tasks.

- Group 559 was directed to construct a system of trails to transport troops, weapons and supplies from north to south.
- Group 759 facilitated the shipment of goods and personnel down the undefended South China Sea coast.
- Special units called the Bo Doi Truong (Central Mountains Troops) carried equipment, first by foot or on bicycle, later by truck as the trails were developed, and transported some 5000 party activists from the north to the south.

In contrast to Diem's government of the regions, the NLF exploited the peasants' grievances, in particular the land issue, and behaved in a largely exemplary way towards the peasants by putting pressure on village councils to lower rents and distribute land to those without any, thus gaining widespread support in the south.

China and the NLF

The Sino–Soviet Summit of 1958 resulted in a major disagreement between the communist leaders Mao Zedong and Khrushchev over a number of important issues:

- the Sino–India border conflict, ongoing since August 1949
- the establishment of a joint Sino–Soviet submarine fleet and the building of a radar station in China
- China not wanting to be seen as a client state of the Soviet Union
- the Soviet Union's reluctance to support revolution in nations struggling for independence and/or against repressive regimes.

This dispute had important consequences for the DRV as both the Soviets and the Chinese competed to win the support of the communists in Vietnam. Both sides sought to 'buy' the loyalty of the DRV by supplying large quantities of military and economic aid throughout the Second Vietnam War 1964–73. In the meantime, Mao, keen to be seen as the leader of international revolutionary communism and concerned about the threat posed to Chinese security, continued to provide economic and military aid to the North Vietnamese. In *Changes in Mao Zedong's Attitude Toward the Indochina War, 1949–1973* (2002), **Yang Kuisong** states that in 1960 China gave US$1.9 billion to the DRV and at the end of 1960 Mao promised Ho Chi Minh that China would send food and weapons to South Vietnam via the DRV.

PRESIDENT KENNEDY AND INDOCHINA

President John F Kennedy came into office in January 1961 with the same worldview and set of assumptions about Indochina as the Eisenhower administration. Despite growing evidence of a serious rift between the People's Republic of China and the Soviet Union over their roles within the communist movement, the forces of communism were still perceived as a united threat that had to be met by the US on a global basis. In January 1961, Kennedy and his administration were faced with deteriorating relations with the communist world due to disagreement over the status of Berlin, the collapse of the Strategic Arms Limitations Talks between the US and the Soviet Union, the result of the U2 spy plane incident in 1960 and the growing crisis in Indochina.

The situation in South Vietnam continued to deteriorate as the insurgency led by the Vietcong steadily increased its territorial grip over large numbers of the peasant population. However, when Eisenhower met John F Kennedy on 15 January 1961, the day before his inauguration as president, it was not South Vietnam that dominated their discussions on south-east Asia but Laos. Eisenhower warned Kennedy that Laos was vitally important to the strategic interests of the US in the region because its fall to the communist-dominated Pathet Lao would provide the Vietcong with a military base from which to launch attacks against South Vietnam, Thailand and Cambodia. Such thinking was framed by the domino theory, which had influenced US foreign policy since just after the end of the Second World War.

The Eisenhower administration had refused to accept the neutralisation of Laos required by the Geneva Accords and ignored the neutralist leader Souvanna Phouma. Instead, US aid had gone to the Laotian government led by General Phoumi Nosovan.

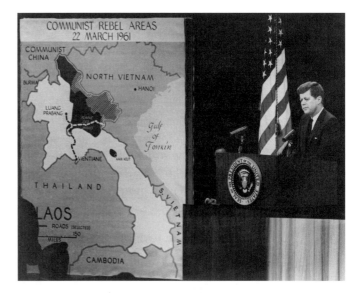

JFK explaining the situation in south-east Asia, 23 March 1961

However, the oppressive policies introduced by Phoumi Nosovan led to the neutralist factions moving to side with the Pathet Lao, Laotian communists supported with aid from the Soviet Union. The influence of the Soviets in Laos convinced the Kennedy administration that the only feasible choice was a negotiated settlement on Laos. In May 1961, Kennedy told the British that he would back a Soviet–British initiative to convene a Geneva Conference on Laos. The final agreement in July 1962 created a neutral and independent Laos. But Kennedy, fearful of being accused of the loss of south-east Asia, did not want to commit military forces to Laos because of the geographical difficulties in engaging in any type of warfare in this region. As far as Kennedy and his advisers were concerned, South Vietnam was logistically and strategically a better place to make a stand against a communist threat.

Kennedy's foreign policy

In Kennedy's view, the Laotian problem reflected the failure of the Eisenhower administration to deal successfully with revolutionary nationalist movements in Asia, Africa and Latin America. The policy of **massive deterrence** developed by John Foster Dulles was criticised because it could be said to restrict other means of dealing with adversaries by offering two choices: nuclear war, or humiliation as the US withdrew from these situations. In February 1960 before his election as president, Kennedy had stated:

> Both before and after 1953 events have demonstrated that our nuclear retaliatory power is not enough. It cannot deter communist aggression that is limited to justify atomic war. It cannot protect uncommitted nations against a communist take-over using local or guerrilla forces. It cannot prevent the communists from gradually nibbling at the fringe of the free worlds territory and strength, until our security has been steadily eroded in piecemeal fashion, each Red advance being too small to justify massive retaliation.

In effect, after 1961, Kennedy set out to develop a range of methods for dealing with adversaries that were quite different from those of his predecessor Eisenhower. This strategy, worked out with key members of his administration including Secretary of Defence Robert McNamara and Secretary of State Dean Rusk, came to be known as the strategy of **flexible response**. However, at the core of this strategy was still the policy of the containment of communism.

The aims of the strategy of flexible response were to:

- deter war
- convince potential aggressors that attacks against the US or its allies would be futile.

New ways of resolving conflict were to include diplomatic settlements through linkage with financial and limited military aid in the form of advisers and training. The thinking behind this strategy was that in a changing world when many nations were moving towards independence from colonial rule the US needed to guide these emerging nations in a non-communist direction. In other words, the emphasis was on the non-military aspects of containment. Other methods included:

- exchange programmes
- assistance in economic planning
- technical assistance
- the provision of finance.

In this way the US thought it could alter the internal structures of the newly independent states to enable them to withstand pressures for revolutionary change that might ultimately lead to communist revolutions.

KENNEDY AND THE SOUTH VIETNAM CRISIS, 1961–3

In January 1961, Khrushchev, in an attempt to heal the rift between himself and Mao, declared support for the wars of national liberation then emerging in Asia, Africa and South America. However, Kennedy misinterpreted Khrushchev's views and was convinced that the Soviet Union was intent on an aggressive expansionist policy. Kennedy became determined to prevail in Vietnam, otherwise he would lose the confidence of the newly emerging nation states – including Thailand and the Philippines, which were allies of the US.

The decision to negotiate over the Laotian issue had seriously shaken Diem's confidence in the new Kennedy administration. There is no indication that Kennedy considered a negotiated political settlement in Vietnam and in many ways he is responsible for the militarisation of US intervention. Kennedy sanctioned the use of US-piloted helicopters and US military advisers to engage with the Vietnamese insurgents. In January 1961, he authorised the use of 400 US Special Forces, commonly known as the Green Berets, which together with 700 military advisers breached the Geneva Accords on the number of military advisers.

So the emphasis in Kennedy's policy for South Vietnam now shifted towards **counterinsurgency** and the greater use of military advisers. At this time, Kennedy was in many ways still unsure about how to resolve the South Vietnam problem. His indecisiveness was a result of the humiliating defeat of the US-supported **Bay of Pigs invasion** of Cuba in April 1961, planned by the Eisenhower administration and executed when Kennedy had just taken up office. This fiasco served to strengthen Kennedy's conviction that he had to demonstrate toughness against communism everywhere.

In order to reassure Ngo Dinh Diem that the US was unwilling to negotiate a neutrality settlement for South Vietnam, in May 1961 Kennedy sent Vice-President Lyndon Johnson on a fact-finding mission. Following advice from the Joint Chiefs of Staff, Kennedy instructed Johnson to offer Ngo Dinh Diem the use of US regular forces to help crush the communist insurgents. Diem's refusal stemmed mainly from his fear that it would further undermine his position by compromising his reputation as a nationalist in the eyes of the South Vietnamese people. Vice-President Johnson recommended to Kennedy that:

> *Better management of the US military aid programme and an increase of US$50 million in military and economic assistance to build up the ARVN to over 100,000 in strength would be sufficient to sustain Diem's regime. US combat troops were neither required nor desirable; if introduced they would revive anti-colonial emotions, to Diem's detriment.*

During September 1961, the Kennedy administration became aware that mounting insurgent attacks threatened to overrun most of the rural Mekong Delta. The CIA reported that the size of the insurgent armed force was approximately 16,000. In addition, most of the arms used by the insurgents were American in origin, most probably 'lost' during combat by the ARVN. In November 1961, the Kennedy administration began a major reassessment of policy. In *America's Longest War: The United States and Vietnam, 1950–75* (1996), **George Herring** questioned Eisenhower's and Kennedy's fundamental belief that they were in Vietnam to defend democracy. Herring argues that the evidence would suggest their support for Diem's regime was more to do with preventing communism and their own strategic interests. The US devoted little attention to what was actually happening in the south and, despite its massive foreign aid programme, exerted little influence. Diem no doubt took advantage of this situation, and aid intended to support economic and social programmes inevitably ended up being used for the ARVN.

The Taylor–Rostow Report, November 1961

The Vietcong operations in autumn 1961 and the weakness of Diem's forces in deterring these attacks encouraged President Kennedy to send a delegation to Vietnam on 18 October 1961. Led by General Maxwell Taylor, a military adviser and key figure in the administration's counterinsurgency tactics, and Walt Rostow, the Chair of the State Planning Department Policy Committee, its instructions were to report on the situation in Vietnam. The Taylor–Rostow Report of November called for:

- improved training of the ARVN troops
- greater use of helicopters for counterinsurgency missions
- strategic bombing of parts of North Vietnam
- increased use of US combat troops to counter the activities of the Vietcong and to act as a morale boost for the South Vietnamese people and their government.

The Taylor–Rostow Report provided a great insight into the era as it showed a complete misunderstanding of the nature of the war in South Vietnam and a contempt for the communists who already had a distinguished and impressive record against France. Finally, the authors of the report made the assumption that the people and government of South Vietnam were fighting for the same aims. The real problems in South Vietnam, however, were political – growing discontent with Diem and his administration and discontent among the peasantry. The response from the US administration, however, viewed the insurgency as being activated by the communists in the north. This helped to reinforce Diem's arguments that political reform in the south was unnecessary, since the insurgency was not a southern-based reaction to Diem's government but one directed by Ho Chi Minh in the north.

In a letter to Ngo Dinh Diem in December 1961, President Kennedy assured him of continued US support against the communists.

> *In accordance with the declaration made by Eisenhower to support the people of South Vietnam in 1954, and in response to your request, we are prepared to help the Republic of Vietnam to protect its people and to preserve its independence. We shall promptly increase our assistance to your defence effort as well as help relieve the destruction of the floods that you describe.*

Interestingly the Taylor–Rostow Report calculated the US could bring a further 8000 US troops into South Vietnam under the guise of a logistical task force whose aim was to repair the flood damage just suffered in the Mekong Delta. However, Kennedy blocked this proposal.

The Taylor–Rostow Report opened up a debate among the Kennedy administration about the level of military commitment in South Vietnam and the desperate need for further political reforms by the Diem government. There were a number of important men in Washington, including President Kennedy, who had grave misgivings about sending in combat troops to South Vietnam. His fears were based on the notion that once combat troops were committed to defend South Vietnam their numbers would escalate. If, on the other hand, he failed to send in adequate numbers and South Vietnam was lost, Kennedy would be accused of not giving enough aid to save an ally in south-east Asia and this would lead to criticisms within the US of his position. In the end Kennedy compromised. His caution about combat troops was well placed, but his decisions marked yet another crucial turning point and increased direct US involvement in Vietnam.

Military Assistance Command

In February 1962, the Kennedy administration agreed to send additional military aid under the newly formed Military Assistance Command, Vietnam (MACV) led by General Paul Harkins. The MACV was formed to coordinate all US military activity in South Vietnam and replace the MAAG. New techniques to reduce the insurgent threat included the use of napalm and defoliants dropped by helicopters to remove the cover and food available in the jungle to the Vietcong. These methods further alienated the Vietnamese peasants from both the Diem regime and the USA, who were now perceived to be destroying the livelihoods of the peasants. The number of US advisers rose from 3205 in December 1961 to more than 9000 by the end of 1962.

South Vietnamese president Ngo Dinh Diem visiting a strategic Hamlet near Pleiku

The Strategic Hamlet Programme

Early in 1962, the Diem government launched the Strategic Hamlet Programme. This was similar to the agroville project a few years earlier. The idea was to herd peasants into armed and protected villages. In theory, the strategic hamlets were to protect and isolate the peasants from the Vietcong militarily, economically and politically, thereby denying the Vietcong manpower, food and intelligence. The peasants were to be compensated for the discomfort of forced relocation through an extensive array of social services, seed, fertilisers and other agricultural support. The programme was placed under the control of Ngo Dinh Nhu and, by the end of 1962, accounted for 3225 hamlets, extended to 7205 by June 1963. These hamlets accounted for 70 per cent of the South Vietnamese peasant population. Many in the Kennedy administration doubted the success of the programme because the ARVN troops found it difficult to protect them from Vietcong infiltration. The peasants disliked the programme because it uprooted them from their ancestral lands. It did nothing to bind the people to the government of Diem since his brother Nhu lacked qualified people to staff the programme, and many corrupt officials worked on it both at a government and village level.

The ARVN and the containment of the Vietcong threat

With the increase in the number of new weapons and US advisers, the ARVN launched major operations against the Vietcong in the spring and summer of 1962. However, the increased use of helicopters for getting troops into areas where insurgents were known to be active worked against the containment of the threat. The noise of the helicopters gave the Vietcong advanced warning of an attack and they would slip away into the neighbouring countryside or jungle. Ironically, while the ARVN and US advisers were chasing the enemy, the Vietcong was gaining wider support on the ground. Peasants whose livelihoods had been undermined by the activities of the ARVN, in particular the spraying of defoliants that not only destroyed trees but also the rice crops, were now being mobilised in support of the Vietcong.

THE CUBAN MISSILE CRISIS, 1962 AND ITS IMPLICATIONS FOR SOUTH VIETNAM

The Kennedy administration become preoccupied in the summer and autumn of 1962 with the Cuban Missile Crisis. As a result, it devoted little attention to what was happening in Vietnam. The inconsistencies of Khrushchev's foreign-policy aims, which oscillated between the extremes of belligerence (illustrated by his 'Wars of National Liberation' speech) and conciliation (illustrated by the policy of peaceful co-existence which manifested itself in the Nuclear Test Ban Treaty), caused major problems for Kennedy. However, the Cuban Missile Crisis in October 1962 reinforced Kennedy's suspicions of Khrushchev's peaceful co-existence policy. In response to the positioning of nuclear weapons in Cuba by the Soviet Union, Kennedy considered the possible use of nuclear weapons. In his Address to the Nation on 22 October 1962, Kennedy revealed his determination to block Soviet expansion.

> *For many years both the Soviet Union and the US have deployed strategic nuclear weapons with great care, never upsetting the precarious status quo which ensured that these weapons would not be used in the absence of some vital challenge ... Our policy has been one of patience and restraint, as befits a peaceful and powerful nation, which leads a worldwide alliance. We have been determined not to be diverted from our central concerns by mere irritants and fanatics. But now further action is required and those actions may only be the beginning. We will not prematurely or unnecessarily risk the costs of worldwide war – but neither will we shrink from that risk at any time it must be faced.*

Interestingly, whether because of changes in Soviet policy towards the US as a result of the Cuban Missile Crisis and Kennedy's determined actions to block the missiles, or as a result of the Sino–Soviet split in 1958, the Soviets appear to have downplayed their role in Vietnam in the period between1961 and 1965.

SENATOR MIKE MANSFIELD'S REPORT, 1963

Mounting criticism of the Vietnam policy by the US press, including the denunciation of Diem's government as corrupt and unpopular, and of the rise in the number of US troops in Vietnam, concerned the Kennedy administration. As a result Kennedy sent advisers to South Vietnam on a fact-finding mission. One influential report was compiled by Senator Mike Mansfield. This report to Kennedy in February 1963 warned:

- the struggle in South Vietnam was becoming a 'US war' that could not be justified by US security interests in the area
- all the current difficulties existed in Vietnam in 1955, but seven years and US$2 billion of US aid had not made any impact on the situation
- Diem's regime was less (not more) stable, more removed from the people

- the escalation of the conflict with the Vietcong was of greater concern to the USA than it was to the South Vietnamese government and people
- the costs of US involvement in Vietnam would escalate if changes were not made to current policies
- further measures to save South Vietnam had to come from the Saigon government and the Vietnamese. Failure to gain their support should lead to a reduction of US commitment to the area.

In discussions with Mansfield, Kennedy's response to the point of withdrawal was positive. But Kennedy felt he could not withdraw from South Vietnam for another two years; his greatest fear at this time was the loss of the 1964 presidential elections. With the Republican candidate, Nixon, having lost only by a narrow margin in 1960, Kennedy believed that to withdraw from Vietnam at this time would lead to accusations of weakness against communist expansion in south-east Asia and the loss of the presidency.

Hilsman–Forrestal Report, January 1963
In response to growing press and congressional criticisms, Kennedy also sent senior advisers Roger Hilsman and Michael Forrestal to Vietnam to assess the military and political situation. While in Vietnam, Forrestal and Hilsman witnessed how US military advisers were being drawn into the escalating conflict with the Vietcong. Their report concluded that the US and the ARVN were containing the Vietcong threat, but the war would probably last longer than anticipated and would cost more in terms of lives and financial aid.

The Battle for Ap Bac
The event that shattered Kennedy's belief that the situation in South Vietnam was improving was the Battle of Ap Bac, only 80 kilometres from Saigon, in the Mekong Delta, which took place in January 1963. Being confident that Diem's regime was on the point of collapse, the Vietcong engaged in a major battle against the ARVN at Ap Bac. The ARVN outnumbered the Vietcong by ten to one but the operation was a disaster. The commanders of the ARVN delayed their own attack, which gave the Vietcong time to prepare its defences. Some of the ARVN units refused to attack or block escape routes and in the confusion some ARVN units fired on each other. After 61 deaths, (three of whom were US military advisers) and with more than 100 wounded, the ARVN broke off the engagement. In their report on the battle, Hilsman and Forrestal informed Kennedy that it had been a stunning defeat for the MACV-supported ARVN units. However, General Harkins called it a great success for the ARVN and indicated that with additional US military support the ARVN stood a good chance of controlling the insurgency. In his State of the Union speech in January 1963, Kennedy indicated that the military struggle was going favourably.

However, the victory at Ap Bac was a significant step forward for the Vietcong. The battle proved that it could be militarily successful in a battle against the ARVN and its US military advisers, despite having inferior weaponry. The communists learned two key lessons from the battle.

- It convinced them that the strategy of well-organised and equipped troops was correct.
- The Vietcong's firmly held belief that the art of winning a guerrilla war was to work hand in hand with the masses was reinforced. This strategy was to trouble the US troops in Vietnam throughout their stay from 1959 to 1973.

The Buddhist Crisis, 1963

Following the Ap Bac defeat, the Buddhist Crisis of May 1963 was triggered by the actions of Catholic Archbishop Ngo Dinh Thuc, brother of President Diem. On 8 May 1963, Thuc ordered that the carrying of flags on Buddha's birthday in Hué was forbidden. When the mass meeting of Buddhists refused to obey the law and the order to disperse by local officials was ignored, the deputy province chief ordered his troops to fire on the crowd. Nine people, including children, were killed. Rather than taking action to remedy the unrest, Diem accused the Vietcong of causing the deaths by using grenades. Despite being shown film of the incident, he refused to retreat from his views.

These actions and the protest of 10,000 in Hué on 10 May triggered yet more attacks against the Buddhists. In response, the Buddhists monks issued a manifesto demanding:

- legal equality with the Catholic Church
- an end to the arrests of the more politically active monks, who were accused of being communist agents
- greater freedom for Buddhists to practise their faith
- compensation for the families of victims of the 8 May shooting.

The Crisis confirmed to the US administration the unpopularity of the Diem regime. The ARVN attacks on Buddhists gathered in Hué further aggravated an already sensitive issue. Buddhist leaders who represented the majority of the South Vietnam population accused Diem's government, which was predominantly Catholic, of religious persecution. The protests culminated in June 1963 with the public self-immolation of Buddhist monk Thich Quang Duc in protest against the anti-Buddhist policies of Diem.

The international press spread photos of the burning monk around the world. This event led to widespread protests throughout South Vietnam and the growing discontent spread to the army. The situation was not helped when Madame Nhu, Diem's sister-in-law, publicly dismissed the burning as a 'Buddhist barbecue' and offered to supply the matches and gasoline to those who wished to imitate the actions of Duc.

Thich Quang Duc's self-immolation at a Saigon intersection, 11 June 1963

Throughout the summer of 1963, the US administration sought to reconcile the two sides but the situation deteriorated further when, on 21 August 1963, Ngo Dinh Nhu ordered the Special Forces to carry out massive raids on Buddhist monasteries in Hué and Saigon, and arrested more than 1400 Buddhists. This action by Nhu and reports filtering back to the White House that Nhu had entered into negotiations with North Vietnam reinforced Kennedy's conviction that something had to be done about Diem's regime. In his book *Intervention: How America Became Involved in Vietnam* (1986), **George McT. Kahin** argued that the Buddhist Crisis of 1963 provided the Kennedy administration with the opportunity to disengage from Vietnam. The US public, outraged by the actions of Diem and his brother Nhu against the Buddhists, would have supported the withdrawal of aid and the military advisers. Instead, Kennedy chose to continue in Vietnam, but now looked to ways of replacing Diem's government with one more acceptable to the Vietnamese.

THE OVERTHROW OF DIEM'S REGIME

From August 1963, the US administration was even more divided on Vietnam and was faced with two choices: continue to work with Diem and move towards a negotiated settlement with the north; or a military coup and the removal of Diem and his regime. The international situation and the relaxing of Cold War tensions after the Cuban Missile Crisis opened up an opportunity to begin negotiations for the proposed neutralisation of South Vietnam. However, Kennedy and his advisers argued against this proposition by French President Charles de Gaulle because the neutralisation of Laos had failed within a year and the North Vietnamese were once again using Laos as a supply route for insurgents in South Vietnam. In October 1963, a delegation led by General Maxwell Taylor and Secretary of Defence McNamara recommended to Kennedy that selective pressures including cuts in financial and military aid might persuade Diem to reduce his oppression of political dissenters. This action by the US administration encouraged the ARVN generals who had become disaffected to continue their plans for a military coup and the overthrow of Diem and his brother Nhu. The Kennedy administration was itself deeply divided over Diem's removal. Ambassador Averell Harriman, the Department of State's chief intelligence officer, Roger Hilsman and others, felt Diem should go, whereas Vice-President Johnson and top CIA and Pentagon officials insisted that his removal would bring chaos to South Vietnam. Kennedy himself was indecisive: his major fear was that should a coup fail Diem would order US troops out of South Vietnam and this would bring humiliation for the US.

On 1 November 1963, the ARVN generals carried out a coup, and Diem and Nhu were killed the next day. Those close to Kennedy, including General Maxwell Taylor, spoke of his shock at their deaths and speculated that this was more to do with the failure of his Vietnam policy than the loss of Diem as an ally. Three weeks later, President Kennedy was himself assassinated. He left to his successor, Lyndon Johnson, a US advisory military force in Vietnam of 16,000 and the belief that a non-communist South Vietnam was vital to the global interests of the US. With the coup, the US now assumed direct responsibility for the South Vietnamese government, a situation far more dangerous than the one Kennedy had inherited from Eisenhower. Secretary of State Dean Rusk and others in Kennedy's administration initially assumed that the new government led by General Duong Van Minh would be anti-communist and opposed to any compromise with the NLF and the Vietminh, and would provide a more aggressive military challenge to the insurgents. They also assumed that the new government in South Vietnam would accept greater US direction of the fighting, and possibly the bombing of North Vietnam. However, when President Johnson came to power, the struggle between the Military Revolution Council (MRC) and the US administration over control of the war led to a further deterioration in the relationship between the US and the South Vietnamese government.

KENNEDY AND THE WITHDRAWAL OF TROOPS DEBATE

Since Kennedy's death, one of the major questions about his presidency concerns his commitment to the struggle against the communist insurgency in South Vietnam. At the moment of his death, was Kennedy at the point of withdrawing US troops from South Vietnam? Secretary of State for Defence Robert McNamara, in his memoir *In Retrospect* (1996), stated that the period 24 August to 22 November 1963 was a pivotal period of US involvement in Vietnam.

> *Three important events occurred in this period; the overthrow and assassination of South Vietnam's president Ngo Dinh Diem, President Kennedy's decision on October 2 to begin the withdrawal of US troops, and Kennedy's assassination 50 days later.*

This section explores the evidence for and against the question: Did President Kennedy seriously wish to withdraw from Vietnam?

Evidence for withdrawal

From April 1963 onwards, Kennedy and his administration became aware that the war against the insurgency in Vietnam was going badly. Congress was reluctant to continue aid to Diem's regime when more pressing issues within the US were in desperate need of additional funding (for example, the social and welfare programme, including a Medicare Plan that Kennedy was struggling to put in place). In May 1963, Ngo Dinh Nhu, Diem's brother and director of the Strategic Hamlet Programme, complained that there were too many US military advisers in Vietnam and that at least half could be safely withdrawn. Early in May 1963, at the Honolulu Conference, Kennedy and his National Security Adviser McGeorge Bundy, together with McNamara and General Maxwell Taylor, began to plan the phased withdrawal of US troops from Vietnam. The first phase was a withdrawal of 1000 troops, to be completed by December 1963; further phasing out of troops would be completely by early 1965.

The initial planning for the phased withdrawal had begun as early as July 1962 at the same time as the fourteen-nation neutralisation declaration on Laos was signed. It was perceived by the Kennedy administration that this action and the progress made in pacifying the insurgency had led to a more stable society in South Vietnam. General Harkins and the MACV were directed to draw up a Comprehensive Plan for South Vietnam designed to ensure that the military strength of the Republic of Vietnam was capable enough to defend itself against attack by the PLAF/PAVN. In response to this directive, Diem began the reorganisation of the Republic of Vietnam's air force, the establishment of four Corps Zones of Control (CTZs) and a joint operations centre to centralise control over military operations. By offering additional training to the ARVN troops and officers, and building up the military equipment necessary to support these changes, it would cut the cost of US aid while at the same time moving the Republic of Vietnam towards self-determination and independence, thereby fulfilling the Geneva Accords of 1954.

The withdrawal plans put together by McGeorge Bundy, McNamara and Maxwell Taylor throughout 1962 and 1963 have been used by **Arthur M Schleisinger** in *Robert Kennedy and his Times* (1979) and **John M Newman** in *JFK and Vietnam* (1993) to support the notion that Kennedy was about to withdraw US troops and advisers from Vietnam. Kennedy's faith in the government of Diem was further weakened over the Buddhist Crisis that broke out in May 1963 and continued through to August 1963, when Diem introduced martial law and the forcible arrest of Buddhist leaders. This crisis, followed by the Taylor–McNamara Report that was fairly optimistic about the abilities of the ARVN to contain the insurgency, further reinforced Kennedy's belief that now was the time to start a withdrawal.

On 2 October 1963, the Taylor–McNamara Report was optimistic about the military situation and saw little direct effect of the political crisis surrounding Diem on the prosecution of the fight against the Vietminh-led insurgency. The report stated:

1 *The military program in South Vietnam has made progress over the last six months.*
2 *Major US support is only needed until the insurgency has been suppressed.*
3 *The political situation in South Vietnam remains deeply serious.*
4 *It remains the policy of the US … to support the efforts of the people of the country to defeat aggression and to build a peaceful and free society.*

Finally, the military recommendations of this report included:

A program be established to train Vietnamese so that the essential functions now performed by US military personnel can be carried out by Vietnamese by the end of 1965. It should be possible to withdraw the bulk of US personnel by that time.

This statement in many ways revalidated what had been agreed at Honolulu in July 1962, the phased withdrawal of US troops and advisers from Vietnam. However, Kennedy was reluctant to make public any decisions regarding withdrawal of troops because he knew it could not be justified on the grounds that real progress had been made towards the goal of a self-sufficient South Vietnam.

At this time there appeared to be a real commitment by Kennedy and his advisers to quietly withdraw from Vietnam in recognition that the insurgency was of a political nature and war was not the way in which to resolve it. It has been asserted by some that Kennedy was thinking of adopting a similar policy to that of the neutralisation of Laos, but others have argued that he was unconvinced that this would work. The whole situation changed again on 1 November 1963 when Diem and his government were overthrown and Diem assassinated.

At the Honolulu Conference of 20–21 November 1963, National Security Adviser McGeorge Bundy prepared a draft of what became known as NSAM 273. Paragraph 7 stated:

With respect to action against North Vietnam, there should be a detailed plan for the development of additional government of Vietnam resources, especially for sea-going activity, and such planning should indicate the time and investment necessary to achieve a wholly new level of effectiveness in this field of action.

In other words, Kennedy was about to pass the fighting of the war over to the ARVN, a form of **Vietnamisation**, and allow it to continue the action against North Vietnam. To support this decision, OPLAN 34-63 was prepared. This called for intensified sabotage raids against the North using ARVN commandos under US control. Therefore, according to **James K Gailbraith** (2003), **Newman** (1993) and **Schleisinger** (1979), document

NSAM 273 clearly showed Kennedy's determination to withdraw from South Vietnam by 1965, whether the USA was winning or not, and certainly he was not prepared to enter into a protracted war.

On 26 November, four days after Kennedy's assassination, Johnson signed the final version of NSAM 273. In the final document, paragraph 7 had been struck out and OPLAN 34A goals amended. The change in the wording of the document, according to James K Gailbraith in *Exit Strategy: In 1963, JFK Ordered a Complete Withdrawal from Vietnam* (2003), was responsible for the decision to implement **OPLAN 34A**: the sabotage raids against North Vietnam that led to the Gulf of Tonkin Incident (see page 125) and eventually to war in 1964.

Evidence against a decision by Kennedy to withdraw

On the other hand, many historians, for example **Frederik Logevall** in *Choosing War: The Lost Chance of Peace and the Escalation of the War in Vietnam* (1999) and **George C Herring** in *America's Longest War: The United States and Vietnam 1950–75* (2002), have asserted the continuity between President Johnson's and Kennedy's Vietnam policy and usually claim that neither president wanted war. The debate seems to centre on a number of issues for Kennedy at this time.

Kennedy would not wish to leave South Vietnam without first achieving a victory in the presidential election. As with Truman in 1949, Kennedy did not relish facing the radical right wing of the Republican Party and be accused of 'losing' south-east Asia. He would not wish to lose electoral support in his bid for a second period in office. Throughout 1963 his approval ratings fell from 76 per cent in January to 59 per cent by November at the start of the presidential campaign. It would be in Kennedy's interest to delay any form of withdrawal from Vietnam until after the elections in November 1964.

In 1963, the Kennedy administration opposed any move to bring about a diplomatic settlement. For the administration the defeat of the insurgency was the priority; in other words, negotiations would be entered into when the US/Republic of Vietnam were in a strong enough position to dictate the terms. In the international context, pressure was building on the US from Britain and France to seek a negotiated settlement. French President De Gaulle proposed the neutralisation of South Vietnam based on a US withdrawal and economic and cultural exchanges between north and south prior to a political settlement. But these moves were rejected by the Kennedy administration because the agreement on Laotian neutrality broke down within months of the removal of US military advisers. However, it is possible Kennedy rejected these moves because he suspected De Gaulle may have been motivated by anti-Americanism.

With Diem's government self-destructing over the Buddhist Crisis, Kennedy wanted to keep his distance from the regime. Rather than withdraw,

Kennedy considered options for improving the political situation in South Vietnam. Within the administration there appeared to be no consensus on the way forward in South Vietnam. Unsure about the loyalty of Diem and his brother Nhu, it was decided to give US Ambassador Cabot Lodge 'enough sanctions to bring changes that would permit successful resistance by the Vietnamese people to communist expansion'. In other words, the Kennedy administration, frustrated by Diem's resistance to the introduction of democratic changes in South Vietnam, was now sanctioning the removal of Diem and Nhu with the support of the ARVN generals.

The first plot against Diem in August 1963 failed due to uncertainty about the support for the coup by Colonel Le Quang Tung, head of the Special Forces battalion. The Kennedy administration was now more divided over Vietnam than it had been over any other issue. Kennedy convinced himself that the removal of Diem and Nhu and their replacement by indigenous leaders, possibly drawn from army officers, could actually hasten US withdrawal from South Vietnam. On 1 November, Diem and Nhu were removed from their positions by the army and murdered. It would appear Kennedy had not really thought through the implications of this action. The removal of Diem now led to South Vietnam becoming more dependent on US military and economic aid if it was to resist a communist takeover. In a cable to Ambassador Lodge on 6 November 1963, Kennedy acknowledged US complicity in the coup as he stated:

> ... *your own leadership in pulling together and directing the whole US operation in South Vietnam in recent months has been of the greatest importance ... As you say, while this was a Vietnamese effort, our actions made it clear that we wanted improvements, and when these were not forthcoming from the Diem government, we necessarily faced and accepted the possibility that our position might encourage a change of government. We thus have a responsibility to help this new government to be effective in every way that we can, and in these first weeks we may have more influence and chance to be helpful than at any time in recent years.*

In other words, the US government would have more influence over the internal policies of South Vietnam including military and political actions.

Certainly, in the last months of his life, Kennedy was plagued with nagging doubts of ever achieving a stable regime in South Vietnam. In his last press conference on 14 November 1963, he made it clear that his key objective was to bring Americans home, but also 'to permit the South Vietnamese to maintain themselves as a free and independent country'. He expressed the view that the recent coup would lead to 'an increased effort in the war'. The administration had worked hard to conceal the truth about Vietnam from the public while at the same time increasing advisers and military presence in the south from hundreds in 1961 to almost 17,000 by November 1963. Kennedy had left an excellent government team to

Johnson but a situation in Vietnam where US policy on how to negotiate with the North Vietnamese had not been fully thought out.

Recent evidence from **Ang Cheng Guan** in *The Vietnam War 1962–64* (2000) also begins to challenge the notion that Kennedy intended to leave South Vietnam. In this work Guan quotes a senior researcher in North Vietnamese history, Luu Doan Huynh, who disclosed that 'Diem's assassination on the 2 November was viewed with alarm in Hanoi because it substantially raised the odds of direct US intervention'. The North Korean Politburo raised its troop strength from 173,500 in 1963 to between 350,000 and 400,000 in 1964–5. Therefore, it would appear that in North Vietnam there was no perceived change in Kennedy's foreign policy goals in the latter part of 1963 and, if anything, there were preparations for an escalation of action by the US and ARVN troops.

CONCLUSION

The opposition of the Vietminh and later the Vietcong throughout the period 1945–63 reveals at one level a struggle for self-determination and the right to independence from the French and, after the Geneva Conference of 1954, from the US. However, the administrations of both Presidents Eisenhower and Kennedy viewed the struggle in the context of the Cold War. Both sought to contain the expansion of communism by initially agreeing the partition of Vietnam along the 17th Parallel and then by supporting the corrupt regime of Diem and eventually turning what was a civil war between the north and south into a military conflict that could have been avoided. The Kennedy administration was presented with a number of opportunities to reduce military escalation:

- the call for an international conference in 1962 by the Vietminh, supported by China, on the neutralisation of Vietnam
- the successful resolution by Kennedy of the Cuban Missile Crisis in late 1962, greatly increasing his international prestige and popularity with the American public
- the Buddhist Crisis in South Vietnam of 1963.

All these events presented the Kennedy administration with excellent opportunities to withdraw from South Vietnam and still retain the support of the US politicians and public.

However, Kennedy chose to defend South Vietnam because he believed that the communists posed a real challenge to the global position of the US in the 1960s; to withdraw from Vietnam, he feared, would be tantamount to surrender to the Soviet Union and China. In 1961, with the introduction of the strategy of counterinsurgency Kennedy hoped to contain the communist threat, but the long-term effect of this strategy was the opposite. Instead of abandoning South Vietnam, the PLAF with Chinese support escalated the war, forcing Kennedy's successor, President Lyndon Johnson, to do the same.

CHAPTER 8

US foreign policy, Johnson and the Vietnam War, 1963–5

AN OVERVIEW

Following the assassination of President John F Kennedy, Lyndon Johnson was sworn in as president of the United States of America on 22 November 1963. Johnson inherited from Kennedy a rapidly deteriorating situation in South Vietnam following the overthrow of Ngo Ding Diem on 1 November 1963 and the establishment of the Military Ruling Council.

Afraid that large-scale involvement might jeopardise his chances in the presidential elections of November 1964 and thus threaten his political and social welfare programme, Johnson cautiously expanded US assistance to South Vietnam in the period January 1964 to August 1965. He increased the number of military advisers and the amount of economic assistance to the South Vietnamese in the hope that an improved version of Kennedy's Vietnam policy might prevent an escalation of the insurgency in South Vietnam. In August 1964, the Gulf of Tonkin Resolution, passed unanimously by the US Congress, provided Johnson with a solid foundation on which to construct future policy on Vietnam. Public support for Johnson also rose as he took firm and decisive action against the North Vietnamese in response to their 'provocative' attacks on the USS *Maddox* in August 1964.

In the early years of the war, 1965–7, the US adopted an intensive bombing campaign, '**Rolling Thunder**', to weaken the military potential of the People's Army of Vietnam (PAVN) before it could be used in the war against South Vietnam.

In June 1965, the first US combat troops were sent to South Vietnam, and in the period June 1965 to December 1967 the number of US troops in Vietnam grew from 59,900 to almost 500,000. At the same time, the PAVN matched the US escalation of the war with the help of the Chinese and Soviets who were willing to supply the North Vietnamese with military equipment, aircraft and troops. The North Vietnamese were surprised by the willingness of the US to fight for South Vietnam. But, the north had invested so much in the struggle and was so deeply committed to the reunification of Vietnam under the leadership of the Vietminh that it saw no choice but to meet the challenge.

The mountainous terrain of Vietnam, of which three-quarters is covered in forest, combined with the tropical climate and monsoon weather – humidity averages 84% throughout the year – had severe affects on the motivation and performance of the US troops fighting a counterinsurgency war. The training they received in the US did not prepare them for the climatic conditions they faced. Also the tactics adopted, such as 'search and destroy', were counter productive as the US troops were frequently forced to fight in these densely forested and mountainous regions where the communists were able to establish bases from which to attack.

Under the presidency of Johnson, US involvement in the war in Vietnam had escalated. The use of air power to bomb North Vietnam was to necessitate land forces to secure American bases. Therefore, the air and land campaigns were linked and this was to lead to a considerable escalation of US military involvement. Yet, despite the increased military commitment, there was little sign of an American victory against the Vietcong and its PAVN supporters.

BIOGRAPHIES

Lyndon B Johnson (1908–73) Vice-President to Kennedy 1961–3, he was appointed president in November 1963 following the assassination of Kennedy. President in 1964–8, he was famous for his role in taking the US into the Vietnam War. However, he was an important figure in ensuring the passing of over 200 pieces of legislation related to economic, social, educational and political reform in the period 1964–8, including the Civil Rights Bill and the Education Reform Bills of 1964.

Le Duan (1908–86) Secretary-General of the Communist Party of Vietnam 1959–69. In 1969, after the death of Ho Chi Minh, he became head of the Communist Party of Vietnam 1969–86.

General Nguyen Van Thieu (1923–2001) He was a member of the group that overthrew Diem in 1963. In July 1965, he became part of the National Leadership Committee responsible for governing South Vietnam after the overthrow of General Nguyen Khanh. In 1967, he was elected as president of the Republic of Vietnam.

HISTORICAL DEBATES

Since the end of the Vietnam War in 1975, there has been a debate about the role of President Lyndon Baines Johnson and his policies and the war. The traditional view tended to suggest that the war was a response by the Americans to the aggressive actions of the North Vietnamese (supported by the Soviet Union and China) against the newly independent Republic of Vietnam. On the other hand, there were those who argued that Johnson chose to enter the Vietnam War in order to win congressional support for his political and social welfare reforms. In *Planning a Tragedy* (1982), **Larry Berman** argued that Johnson heard but ignored advice against entering a war and that Johnson was simply using his advisers in order to legitimise his escalation decisions. In *Vietnam: A History* (1983), **Stanley Karnow** agreed with Berman and stated that in discussions with

Senate majority leader, Mike Mansfield, Johnson listened to his objections to the escalation to war but failed to act on them.

In contrast to the earlier debates on the role of Johnson and the reasons for the War, historians writing in the early 1990s began to explore the role of his advisers and the escalation to war. In *Uncertain Warrior: Lyndon Johnson and his Vietnam Advisers* (1993), **David M Barrett** argued that Johnson was overly influenced by the policy advisers he inherited from Kennedy: 'In the matters of foreign policy Lyndon Johnson was unusually susceptible to the influence of the so-called intellectuals in the administration who were members of the Kennedy presidency.' These intellectuals included National Security Adviser McGeorge Bundy and Secretary of Defence Robert McNamara. In addition, Barrett argued that Lyndon Johnson was desperately and sincerely attempting to continue the Kennedy mandate, 'to reassure the Kennedy people and to be the heir to the affection of the Kennedy insiders as well as the nation'. In *Intervention: How America Became Involved in Vietnam* (1986), **George McT Kahin** has offered a similar view of Johnson, emphasising the impossible dilemma bequeathed to him by Kennedy; Johnson is depicted as a reluctant president being dragged into a war by McNamara and McGeorge Bundy.

Lloyd C Gardener, in *Pay any Price: Lyndon Johnson and the Wars for Vietnam* (1995), further developed these arguments. The overthrow of Diem, which Johnson opposed and Kennedy authorised, placed an inescapable burden of responsibility on the US, and ironically on Johnson himself. 'Kennedy's spirit … expressed itself over and over again through the counsel of McGeorge Bundy and Robert McNamara, both of whom carried forward the myth of Kennedy and America's special mission to the world.' Therefore, Gardener argues, Johnson had to stress Kennedy's commitment to the War as a way of protecting himself from the charge that he was responsible for it. Like most of the earlier studies on the Vietnam War, Gardener's work focuses on the role of the president and his advisers in taking the USA to war and notes the role played by China, the Soviet Union and the Vietnamese in passing.

Recent studies have explored the lack of diplomatic initiatives to end the war. **Frederik Logevall**, in *Choosing War: The Lost Chance for Peace and the Escalation of the War in Vietnam* (1999), has argued that US policymakers did have options to avoid war before the 1965 decision to escalate the conflict following the Gulf of Tonkin Incident. Logevall is especially critical of Secretary of State Dean Rusk, who ignored his responsibility to seek a diplomatic solution and instead viewed the conflict in Vietnam as a military problem which required a military solution. In exploring the lost opportunities for peace, Logevall argues that the Johnson administration should have taken French President Charles de Gaulle's neutralist stance more seriously. However, documents from China, the Soviet Union and Vietnam reveal that the fears of Rusk, McNamara and Johnson were justified. Secretary Le Duan of the Communist Party of Vietnam viewed a coalition government in Saigon as a step towards reunification of Vietnam.

Explorations of the Vietnam War as an international phenomenon have coincided with efforts by historians to make the Vietnamese central to any consideration of the US–Vietnamese War of 1965–75. This research has benefited from the release of important Chinese and Soviet primary sources and the publication of these in the Working Papers of the Cold War International History Project (CWIHP), for example, **Yang Kuisong**'s Working Paper 34, and **Qiang Zhai**'s *Changes in Mao Zedong's Attitude Towards the Indochina War, 1949–73* (2002) and *China and the Vietnam Wars, 1950–75* (2000). These studies explore the influence of Mao on the North Vietnamese from the First Vietnam War against the French through to the struggle with the US after the Geneva Conference in 1954. They show clearly how the Vietnam War was more than a civil war for the Vietnamese. The Soviets and Chinese both sought to assert their control over south-east Asia and, more importantly, the international communist community. These views are supported by **Ilya Gaiduk** in CWIHP Bulletin 6–7, *The Vietnam War and the Soviet–US Relations, 1964–73: New Russian Evidence* (1995), in which he argues that after the overthrow of Nikita Khrushchev in October 1964 the Soviet Union began to actively support the North Vietnamese with military and economic aid in order to counter the influence of the Chinese.

JOHNSON AND THE US GOVERNMENT, 1963–4

The fall of Diem in November 1963 created even greater instability in South Vietnam because there was no effective political force to pull the Vietnamese together. In this situation, the generals who had been responsible for the overthrow of Diem now responded with the creation of a Military Ruling Council (MRC). In the USA, Lyndon Johnson, who had become president after the assassination of Kennedy in late November 1963, set as his first task the orderly transition of government and the restoration of national calm within the US. Of greatest importance to Johnson was the passage of Kennedy's legislative agenda for civil rights, political reform, the Medicare health insurance programme for the elderly and educational reforms, both as a memorial to Kennedy and a platform on which to launch his own social reforms and campaign for election in his own right. In terms of foreign policy, Johnson continued Kennedy's policies, particularly in Vietnam.

From the beginning of his presidency, Johnson believed that a firm stand would discourage any Soviet tendency to intervene in South Vietnam and encourage the continuation of the trend toward détente. Of greater concern to Johnson and his foreign policy advisers was the clear support for Ho Chi Minh and the Vietcong from the Chinese. In September 1962 at the Tenth Plenum of the Chinese Communist Party, Mao announced that: 'China must support the armed struggles in South Vietnam and Laos without conditions because they were excellent armed struggles.'

Not fully confident in foreign affairs, Johnson chose to retain Kennedy's foreign and military policymakers, Secretary of Defence Robert McNamara, Secretary of State Dean Rusk and National Security Adviser McGeorge Bundy, who were committed to containing the communist threat in South Vietnam. In January 1964, Secretary of Defence McNamara argued that the consequences of a communist-dominated Vietnam would be extremely serious, both for the rest of south-east Asia and for the US. Any surrender of territory to communism was in the view of US foreign policymakers an indication of US weakness that would be noticed by its allies. After the Cuban Missile Crisis, there was a determination among the Johnson administration to finally block any further communist expansion. As Robert McNamara wrote in a January 1964 memorandum to President Johnson:

> *In the eyes of the rest of Asia and of key areas threatened by communism in other areas as well, South Vietnam is both a test of United States firmness and specifically a test of our capacity to deal with 'wars of national liberation'. Within Asia there is evidence – for example, from Japan – that US disengagement and the acceptance of communist domination would have a serious effect on confidence. More broadly, there can be little doubt that any country threatened in the future by communist subversion would have reason to doubt whether we would really see the thing through … My assessment of our important security interests is that they unquestionably call for holding the line against further communist gains.*

Johnson's greatest fear was that if South Vietnam should fall to the communists he would be subject to a politically crippling attack equivalent to that against Truman in 1951, and the opportunity to implement the political, social and welfare legislation developed by himself, his predecessor Kennedy and their advisers would be lost.

THE SITUATION IN SOUTH VIETNAM, 1963–4

After the assassination of Diem, the situation in South Vietnam worsened. The Kennedy and Johnson administrations had believed that once Diem was removed the new leadership in South Vietnam would ensure a more vigorous prosecution of the war against the National Liberation Front (NLF) and its military arm, the Vietcong. It was believed that the Military Ruling Council (MRC) under General Duong Van Minh would accept greater US participation in the fighting. However, the MRC had a different set of priorities.

- It looked to a negotiated settlement by South Vietnamese political groups.
- It perceived the NLF as the prime opposition to Diem's repressive policies.
- The NLF had been the only effective channel of opposition; with the removal of Diem the NLF would lose potential political support.

General Minh also opposed any greater US role in directing the ARVN operations against the insurgents. Minh argued that an increased US presence would remove any level of legitimacy of the MRC. In the period December 1963 to the end of January 1964, General Minh promoted the notion of a government of reconciliation and the MRC launched a rural welfare programme and encouraged the peasants to form their own local defence units. The pilot area was Loc An province where the peasants were heavily influenced by the NLF. General Minh's refusal to allow US officials to participate in the project further aroused the belief that the new government was uncooperative.

Neutralisation and the USA

In December, General Minh called for a policy of neutralisation for South Vietnam. This was supported on 8 December 1963 when the NLF reiterated its demand for a coalition government, gradual reunification, a separate neutral foreign policy and the removal of any military alliances. An article in December in the *New York Times* by Walter Lippmann, a well known critic of the US policies in Vietnam, also advocated a 'negotiated settlement and neutralisation of Vietnam'. In addition, a neutralisation scheme proposed by French President De Gaulle and endorsed by Senate majority leader, Mike Mansfield, and other Democrats was rejected without any serious consideration

The call for neutralisation by some Democrats, the NLF and De Gaulle concerned the US administration because it would end all military ties and any foreign military presence in South Vietnam. The US administration believed that without US support the MRC would collapse and this would lead to a victory for the NLF. **Kahin** (1986) has argued that: 'Presidential advisers who had so vigorously championed an interventionist policy under Kennedy had reason to fear that their own credibility and careers would be open to attack at home, this outcome would provide the clearest evidence of the error of their past recommendations.' **Frederik Logevall**, in *Choosing War: The Lost Chance for Peace and the Escalation of the War in Vietnam* (1995), supports this view. He argues that credibility included a domestic political component and even a personal one for the decision makers involved in formulating US policy. Policymakers remained committed to escalation in Vietnam because they had supported this policy earlier. To advance a political solution or military withdrawal would be to 'expose themselves to potential humiliation and to threaten their careers'.

Removal of General Minh

General Minh's neutralist stance therefore seriously threatened the US position on South Vietnam and this subsequently led to his overthrow on 30 January 1964 by General Nguyen Khanh with the support of US Colonel Jasper Wilson, liaison officer to US General Paul Harkins. The reason given for Minh's removal was his pro-French and pro-neutralist stance. The real reasons appear to be as follows.

- Minh had ordered an investigation into the corruption that existed among officers of the ARVN.
- Many of the officers involved in the coup against Diem felt they had been under-rewarded for their efforts.
- Secretary of Defence McNamara had criticised the absence of any pacification plans by Minh's government and the expansion of NLF/Vietcong activities.
- The US could no longer tolerate Minh's neutralist stance, which posed a threat to the US military role in South Vietnam.

Government of General Nguyen Khanh

The ARVN was now a major political force in the political structures of South Vietnam due to the expansion of its numbers, its direct involvement in government, and increased aid and equipment from the US. Many of the officers who had supported Khanh were now given key positions in the revamped MRC. General Tran Thien Khiem, a key figure in the overthrow of Minh, was appointed minister of defence. In order to ensure the support of the ARVN troops, Khanh ordered a 20 per cent increase in pay for the privates and corporals. Despite the increase in pay the number of desertions from the ARVN continued to rise, while the Vietcong was able to recruit effectively from among the villages, towns and cities.

General Khanh's government faced staggering problems. According to a report by McNamara to Johnson in March 1964, 40 per cent of the countryside, including the Strategic Hamlets, was under the control of the NLF-Vietcong. Replacing Minh with Khanh had not stemmed the growth of anti-war and neutralist sentiment among the Vietnamese population. In March 1964, Secretary of Defence McNamara toured South Vietnam with Khanh in an effort to boost his public image. This public relations exercise failed to make Khanh more acceptable to the Vietnamese and, if anything, it increased the appeal of the NLF. Khanh's willingness to cooperate with the US and allow the increase of military advisers to 22,000 and the use of US economic aid to expand the ARVN and paramilitary forces by 144,000 did not lead to an increase in support for his regime. In fact, in 1964, the US averted three separate coups to oust Khanh from office.

THE SITUATION IN NORTH VIETNAM, 1963–4

The Diem coup was viewed with alarm in the north because Ho Chi Minh and the Vietminh believed it substantially raised the odds of direct US intervention in South Vietnam. At the Ninth Plenum of the Vietnamese Communist Party in November 1963, war preparations were announced. Three areas were given immediate attention: protecting the north, intensifying the struggle in the south and supporting the ongoing struggle in Laos. At the end of 1963, according to **Ang Cheng Guan** in *The Vietnam War, 1962–64: The Vietnamese Communist Perspective* (2000), the north had already begun to send troops to the south in an effort to achieve a quick victory after Diem's assassination and before the US could take over the war.

According to **Bui Tin**, in *Following Ho Chi Minh: Memoirs of a North Vietnamese Colonel* (1995), full-scale war preparations began after the Ninth Plenum when the size of the PAVN was increased from 173,500 to between 350,000 and 400,000 in 1964–5 and to 500,000 by 1966–7. Bui Tin, along with eleven other high-ranking officers, was sent to the south to make reconnaissance trips in early 1964. Equipment and reinforcements for the NLF had been entering the south since 1961 via the Ho Chi Minh Trail and over 40,000 cadres, fighters trained to be regular soldiers in the north, moved to the south. According to a US report on 2 March 1964, there was mounting evidence that infiltration from the north to the south was of such proportions to constitute an increasing threat to Khanh and the MRC.

In the north, Ho Chi Minh urged his colleagues to take advantage of the disorder in the south by escalating military and political pressure on the Saigon government. The problem for the government in North Vietnam was that its members were split about how to achieve unification. Should they expand support for the NLF in the south or engage in a war against the ARVN and by implication the US? The main problem for the Vietminh was the lack of military resources to engage in any kind of fighting with the US-supported ARVN. Therefore, in January/February, Le Duan, the Vietnamese Communist Party's Secretary-General, went to Moscow to seek support for the war against the south.

A Viet Cong booby trap being put in position

However, as it turned out Le Duan failed to gain the support of Khrushchev. During talks with the Soviets, Le Duan criticised them for pursuing peaceful coexistence with the US, for failing to support national liberation movements, and for favouring India against China in the Sino–Indian border dispute. In fact, according to **Ilya Gaidak** in *The Vietnam War and Soviet–US relations, 1964–73: New Russian Evidence* (1995), the Soviets warned Le Duan about the possible consequences these views would have for the 'Vietnamese friends' relations with the Soviet Union. Following these talks in July 1964, an NLF delegation went to Moscow and requested supplies and arms, and asked that a permanent mission of the National Liberation Front of South Vietnam be opened in the Soviet Union. However, the Soviets chose to ignore these requests. This clearly showed that in 1964 the Soviet Union had isolated itself from the struggle in Vietnam. But all this was to change as a result of the Gulf of Tonkin Resolution, passed by the US Congress in August 1964.

US POLICY IN SOUTH VIETNAM

In the early months of 1964, Johnson adopted a cautious approach towards further escalation in South Vietnam. He did not want to appear weak, nor did he appreciate the fact that the US was bogged down in Vietnam, but it was there, he concluded, that 'we have got to conduct ourselves like men'. In an attempt to gain international recognition for its attempts to prevent the Republic of Vietnam falling to communism, the US began a 'many flags' campaign. The purpose of the campaign was to encourage US allies to provide troops and military support for the ARVN. Unfortunately, few countries responded to this initiative and of these Australia sent 8000 troops, New Zealand sent an artillery battery, Thailand sent a small volunteer contingent, the Philippines an engineering battalion and Taiwan small highly trained units for covert operations. Canada sent medical supplies and personnel. Britain refused to commit troops arguing that it had to fight insurgents in Malaya.

Covert operations in North Vietnam were also expanded in early 1964 with intelligence over flights, the dropping of propaganda leaflets and OPLAN 34A commando raids. OPLAN 34A was first approved by Secretary of State Dean Rusk and Secretary of Defence Robert McNamara in November 1963, and consisted of commando and diversionary raids in North Vietnam. The Special Observation Group (SOG), an ultra-secret 'unconventional war task force' and CIA personnel who hired Vietnamese mercenaries were responsible for manning the raids, but the Secretaries of State and Defence had to give approval for their activities.

In March 1964, NSAM 288, the result of a major policy review by Johnson and his administration, outlined US objectives in sweeping terms.

- It emphasised the desire to preserve the independence of a non-communist South Vietnam.
- It called for a national mobilisation plan to put South Vietnam on a war footing and increasing the size of the ARVN.
- General Westmoreland was to replace General Harkins as commander of the US Military Assistance Command Vietnam (COMUSMACV).
- The number of military advisers was increased from 16,300 to 23,300 and there was further expansion of economic assistance by US$50 million.

In the spring and summer of 1964, although the US administration did little more than affirm existing policy on South Vietnam, its attention was moving increasingly towards North Vietnam. The change reflected a growing US concern over the increased infiltration of insurgents and supplies from the north to the south. The OPLAN 34A activities, the propaganda and the expansion of MACV advisers in the south, it was believed, would undermine the north's activities and provide South Vietnam with the time to develop democratic forms of government. At a conference in Honolulu in early June 1964, the key US advisers on Vietnam approved a variety of contingency plans for air strikes against North Vietnam on a sustained basis and the increased build-up of US troops. It was at this time that the US resumed its OPLAN 34A and DE SOTO, special electronic intelligence gathering activities in the coastal areas of North Vietnam.

Gulf of Tonkin Resolution, August 1964

On 22 June 1964, Secretary of State Dean Rusk advised the president that an armed attack against the US by the North Vietnamese would give him the legal basis for sending US forces to Vietnam providing that he had the support of Congress. Incidents in the Gulf of Tonkin, which involved attacks against the USS *Maddox* on 2 August 1964 and against the USS *Turner Joy* on 4 August from North Vietnamese torpedo boats, gave Johnson the opportunity to escalate the war in Vietnam. On 7 August, they led to the unanimous approval of the Tonkin Resolution by the US Congress. It authorised the president 'to take all necessary measures to repel any armed attacks against the forces of the US and to prevent any further aggression' and to 'take all necessary steps, including the use of armed forces, to assist any member or protocol state of the south-east Asia Defensive Treaty requesting assistance in defence of its freedom'.

Johnson and his advisers used this opportunity to show the Republican challenger for the presidency, Senator Barry Goldwater, who had vigorously urged escalation of the war, and the American population that Johnson could be firm in the defence of US interests without recklessly turning to war. On 8 August, Johnson authorised retaliatory attacks against North Vietnamese gunboats and oil storage dumps at Vinh. From a domestic standpoint, Johnson's handling of the Gulf of Tonkin incident won him widespread support. A Louis Gallup poll showed his personal ratings rose from 42 to 72 per cent overnight. This, together with overwhelming support from Congress for the Gulf of Tonkin Resolution, gave Johnson a solid foundation on which to base his future presidency.

However, many historians including **George McT Kahin** (1986) and **Gabriel Kolko** (1985) argue that the attack on the USS *Maddox* was not unprovoked, and that the *Maddox* had been engaged in a patrol involving electronic spying. Further, Kahin (1986) and Kolko (1985) argue that the evidence now shows that the second attack never took place. Their arguments are supported by **Ang Cheng Guan** (2000), whose research in the North Vietnamese archives confirms that an attack was made against the *Maddox* by a North Vietnamese torpedo boat on 2 August 1964; however, the North Vietnamese deny the second attack on 4 August against the *Turner Joy*. The Gulf of Tonkin incident in August 1964 and the resolution passed by Congress was a major turning point in the escalation to war because it strengthened the commitment of China and later the Soviet Union to the North Vietnamese communists and their struggle against the USA.

CHINA AND SUPPORT FOR NORTH VIETNAM

On a visit to China shortly after the Gulf of Tonkin incident, Le Duan was told by Mao that China would be prepared to intervene in the conflict should the USA decide to invade the DRV. In September 1964, Mao deployed between 300,000 and 500,000 troops in southern China, and began the construction of two large airfields in the Mengzi region. Mao also informed Le Duan at this meeting that one North Vietnamese air regiment equipped with 36 aircraft had been returned to the DRV after receiving training in China. In December 1964, a bilateral agreement was signed between China and the DRV which provided for military supplies and, from June 1965, the introduction of PRC support troops to North Vietnam. According to **Chen Jian** in *China's Involvement in the Vietnam War* (1995), aid to North Vietnam in the period 1964–9 took three main forms:

- engineering troops for the construction and maintenance of defence works, air fields and railways in North Vietnam
- anti-aircraft artillery troops in the defence of important strategic areas in North Vietnam
- supply of military equipment and materials.

Table 8.1 highlights the type of equipment that China was supplying to the DRV in the period 1964–9.

Table 8.1 Equipment supplied by China to North Vietnam, 1964–9

Materials	1964	1965	1966	1967	1968	1969
Guns	80,500	220,767	141,531	146,600	219,899	139,900
Artillery	1205	4439	3362	3984	7087	3906
Artillery shells	335	1800	1066	1363	2082	1357
Radio transmitters	426	2779	1568	2464	1854	2210
Bullets (000s)	25,420	114,010	178,120	147,000	247,920	119,170
Telephones	2941	9502	2235	2289	3313	3453
Tanks	16			26	18	
Military vessels		7	14	25		
Automobiles	25	114	96	435		162
Planes	18	2		70		
Uniforms (thousand sets)			400	800	1000	1200

THE SOVIET UNION AND SUPPORT FOR NORTH VIETNAM

The fall from power of Khrushchev in October 1964 marked a turning point in Soviet–North Vietnamese relations. The new leader of the Soviet Union, Leonid Brezhnev, now began to offer support to the DRV. It is possible that this support was offered because the Soviet Union feared a loss of Soviet influence in south-east Asia, particularly in the context of the mounting differences between China and the Soviet Union. On the other hand, the Soviet change of attitude might have occurred because of the consolidation of China's position in south-east Asia and the threat China now posed to the Soviet Union's authority in the world communist movement. Furthermore, the assassination of Kennedy and the coming to power of Johnson reduced Soviet hopes of an improvement in Soviet–US relationships.

In late 1964, therefore, the Soviets reverted to a policy of confrontation with the USA as a result of the US bombing of North Vietnam in retaliation for the attacks against the USS *Maddox*. According to **Ilya V Gaiduk**, in *The Vietnam War and Soviet–US Relations, 1964–73: New Russian Evidence* (1995), Soviet policy from November 1964 onwards now focused on several goals.

- The Soviets emphasised moral and political support for the Vietnamese struggle against US aggression.
- The Soviet media frequently carried official statements by the Soviet leadership denouncing US attacks.
- Contacts were expanded with the DRV and the NLF in South Vietnam and the Communist Party of the Soviet Union, Central Committee (CPSU CC) approved the opening of a permanent mission for the NFL in Moscow.
- The Soviets supplied the latest surface-to-air missiles, jet planes – including the MiG-21 jets – rockets and Grad field artillery shelling systems, which were highly effective in attacks on US bases, airfields and ammunition dumps.

Ho Chi Minh, who unlike Le Duan had always favoured the Soviet side in the Sino-Soviet dispute, welcomed such a turnaround in Soviet policy. However, the North Vietnamese took steps to secure maximum gains by exploiting both China and the Soviet Union as they competed for influence in south-east Asia.

POLITICAL UNREST IN SOUTH VIETNAM

In South Vietnam, General Khanh did not reap the domestic political benefits that both he and the Johnson administration had expected to receive from the US retaliatory air attack against the north and the Gulf of Tonkin Resolution committing the US to the defence of the Republic of Vietnam. In fact, these actions together with the fear of reprisals from the north and the declaration of a state of emergency by Khanh further added to the unpopularity of the MRC. In an attempt to restore order in the south, Khanh introduced a Constitution on 16 August 1964. The Vungtau Charter included:

- the new post of president to be given to Khanh
- civilian representation in the government to be reduced; this included the removal of the Dai Vet nationalist representatives
- the ability of the MRC to decree a state of emergency
- the introduction of press censorship.

When Khanh announced his assumption of the presidency and the curtailment of civil liberties, major protests occurred in Saigon. On 24 August 1964, the Buddhists and their student allies led massive demonstrations against the new constitution and the self-appointment of Khanh as president. The mounting demonstrations by the Buddhists against Khanh and the new constitution along with indications that he was about to abdicate seriously alarmed the Johnson administration. General Westmoreland was also concerned that a coup against Khanh was being planned by Dai Vet Catholic generals.

The fact that US intervention was needed to maintain Khanh in power made it even clearer that the Tonkin Resolution and the bombing of the DRV had not created unity among the South Vietnamese military forces. In the face of stiff opposition, US Ambassador Maxwell Taylor pressed hard for a compromise. The outcome was the formation of a three-man leadership of Khanh, General Minh and the pro-Dai Vet Catholic leader General Tran Thien Khiem. Khanh was to serve as prime minister until the elections promised to the Buddhists. However, this uneasy alliance failed to provide stability in the government. On 26 September 1964, a seventeen-member High National Council was installed as a government for South Vietnam. This council was anti-communist, anti-neutralist and consisted mainly of civilian members. Tran Van Huong was appointed prime minister but Khanh, as ARVN commander-in-chief, retained the real power.

The weakness of the government in South Vietnam continued to worry the Johnson administration. In December 1964, US Ambassador Maxwell Taylor was instructed by the National Security Council to tell Khanh and the council that there would be no US military intervention against North Vietnam until they demonstrated the qualities of political cohesion, governmental stability and effectiveness in their campaign against the Vietcong. It was clear to the US policymakers that the political situation in Saigon had deteriorated even further with the Buddhists continuing to demonstrate against the government and the military officers still engaged in internecine warfare.

The fall of General Khanh
The split between the US and ARVN Commander-in-Chief Khanh deepened when, on 21 December 1964, Khanh called a press conference

to announce the dissolution of the High National Council and declared US Ambassador Maxwell Taylor *persona non grata* and would therefore no longer be diplomatically welcomed by Khanh's regime. By the end of December 1964, the Johnson administration had decided that if any progress was to be made against the NLF insurgency, Khanh, who was now heavily influenced by the Buddhist opposition and moving towards an accommodation with the NLF, had to be removed. It was not only the political character of the Khanh regime that was at stake, but also the possibility of launching a retaliatory campaign against the North Vietnamese.

On 24 February 1965, Khanh was removed from power and replaced by a new military leadership of the Armed Forces Council led by Air Marshall Ky, General Nguyen Chanh Thi and General Nguyen Van Thieu, who were more sympathetic towards the escalation of bombing of the north. On 1 March 1965, Prime Minister Phan Hug Quat announced that 'the war in South Vietnam was obviously a case of self-defence and that there could be no peace until the communists end the war they have provoked and stop the infiltration'. Air Marshal Ky, now spokesperson for the Armed Forces Council where the real political power lay, declared that 'the council would replace any government that in its judgement threatened to betray the country'. On the same day, Prime Minister Quat sacked 300 hundred civil servants who were members of the Buddhist Peace Movement Committee and arrested nearly 100 of them. On 2 March 1965, the USA launched 'Operation Rolling Thunder', a sustained bombing of the north.

JOHNSON AND THE MOVE TO WAR, 1965

There was a growing belief among the Johnson administration that a gradual build-up of US forces in South Vietnam combined with the increased bombing of North Vietnam would coerce North Vietnam into negotiations. This strategy of gradual escalation was based on the assumption that North Vietnam would give up its goals rather than risk total destruction. Johnson stressed he was continuing Kennedy's flexible approach by giving equal attention to military measures and negotiation, in this way keeping both the 'hawks' and 'doves' in Congress quiet. Plans to bomb North Vietnam continued into 1965, supported by Ambassador Maxwell Taylor's 'Fork in the Road' memo of 27 January 1965:

> *I am now pretty well convinced that our current policy can lead only to disastrous defeat. What we are doing now, essentially is to wait and hope for a stable government … In the last six weeks that effort has been unsuccessful … there is no real hope of success in this area unless and until our own policy and priorities change.*

> *The underlying difficulties in Saigon arise from the spreading conviction there that the future is without hope for anti-communists … The*

Vietnamese know just as well as we do that the Vietcong are gaining in the countryside. Meanwhile they see the enormous power of the US withheld. And they get little sense of firm and active US policy. They feel we are unwilling to take serious risks …

There are two alternatives. The first is to use military power and to force a change in communist policy. The second is to deploy all our resources along a track of negotiation, aimed at salvaging what little can be preserved with no major addition to our present military risks. Bob [Robert McNamara] and I tend to favour the first course.

In 1965, Johnson had to make a decision – escalate the war, or continue negotiations with the north in order to give the South Vietnamese government time to quell the political unrest and restore order.

Pleiku incident and escalation

On 6 February 1965, National Liberation Army units attacked a US army barracks and helicopter base in Pleiku, killing nine US service personnel and destroying five helicopters. In effect, this action gave Johnson a reason to begin a retaliatory bombing campaign against North Vietnam. Code named 'Flaming Dart', it followed a plan of reprisals that had already been drawn up by the Joint Chiefs of Staff. On 10 February 1965, a further attack by the NLF against army quarters at Qui Nhon, where 23 US service personnel were killed, led to even heavier bombing attacks against North Vietnam. However, Johnson was still cautious about initiating sustained bombing against North Vietnam. But among Johnson's senior advisers, including Secretary of State Rusk, National Security Adviser McGeorge Bundy and Secretary of Defence McNamara, there was a strong desire to escalate the bombing in order to be able to negotiate with the North Vietnamese from a position of power. On 25 February, Secretary Rusk clearly outlined the aims of the US policymakers for South Vietnam at this time when he said that he was:

…determined to deflect pressures for unconditional negotiations and to maintain pressure on North Vietnam begun by the air raids. There could be no negotiations until Hanoi first agreed to respect the security and independence of South Vietnam. The heart of the problem is an assault upon the safety and the territorial integrity of South Vietnam. If that is relieved and removed, then things can begin to move.

Divisions between and within the Democrats and the Republicans in the civilian and military elements of the administration and Congress reflected the point that Johnson, like his predecessors, had not fully thought through the US role in South Vietnam; nor had any full consideration been given to how victory would be achieved. Kennedy's flexible response strategy – negotiation followed by armed intervention – had not been clearly worked out in response to South Vietnam. Therefore, by continuing Kennedy's policies Johnson now found himself in a situation whereby the only way to retain credibility as a world power was to defeat militarily the People's Army of Vietnam (PAVN) and drive it to the negotiating table. However, this task proved to be incredibly difficult. In April 1965, the fact that the US troops were now undertaking offensive as opposed to defensive operations came out in the press, and widespread criticism followed. There was also criticism from prominent senators such as the Senate majority leader, Mike Mansfield. In a letter to Johnson on 24 March 1965, Mansfield stated:

> The US does not have interests on the south-east mainland to justify the costs in US lives and resources which would be required if we were to attempt to exercise primacy over what transpires in that region. In the end this course will win us widespread difficulties which will play havoc with the domestic programme of the administration.

In 1965, Johnson faced a dilemma. If he failed to counter the aggressive actions of the North Vietnamese against the south, Congress would refuse to fund his civil rights, Medicare and education legislation. In reply to his critics, Johnson stated in a speech at Johns Hopkins University in Baltimore, on 7 April 1965:

> Vietnam is far away from this quiet campus. We have no territory there, nor do we seek any. The war is dirty and brutal and difficult. We fight because we must fight if we are to live in a world where every country can shape its own destiny. And only in such a world will our own freedom be finally secure ...

> Over this war and all Asia is another reality: the deepening shadow of Communist China. The rulers in Hanoi are urged on by Peking ...

> We are also there to strengthen world order. Around the globe, from Berlin to Thailand, are people whose well-being rests, in part, on the belief that they can count on us if they are attacked.

Throughout April and May 1965, Johnson sought to disarm his critics through peace initiatives, even to the point of approving a five-day bombing pause. Johnson stated that he was prepared to enter into unconditional discussions, and even offered Hanoi a US$1billion development programme for the Mekong River Valley. However, these initiatives by Johnson, sincere in a desire for peace, were designed primarily to silence domestic and international critics. On 4 May 1965, Johnson requested US$700 million for military operations in Vietnam. Congress approved the request quickly even though Johnson had not actually clarified the policy he was following.

THE BOMBING CAMPAIGN

Among Johnson's policymakers there was a broad consensus about the aims of 'Operation Rolling Thunder'. It was designed to coerce the North Vietnamese into stopping the infiltration of troops and supplies into

South Vietnam and into negotiations for a peace settlement. In addition, it was one way of getting around the need to send US troops into Vietnam. The bombing was conceived as a campaign of graduated escalation. At each stage, targets were identified as an active deterrent against North Vietnamese support for the insurgency in the south.

- Stage 1: In 1964 and 1965, bombing was limited to North Vietnam's industrial economy
- Stage 2: In May 1965, bombing commenced against air defences and transportation, railways, roads and airfields
- Stage 3: In August 1965 to winter 1966–7, air power was used to limit infiltration from the north of men and supplies to the NLF and the PAVN divisions operating in the south. In this period, attacks against petroleum refineries began. Most of the operations were concentrated at the DMZ and into North Vietnam as far as Thanh Hoa.
- Stage 4: In 1967 to April 1968, attacks in and around Hanoi, Haiphong the main North Vietnamese port and the buffer zone along the Chinese border involved the highly controversial bombing of civilians in the major northern cities.
- Stage 5: From April to November 1968 there was a de-escalation of bombing as Johnson had begun talks in Paris with the DRV. Bombing was now focused around the DMZ line and in the northern parts of South Vietnam.

The air war assumed massive proportions as bomb tonnage rose from 63,000 in 1965 to 136,000 in 1966 and to 226,000 in 1967. The average weekly bombing sorties also rose from 883 in 1965 to 3150 in April–June 1967. Yet studies by systems analysts working in the Secretary of State's department showed that while bombing raids against North Vietnam had increased four times between 1965 and 1968, they had not significantly impaired Hanoi's ability to supply its forces in the South.

However, according to **Robert Pape**, in *Coercive Air Power in the Vietnam War* (1990), 'Operation Rolling Thunder' failed not because it was poorly executed but because most of the supplies to the insurgents in the south were not manufactured in North Vietnam but were coming from China after 1964 (see Table 8.1) and the Soviet Union after 1966. Military supplies were also being transported via the Ho Chi Minh Trail and the waterways, difficult

Village of Ben Suc after its destruction by US troops, 8 January 1967

targets for strategic bombing. In addition, the air attacks had a limited impact on guerrilla warfare and therefore no impact on the policies of the north. Insurgent attacks in South Vietnam in the period July 1965 to December 1967 increased on average five to eight fold.

The bombing is estimated to have done US$600 million worth of damage in the north, but at a cost of lost aircraft alone of US$6 billion. Sixty-five per cent of the bombs and artillery rounds expended in Vietnam were being used against unobserved targets at a cost of US$2 billion per year. In 1966, 27,000 tonnes of dud bombs and shells were used by the PAVN/Vietcong to make booby traps, and these accounted for 1000 American deaths in that year. In early 1968, systems analysts showed that despite 500,000 US troops, despite the expenditure on bombs and enemy casualties (many of whom were civilians) of up to 140,000, the PAVN could still send 200,000 men into South Vietnam. Major problems faced by Johnson's administration were the lack of objective evaluation of the progress of the war and limited accurate intelligence.

CONCLUSION

When Johnson became president in 1963 he was faced with the same choices as Kennedy. He could either increase US commitment and resources to help the South Vietnamese regime and risk a heavy cost in US lives and dollars or withdraw from South Vietnam and see another country fall to the spread of communism. There is evidence that Kennedy was ready to withdraw US advisers from Vietnam just before his death. This action was rejected when Johnson became president. Johnson believed that a firm stand was needed against communism promoted by China and the Soviet Union. This would safeguard America's reputation as the defender of freedom and democracy and secure Johnson's own domestic agenda of social welfare reforms. The Gulf of Tonkin incident gave Johnson the excuse needed to increase US involvement in Vietnam and provided support from the US Congress for such action. By 1965, the US was undertaking 'Operation Rolling Thunder', a campaign of heavy air bombardment of North Vietnam, in support of the regime in the south. It was an action that was to lead to further entanglement and greater involvement in the conflict.

CHAPTER 9

Johnson and the escalation of the Vietnam War, 1965–8

AN OVERVIEW

Under the presidency of Lydon B Johnson, US involvement in the war in Vietnam had escalated. The use of air power to bomb North Vietnam was to necessitate land forces to secure American bases. Therefore, the air and land campaigns were linked and this was to lead to a considerable escalation of US military involvement. Yet, despite the increased military commitment, there was little sign of an American victory against the Vietcong and its People's Army of Vietnam (PAVN) supporters.

In January 1968, the Tet Offensive, a massive and coordinated assault by the National Liberation Front (NLF) and the PAVN against the US and Army of the Republic of Vietnam (ARVN) troops in South Vietnam became a major turning point in the war for the US. Despite winning the battle, the American public and media were now concerned that the US had no role to play in Vietnam, and began to demand the end of the war and the return of US troops. This public mood was reflected in the presidential elections of November 1968 when Richard Nixon, the Republican candidate, won the presidency with the promises of a reduction in the number of US troops in Vietnam and 'Peace with honor'.

BIOGRAPHIES

General William Westmoreland (1914–2005) The US general who oversaw the build up of US forces in Vietnam between 1964 and 1968. He was often criticised for favouring traditional methods of warfare and not understanding the nature of guerrilla warfare. After retiring from the army in 1972 he vigorously justified his tactics in Vietnam and blamed the political leaders and their advisers for US failures in the war.

THE LAND WAR

Problems in South Vietnam and the move to open-ended commitment

As the bombing campaigns got underway, the US realised it needed to secure the airfields and its other major installations in South Vietnam. But the disintegration of the ARVN, because of political infighting among the senior officers together with the unwillingness of ARVN troops to carry out patrols or confront the Vietcong, meant it was ineffective in the protection of US bases.

With the air war well underway in mid-1965, General William Westmoreland, now commander of US forces in Vietnam, called for the expansion of ground troops, initially to defend Da Nang, an important supply air base. Further differences within Johnson's administration about the way the war should go were revealed by this request. Ambassador Maxwell Taylor, National Security Adviser to Kennedy, argued that US troops were inadequately trained for guerrilla warfare – a factor that became more obvious as the war progressed. However, Maxwell Taylor's greater fear was that the introduction of US forces would encourage the ARVN to pass military responsibility to the USA.

Taylor's predictions proved to be accurate as, throughout 1965, General Westmoreland, supported by the JCS, requested more and more troops. By June 1965 the number of US troops in South Vietnam amounted to 220,000 and yet at this period the US was still not officially at war with North Vietnam. President Johnson had not consulted Congress about a declaration of war; he had sanctioned the escalation in troop numbers in his role as chief of the armed forces.

Government of Air Marshall Ky
The problems of the ARVN were further compounded by the continued instability of government in South Vietnam. In mid-May 1965, the fifth government to take office in less than eighteen months was led by Prime Minister Air Marshall Ky and General Nguyen Van Thieu in command of the army. This now reinforced the belief that civilian rule in South Vietnam was non-existent and, although Johnson's administration welcomed the new government's commitment to the war effort, it had little faith in its abilities.

From July 1965 onwards, Johnson made an open commitment to supply US forces to South Vietnam as the situation demanded. Significantly, in coming to this decision Johnson's administration had all but ignored the object of its concern, South Vietnam. The Saigon government was not consulted about the escalation in bombing or the increase in combat troops. The Americanisation of the war came with limited dissent from the South Vietnamese despite having just emerged from years of domination by foreign powers. Ambassador Taylor urged Johnson to increase the level of bombing to convince the Democratic Republic of Vietnam (DRV) they faced a progressively severe punishment if they continued to support the insurgency in the south.

On the other hand, despite the scale of escalation Johnson was reluctant to openly declare war and to mobilise the reserves or the National Guard. He feared that a declaration of war would provoke the Soviet Union and the People's Republic of China (PRC) into taking military action to support the North Vietnamese, and appeared to be unable to take advantage of the deep split between the Soviet Union and the PRC in their struggle to assert themselves as leaders of international communism. Johnson was also aware that a declaration of war would jeopardise the passing of his domestic legislation and destroy his dream of a Great Society in the US as money would be diverted to the struggle in Vietnam.

Several US officials worked hard to head off the impending war but the momentum was too strong. In the months preceding escalation, the *New York Times* attempted to alert the American public of the deepening crisis. But the Johnson administration endeavoured to keep the public in the dark. Many key decisions were kept secret and it was argued that the increase in troop numbers was to prevent escalation into war. By July 1965, Vietnam had become a US war with a further 180,000 US troops deployed there, bringing the number of troops to 220,000 and the introduction by General Westmoreland of the offensive search-and-destroy strategy. The first operation, code-named 'Operation Starlite', in Quang Tri province produced a favourable kill ratio of more than 13:1 for the US marines and caused optimism for US military leaders.

Military tactics and their implications

It could be argued that the Americans fought the wrong type of war, in the wrong place and at the wrong time. The problem for the US military was that it never developed a strategy appropriate for the war it was fighting. It assumed that the application of its military and technological power would be sufficient to destroy the insurgents and dissuade the North Vietnamese from continuing their support for the NLF/Vietcong. In addition, the operational parameters of the war were set by Johnson: his decision to confine US ground forces to South Vietnam in effect meant that the North Vietnamese could continue to support the south without fear of the ground war expanding to North Vietnam.

As Field Commander of US forces in Vietnam, General Westmoreland played a significant role in shaping the ground war in Vietnam. His strategy was one of attrition, the major aim being to locate and destroy People's Liberation Armed Force (PLAF, or Vietcong) and PAVN units. This aggressive strategy relied on a steady increase in the number of personnel but the only additional resources available were the reorganised US Army Reserves (USAR) and the Army National Guard (ARNG). Johnson realised that a full mobilisation of the USAR or ARNG would appear provocative to the Soviet Union and China, and so the draft system was used to increase the number of regular troops for the war. In addition to the draft, Secretary of Defence Robert McNamara announced in 1965 the formation of a Select Reserve Force (SRF) of 150,000 men. The goal of the SRF was to prepare units for a rapid mobilisation and deployment to Vietnam if needed.

The standard Vietnam tour of duty for men drafted into the army was one year. This action was perceived to be fair on draftees because they knew exactly when they would be leaving Vietnam. However, the policy of one-year tours was flawed because as men became skilled jungle fighters they were rotated out of combat assignments and replaced by inexperienced men. The policy was particularly harsh on the non-commissioned officers (NCOs). As a result of the short officer command tours in Vietnam the NCOs had to serve as the leaders, and pass on their knowledge and experience to their superiors and subordinates. Officers were required to serve only six months for two reasons. First, it expanded the number of officers in the US army with combat experience. Second, the rapid turnover prevented the 'burn out' of commanders. In a study in 1976, most officers felt the policy had a negative effect on discipline and morale among the troops; they also felt they were just getting proficient at their jobs when it was time to leave.

Using their technological superiority, the US troops set out to destroy as many of the enemy as they could find. Herbicides were used to destroy natural cover. More than 50 million kilos of chemicals such as Agent Orange were sprayed over millions of hectares of forests. Heavy artillery fire, bombing and the use of napalm were key elements in the search-and-destroy tactics. It was estimated that from 1965–7 South Vietnamese and US air personnel dropped over one million bombs on South Vietnam–double that dropped on North Vietnam.

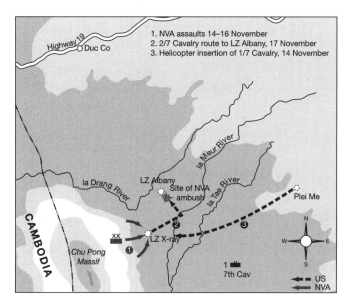

Battle of la Drang, 14–20 November 1965

The Americans chose to fight a conventional war in Vietnam believing the superiority of their armed forces would eventually wear down the Vietcong and the PLAF. The Battle of Ia Drang Valley of 14–26 November 1965 was a major turning point for the war. This was the first time the US called in B52 bombers, as it became apparent that the US troops were being overrun.

In the build-up to the battle, US forces had destroyed a number of PLAF bases. The North Vietnamese army chose to make a stand against Westmoreland's troops at LZ X-Ray, an area that was no larger than a football pitch. During the struggle over the next eleven days the US forces suffered 305 deaths. The NVA had greater losses with an estimated 3561 deaths from a total of 6000 troops. Westmoreland believed that the battle justified his strategy of attrition because of the high mortality rate experienced by the NVA. However, General Giap realised that in some ways the battle had been a victory for the NVA because it had proved it could fight the US army. But the high level of losses convinced Giap that guerrilla warfare was a far more appropriate method of wearing down the US troops.

Throughout 1966–7, Westmoreland concentrated on large-scale search-and-destroy missions against the bases of the Vietminh and the PLAF. 'Operation Cedar Falls' in January 1967 was one of these major campaigns. Some 30,000 US troops were sent into the 'Iron Triangle' just north of Saigon. They removed the local population, flattened the villages, and then bombed and burned the tunnels of the NLF and Vietcong. One of the main measures of success in these campaigns was the 'body count'. But the sheer destruction made it difficult to distinguish between the 'enemy' and the local Vietnamese population. As **Philip Caputo** recounts in *A Rumour of War* (1977), 'If it is dead and Vietnamese, it's VC.' Many of these counts were inaccurate and by the time the statistics reached Washington they bore little resemblance to reality.

North and South Vietnam

This action was followed up in February 1967 by 'Operation Junction City', one of the largest operations of the war. During the battle large numbers of NLF/PAVN units launched suicide night attacks against US positions. Afterwards US troops left the area believing they had inflicted heavy casualties, estimated at 2700 NLF deaths supported by the 9th Division of the PAVN. These major encounters encouraged General Giap to move the NLF/PAVN troops to safe havens in Cambodia as the US and ARVN troops disrupted operations and inflicted heavy casualties.

However, the war of attrition pursued by Westmoreland was flawed. It was assumed by US planners that it would eventually wear down the enemy and encourage a push for a negotiated settlement favourable to the USA and South Vietnam. The reality was

The NLF tunnel system

that in the north around 200,000 North Vietnamese reached draft age every year allowing Hanoi to replace its losses and match US escalation. An ability to exploit the geographical conditions present in Vietnam and the use of the widespread tunnel network developed over the last 20 years allowed the PLAF/VC and the NVA to make contact with the US troops when and where it suited them. Therefore, the NVA and the PLAF/VC retained the strategic initiative and could strike sharply and quickly. Westmoreland, on the other hand, did not have sufficient troops to control the countryside or to wage war systematically against the insurgents and the NVA.

NORTH VIETNAM AND THE WAR

In the north, the Vietnamese showed great ingenuity in evacuating civilians away from the bombing. In 1965, evacuation programmes were initiated in all major cities. US intelligence estimated that the population of Hanoi fell from 475,000 in 1965 to 235,000 in 1967, while the main port of Haiphong declined from 220,000 to 55,000. Industry and storage facilities were scattered throughout the north and in many places reassembled underground. But for all its ingenuity the north could not have sustained the continued destruction of its power plants, petroleum depots, transport systems and industrial base without the aid of the Soviet Union and the PRC.

Assistance from the Soviet Union

Under Leonid Brezhnev, the Soviet Union was keen to win over the North Vietnamese from dependence on China, and provided them with jet aircraft MiG-21s and sophisticated air defence weaponry. The expanding war also provided the Soviet Union with the opportunity to tie down its major rival and undermine US prestige, test its own weapons under combat conditions and analyse the latest US military products. **Ilya Gaiduk** (1995) points out that in spring 1965 the Soviets signed an agreement with the North Vietnamese to transfer models of captured US military products to the Soviet Union. Despite this agreement the North Vietnamese did not fully trust the Soviets and often attempted to block access by Soviet Defence Ministry representatives to captured weapons.

The Soviet Ministry of Commercial Shipping made complaints against the North Vietnamese at the height of the US bombing campaign against Haiphong in 1966. The port authorities, the Ministry complained, had artificially delayed the unloading of Soviet vessels, believing that the longer the Soviet flag-flying vessels remained in the port, the less risk of damage it would face from US bombing raids. Furthermore, they usually placed the vessels in close proximity to the most dangerous areas, e.g. next to anti-aircraft guns. In the period 1966–8, the Soviet Union provided 1216 million roubles in economic and military aid. However, the Soviets were keen to support a peaceful resolution to the US–Vietnamese conflict primarily because they found the unpredictability and unmanageability of the North Vietnamese worrying and feared a direct clash with the US.

Assistance from the People's Republic of China

The PRC gave the NVA valuable assistance but mainly for its own gains as it attempted to assert its leadership of revolutionary movements. It also viewed the defence of North Vietnam as essential to its own security and let it be known that should the US invade North Vietnam it would send in military forces. Obviously this was a warning Johnson could not ignore, particularly as the Korea War was still fresh in the minds of many Americans. Agreements made between China and North Vietnam in 1964–5 led to 320,000 Chinese engineering and artillery troops helping the North construct new highways, railroads and bridges to facilitate the transport of supplies from China (see Table 8.1, Page 126).

THE OTHER WAR: PACIFICATION AND NATION-BUILDING

Buddhist protests, 1966

The Honolulu Summit of 7 February 1966 sought to establish political stability in a popular, broadly based government based in Saigon. The military regime headed by Premier Ky was pressed by the US administration to implement political and economic reforms. However, stiff opposition from the Buddhists to Ky's sacking of the popular Buddhist General Nguyen Chanh Thi in March 1966 led to major demonstrations in Hué and Danang. The demonstrators called for democratic elections, social reforms and a civilian-controlled government. The crisis worsened in mid-May when Ky ordered ARVN troops to remove the Buddhist protestors from Danang, Hué and Saigon and take control of the cities. By 19 June 1966, the Buddhist protest had been quashed, and several hundred Buddhist monks and university and high school students were arrested. Many of the Hué University students fled to the mountains, where they joined the NLF.

The challenge mounted by the Buddhist militants and their supporters in spring 1966 was the last that Ky and Thieu had to face. The US administration now moved forward with its plans outlined at the Honolulu Summit. President Johnson, a populist reformer, realised it was necessary to win the hearts and minds of the people of South Vietnam if they were to ever defeat the NLF. The Revolutionary Development (RD) Programme, established in 1966 and supported with US$400 million of US aid, was aimed at nation-building and pacification of the rural population. Teams of workers were introduced into hamlets where they focused on 'economic development' projects of the residents' choosing, such as the building of schools, dispensaries and roads. The RD workers were also there to gauge support for the South Vietnamese government and the NLF, as well as preparing for the national and local elections.

The Revolutionary Development Programme

The fundamental aim of the RD teams was to build up support for the Saigon government. However, like earlier programmes, poor coordination between pacification and offensive operations hampered progress with some villages being bombed by US planes. This, together with the absence of security – in 1966 over a seven-month period 3015 RD workers were murdered or kidnapped – ensured the RD Programme achieved little. In 1967, aware of the problems in the rural areas and the advantages this gave to the NLF, Westmoreland encouraged the ARVN to commit the bulk of its forces to rural security.

South Vietnamese government and land reform

The most successful programme introduced by the South Vietnamese government was that of land reform. The government had in September 1965 begun to issue new landownership certificates to peasants and it also ruled that village communal lands formerly rented to the highest bidder were to be rented at fair rates. In addition, the government went ahead with the distribution of about half a million hectares of expropriated and government land, much of which went to refugees driven from their homes as a result of the flooding in central Vietnam in 1964–5 and the war.

Democratic reforms of Premier Ky

Attempts at democratic reform in South Vietnam floundered. During the 1967 general election, the government, supported by US Ambassador Cabot Lodge, successfully blocked attempts by opposition candidates to stand for election. In the leadership struggle, General Thieu was able to replace General Ky with only 35 per cent of the vote. The second largest group in the election with 17 per cent of the votes had advocated negotiations with the People's Liberation Front. While the Johnson administration supported the elections and hoped they would provide the Saigon government with some respectability, many viewed them as yet further evidence of Saigon's weakness and corruption.

The Thieu government

The Thieu administration lacked credibility with the South Vietnamese and together with the expansion of the war this created equally formidable problems in South Vietnam. Military activities such as 'Operation Cedar Falls' had created a huge refugee problem. It is estimated some four million South Vietnamese left their villages to work in the major cities or for US projects. The US invested US$1 billion in military construction programmes, including barracks, air fields and housing for senior military officers. It also invested in new docking facilities at Cam Ranh Bay and US storage centres at Longbinh. Some Vietnamese found new economic opportunities working in the cities as cab drivers, bar girls and profiteers/importers engaged in selling watches, bicycles and radios to workers employed by the USA. The US administration was concerned by the widespread corruption that emerged in Saigon but failed to take action because it might alienate the government or bring about its collapse.

The rapid build-up of half a million US troops in South Vietnam threatened to overwhelm the Vietnamese traditional way of life, the economy and family structures. According to **George C Herring** in *America's Longest War: The United States and Vietnam 1950–75* (2002), signs of US presence appeared everywhere: 'Vietnamese children wore Batman T-shirts. Long strips of seedy bars and brothels sprang up overnight around base areas. In a remote village near Danang houses were made of discarded beer cans, red and white Budweiser, gold Miller, cream and brown Schlitz.' In addition, US spending had a devastating effect on the vulnerable South Vietnamese economy, with prices of goods and rice increasing by 170 per cent in the period 1965–7. The influx of US goods also destroyed the few native industries, and made the economy even more dependent on the economic aid of the USA.

CHANGE IN US POLICY AND THE CONSIDERATION OF VIETNAMISATION

Towards the end of 1967, in one of his last policy memos to Johnson, Secretary of Defence Robert McNamara proposed a study of US military operations in South Vietnam to find ways of reducing US casualties and forcing the ARVN to assume a greater burden of fighting. This was the start of a consideration of Vietnamisation, the principle that the South Vietnamese would do more to defend themselves against the NLF insurgency. At the same time, a group of leading establishment figures known collectively as the Carnegie Endowment proposed a clear and hold strategy that would stabilise the war at a political level and save South Vietnam without surrender. Johnson was also rethinking strategy in late 1967 and began to consider McGeorge Bundy's advice that Vietnam had now become a critical domestic issue and that the president had an obligation to challenge the field commander in Vietnam, Westmoreland. Although Johnson did not initiate a change in strategy at this point, he was moving towards the position that South Vietnam and the ARVN should take greater responsibility for the war. In public, Johnson vowed to see the war through to a successful conclusion: 'We are going to wind up with a peace with honour which all Americans seek.' These words would take on an ironic ring in the aftermath of the Tet Offensive.

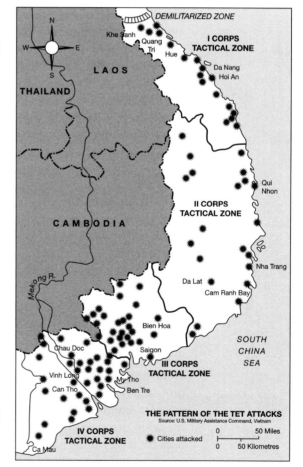

The Tet Offensive, 1968

THE TET OFFENSIVE

At 2.45 am on 30 January 1968, PLAF/VC and PAVN troops launched an attack against the US Embassy in Saigon. This was the start of a massive coordinated attack against six of the largest cities, 36 of the 44 provincial capitals and numerous district centres and villages in South Vietnam. In most of these areas, the insurgents were repulsed quickly with Hué being the only exception to the general pattern. The liberation of the city took nearly three weeks with major damage to the ancient buildings and temples and a heavy loss of life. In Hué, US troops and the ARVN suffered about 500 deaths, while the insurgent deaths numbered around 5000. There were many civilian casualties with mass graves found in and around the city of Hué. In a memo to President Johnson, General Westmoreland calculated the total number of deaths among the Tet insurgents throughout South Vietnam to be approximately 25,000, with more than 5000 detainees. Other sources put the number of those killed as much higher, one even gives a total of 84,000. Arranged to take place during the Tet holiday, this attack became known as the Tet Offensive. It proved to be a tactical defeat for the communists, but the subsequent opportunity to eliminate the VC before they could recover from their losses was missed by the US and the communists ultimately achieved an enormous political and psychological victory.

The Tet Offensive occurred at a crucial stage in the war. It came at the end of a period during which the communists looked to be weakening.

In 1967, the Vietnam War had reached a critical turning point with the success of the search-and-destroy tactics of the US forces. The elections of September 1967 in South Vietnam and the success of President Thieu had seriously worried the communists in the north. Support for the PLAF/VC was beginning to diminish and morale among the insurgents was at an all-time low because of major losses. Throughout the late summer and autumn of 1967, the Politburo in the north sought to change its strategies and believed a general offensive would lead to a general uprising among the Vietnamese in the south. The overall objective was to lure the US troops into the more remote areas of Vietnam while at the same time causing maximum disruption in the cities and urban centres. As part of this strategy, in October and November 1967, PAVN forces attacked US bases including Khe Sanh close to the Laotian border.

In December 1967, the NLF contacted the US Embassy in Saigon with secret offers of peace talks, the purpose being to undermine the confidence of the Thieu government in the US. This could be seen as a response to Johnson's **San Antonio formula** of September 1967. The formula proposed a modified negotiating position: the US would stop the bombing with the understanding that this would lead to prompt, productive discussions. In exchange, it was assumed that North Vietnam would not take advantage of the cessation of air strikes by significantly increasing the infiltration of soldiers and supplies across the 16th Parallel. However, during this period the NLF and PAVN gathered a force of 84,000 near the major cities of the south. The North Vietnamese offensive was timed to coincide with the Tet festival when traditionally the Vietnamese people returned to their villages and families to engage in a week of celebrations. The insurgents found it easy to mingle with the holiday traffic and were able to smuggle weapons in fruit and vegetable carts and even in mock funeral processions.

South Vietnamese volunteers unload ammunition for PLAF/VC forces on the Ho Chi Minh Trail.

In October–November 1967, the Johnson administration was more preoccupied by the siege around Khe Sanh and overlooked the intelligence reports communicated to senior military and political leaders in both Saigon and Washington. These stated that: 'Despite enemy security measures, communications intelligence was able to provide clear warning that attacks, probably on a larger scale than ever before, were in the offing.' Considerable numbers of messages were read. Moreover, these messages indicated a sense of urgency and secrecy not previously seen. However, there was not sufficient evidence in the messages to predict the exact timing of the attack.

When the Tet Offensive began, Johnson's administration was told in reports from the Embassy in Saigon that its aim was to seize as many cities as possible and to undermine South Vietnamese confidence in the government and the US. Documents subsequently seized by US troops showed that the orders from Hanoi were to seize and hold as many centres as possible prior to a general uprising among the people of South Vietnam. Hanoi radio constantly communicated the same message, that the government forces throughout the south were defecting to the communists, and there was to be a coalition government formed in Saigon including elements of the NLF and Thieu's administration. McNamara was convinced that the offensive was probably intended to convey the impression that, despite PLAF/VC problems and despite half a million US troops present in South Vietnam, the communists were still a powerful force and capable of waging war. There was also widespread belief among Johnson's senior advisers that the offensive was related to Hanoi's offer of peace talks.

South Vietnamese reaction to the Tet Offensive

Thieu's government, shaken by the attack during the Tet holiday, attempted to capitalise on the popular revulsion. On 31 January 1968,

Thieu declared martial law and banned all public meetings, demonstrations and activities that might be perceived as helping the communists. In an attempt to achieve national unity, Thieu established a War and Reconstruction Council in May 1968 to re-establish normal administrative operations to the cities and towns and provide immediate relief to the thousands of refugees who had lost their homes. Many of the civilian population were shocked by the excesses of the offensive, and their confidence in the ability of US troops and ARVN to protect them both in the towns and the countryside was severely shaken.

US reaction to the Tet Offensive

Although the attacks subsequently failed, the way in which the US media portrayed them led many Americans to realise that the war in South Vietnam was far more serious than expected, and that the boasts of imminent victory were misguided at best and calculated lies at worst. Walter Cronkite, an influential reporter and opponent of the War, summed up the mood among the media when in a much-publicised broadcast in February he stated:

US Marines patrol Hué during the Tet offensive, 24 February 1968

> *To say that we are close to victory today is to believe, in the face of evidence, the optimists who have been wrong in the past. To suggest that we are on the edge of defeat is to yield to unreasonable pessimism. To say that we are mired in stalemate seems the only reasonable, yet unsatisfactory conclusion.*

On 10 March 1968, the *New York Times* reported that the Johnson administration was considering sending a further 206,000 troops to Vietnam at the request of the US military. On the same day, NBC television reporter Frank McGee questioned whether it would be viable to continue to increase the numbers of US troops: 'Laying aside all other arguments, the time is at hand when we must decide whether it is futile to destroy Vietnam in order to save it.' At the same time as the NBC announcement, public opinion polls revealed a sharp decline in Johnson's popularity from 40 per cent in 1967 to a low of 26 per cent in March 1968.

DOMESTIC OPPOSITION

Throughout the period 1965–7 when military escalation was at its height and troop levels rose in Vietnam, a growing debate emerged among the American population over the desirability of Johnson's commitment to military intervention in Vietnam. The 'hawks' called for a more aggressive military strategy while the 'doves' argued that the war violated US interests and values. The Tet Offensive brought these differences into the open. Reports of the possibility of sending even more troops to Vietnam received a hostile reaction from the American public and reactivated the anti-war movement which throughout 1967 had demonstrated in large numbers against Johnson's policies in South Vietnam. The military draft was among the most divisive issue during the war, and tens of thousands resisted it through legal and illegal means. In October 1967, this had culminated in an anti-draft group called **The Resistance**. It collected 1100 draft cards from men who refused induction, a federal crime. The anti-war activities culminated in a 100,000-strong march against the Pentagon on 21 October 1967. The two-day confrontation, which brought 600 arrests, which, focused public attention on the growing breakdown of national consensus. From March 1968 onwards, support from the 'hawks' for the military escalation in South Vietnam decreased.

The role of Martin Luther King in the anti-war movement

Influential individuals such as Martin Luther King, a respected civil rights activist, joined the anti-war movement and were instrumental in raising awareness of the inequalities generated by the war. On 4 April 1967, Martin Luther King outlined his reasons for joining the anti-war movement in his 'Beyond Vietnam' speech.

- The Vietnam War had a negative impact on the US poverty programme.
- There was a high number of black troops fighting in the war in proportion to their number in the population.
- The black community had been told that violence would not benefit its struggle for civil rights, yet the civil rights of the South Vietnamese had been destroyed by the violence of the war.
- Having received the Nobel Peace Prize for his contribution to civil rights in the US, King now felt that he had to 'work harder for the brotherhood of man', which implied he would now work for the rights of those in Vietnam.
- King maintained that communism would never be defeated by bombs; the best way to win the ideological war was to emphasise the positive values of US society.

On 15 April 1967, Martin Luther King joined 200,000 demonstrators against the war in New York, the biggest peace demonstration in US history. At the rally, his major theme was to stop the bombing. Martin Luther King maintained in subsequent speeches that the US government had the resources to carry on the war and at the same time fulfil its promises of domestic reform. However, in a speech on 11 November 1967 he maintained that: 'This is the inescapable contradiction between war and social progress at home. Military adventure must stultify domestic progress to ensure the certainty of military success. This is the reason the poor and particularly Negroes have a double stake in peace and international harmony.'

Impact of the anti-war movement, 1967–8

Throughout the summer of 1967, the anti-war groups used the media by placing adverts in the major newspapers calling for 'Negotiation Now'. They proposed a halt to the bombing and a general cease-fire. However, the problem for the anti-war movement was its own internal divisions. First, liberal demonstrators distrusted the motives of the left groups and feared that association with them would damage their public credibility. Second, some radicals argued for negotiations with the North Vietnamese while others believed that the Vietnamese had the right to determine their own future.

The anti-war movement nonetheless exerted a powerful agenda-setting force on the federal government and American society. The protests that resulted in injuries or damage to property gained widespread publicity and the attention of Congress. However, there is not enough evidence to support the contention that Johnson's policies or the actions of Congress were influenced to any great degree by the anti-war protests. During his presidency, Johnson worked hard to eradicate poverty and racial discrimination and to improve education. In total, some 200 laws and programmes constituting the Great Society were passed in the period 1964–8. He was not to be distracted to the point where he failed to pursue his social reforms.

REAPPRAISING POLICIES ON THE VIETNAM WAR

It was not only growing public disapproval of Johnson's Vietnamese policies that manifested itself in March 1968. General Earle Wheeler, the Chairman of the Joint Chiefs of Staff, believed that the continuing Vietnam War had seriously weakened US force levels throughout the world, and his pessimistic report to Washington at the beginning of February implied that a denial of the request for the additional 206,000 troops could lead to a military defeat for the USA, or at least an indefinite continuation of the war. Johnson now faced a dilemma: a major escalation of the war would impose additional demands on the American people in an election year and further opposition from an already hostile Congress. On 2 March, Johnson instructed Clark Clifford, McNamara's replacement as Secretary of State for Defence, to carry out a comprehensive reassessment of Vietnam policy. Clifford was supported by a number of senior civil servants in the Pentagon – men such as Paul Warnke, Townsend Hoopes and Paul Nitze, who had long been disenchanted with the Vietnam strategies. At the start, Clark Clifford introduced new procedures. He demanded precise information from Westmoreland and Wheeler on how the additional troops would be used and what results could be expected. The civil servants would study all the implications of these requests, including domestic and international reactions as well as implications for the progression of the war.

The Clifford Report

The Clifford Report stated:

> *The increased level of forces alone would not lead to the achievement of the US political or military objectives in South Vietnam. The enemy would match any increase, the total number of troops would not be sufficient to drive out the communist forces, having 700,000 troops would lead to a total Americanisation of the war which would serve to undermine the effectiveness of and confidence in the South Vietnamese government. The call-up and consequent expenditures would lead to severe domestic problems within the US ... US troops should no longer engage the enemy through search-and-destroy operations. Instead US combat units should confine their operations to providing security for the populace and to support operations undertaken by the ARVN.*

In other words, US policy should return to its original purpose as outlined by Presidents Dwight Eisenhower and John Kennedy – to support the government of South Vietnam through economic and military aid in the form of equipment and training for the ARVN.

In response to Westmoreland's demands, Clifford recommended a small increase in the number of troops and an increase in expenditure on weapons and further training for the ARVN. He also recommended an end to the policy of search and destroy, which he felt was doing more harm than good both in terms of the amount of structural damage and the morale of the people. As a result of his findings, Clifford recommended a move from search and destroy to a strategy of population security; a search-and-hold strategy. At the same time, the ARVN would be encouraged to assume a greater responsibility for the war against the communists. Johnson and his administration accepted Clifford's recommendations and fully endorsed the principle that South Vietnam should do more to defend itself: paradoxical, given it was Johnson and his advisers who had imposed the escalation of the war on the South Vietnamese government in 1965 without full consultations.

In fact, in the aftermath of the Tet Offensive and the assault against Khe Sanh at the end of February, the ARVN had quickly recovered its commitment and fighting ability. According to General Abrams, who had been working with the ARVN since 1967, the general performance of the ARVN had been good, exceeding the expectations of most of the senior US officers, including General Westmoreland. In order to build up the effectiveness of the ARVN, an increase of some 140,000 recruits to join the existing ARVN force of 600,000 after June 1968 would be achieved by the reduction of the drafting age to nineteen. General Abrams reported in February that there had been 7000 volunteers compared to only 1500 in January, a direct result of the Tet Offensive. There was a to be an additional focus on the quality of officer training with some officers being promoted from the ranks as a result of their actions during the Tet Offensive and the battles for Hué and Khe Sanh. In this way, Clifford's proposals supported by the evidence from General Abrams would ensure the ARVN would be capable of defending South Vietnam. The decision to shift greater responsibility for the fighting to the ARVN represented a major shift in US policy, in principle back to the aims of the US governments before 1965.

Restricting the bombing campaign

Secretary of State Dean Rusk, convinced that the bombing of North Vietnam produced only marginal results, now called for a restriction of bombing to the DMZ and supply routes of the PLAF/VC. By adopting this strategy and by relaxing the San Antonio formula the administration hoped it would bring pressure to bear on the North Vietnamese to begin the peace negotiations. This would test whether the North Vietnamese were serious in their offer to begin negotiations that Johnson, believing the Tet Offensive had seriously damaged the North Vietnamese forces, hoped to be able to negotiate from a vastly strengthened position.

Domestic pressure and the gold crisis of March 1968

Pressure on the domestic front, through the activities of the anti-war movement and the media, combined with pressure from the Senate Foreign Relations Committee in mid-March revealed growing disapproval of the way in which Johnson was handling the war. Public disputes among the Democrats and open challenges to Johnson's renomination as their presidential candidate seriously worried party regulars. They urged Johnson to do 'something exciting and dramatic to recapture the peace issue' and to shift his stance from winning the war to securing 'peace with honour'.

Before Johnson could do anything to save the Democrats' chances of regaining public support he had to deal with a severe economic crisis in March 1968. The balance of payments deficit and the rapid expansion of military commitments in 1967 weakened the dollar in international money markets. In order to stop the collapse of the dollar large amounts of gold were sold, thereby depleting the reserves held by the Treasury. Subsequently there was a loss of confidence among Americans as doubts among business and government leaders led to a questioning of the nation's ability to finance the war. The crisis further undermined Johnson's Great Society initiative as Congress refused to raise further revenue to pay for the welfare and social programmes. As a result of the gold crisis it became essential for the administration to conduct a full review of its Vietnam policy in the context of global and national security concerns.

The end of the gradual escalation policy

By the last week of March 1968, Clark Clifford had called for the initiation of the process of de-escalation in South Vietnam. Worried by the damage the Vietnam policies were doing to the US international financial position and the tremendous erosion of support from the nation's business community, Clifford promoted the notion that the US might have to settle with the North Vietnamese and get the deal it could obtain. Johnson was furious about Clifford's perceived defection to the doves. He was deeply opposed to abandoning a policy he had invested so much in but on the other hand he could no longer ignore the protests that were building up around him. When, on 26 March, he met with Generals Wheeler and Creighton Abrams, Westmoreland's successor, he blamed the fiscal situation, panic in Congress and opposition from the press as reasons for the change of policy.

On the same day he also met the 'Wise Men', who included former Secretary of State Dean Acheson, their chair, and others who had close links to the world of finance, corporate law and big business – George Ball, McGeorge Bundy, Cyrus Vance and Arthur Dean. These trusted advisers from outside the government had fully supported his policies in November when the war appeared to be going well. Now, after Tet, they advised him to begin the steps towards disengagement. Most agreed that the goal to keep a free and independent South Vietnam was probably unattainable and that moves should be made to end the war.

When informed by Clifford of the change in policy, the JCS also reluctantly agreed to the initiatives. On 31 March, Johnson met the Soviet Ambassador and informed him of the change in US policy. Johnson stated that he could not call for a total end to bombing because he still needed to protect US troops along the DMZ; but there would be no bombing above the 20th Parallel for the foreseeable future. Johnson further stated that 'it was now up to the Soviet Union as the Geneva Conference co-chairmen and as a major arms supplier to Hanoi to bring its influence to bear for a conference and the making of peace.'

Johnson withdraws from the presidential election

Later on the same day at 9 pm, Johnson addressed the nation. His speech is often cited as the key turning point in US involvement in Vietnam. It marked the culmination of months of debate within the administration over where Vietnam policy was taking the USA. Johnson acknowledged the success of the Tet Offensive for US and ARVN troops and stated his intentions to seek peace by repeating the terms offered in the San Antonio formula: to end the bombing of North Vietnam and, if the North Vietnamese did not take advantage of the situation, to engage in meaningful and productive talks. In the initial phase, all bombing would be contained within the 20th Parallel; should the peace negotiations go well there would follow a complete halt to the bombing. At the end of his speech, Johnson discussed a final decision:

> *With America's sons in the fields away, with America's future under challenge right here at home, with our hopes and the world's hopes for peace in the balance every day, I do not believe that I should devote an hour or day of my time to any personal partisan causes or to any duties other than the awesome duties of this office – the presidency of your country. Accordingly, I shall not seek, and I will not accept the nomination of my party for another term as your president.*

Johnson's speech of 31 March brought a halt to the policy of gradual escalation. Faced by a collapse of support on the home front and increasing hostility from international allies, Johnson hoped to salvage something from the war. The speech therefore did not herald a change in foreign policy, but a change in tactics from a war of attrition to peace talks and Vietnamisation.

Change in military tactics

To improve their position in Vietnam in March and April 1968, the US and South Vietnamese armies conducted the largest search-and-destroy campaign of the war, sending more than 100,000 troops against the communists in and around Saigon. Abrams reduced the scale of military operations in the summer and autumn as part of the **Accelerated Pacification Campaign**. The purpose was to secure as much of the countryside as possible in case serious negotiations should begin. The *Chieu Hoi* programme, which offered amnesty and 'rehabilitation' to defectors from the north, was intensified, as was the Phoenix programme, a direct attack on the NLF through mass arrests. On the other hand, despite the weakening of the NLF forces in the countryside its main units remained intact, and the launch of major operations by the combined NLF/PAVN in May and August 1968 made clear they retained significant strength and the will to fight on.

The policy of Vietnamisation whereby the US passed a larger share of the fighting to the ARVN also progressed. General Abrams increasingly used US and ARVN forces in combined missions. However, despite improved training, better equipment and an increase in the number of officers, problems of desertion and poor leadership continued to affect ARVN performance. The peace talks did, however, influence the relationship between the US forces and the South Vietnamese people. Many Vietnamese felt that they had been railroaded into negotiations before they were ready. There was a growing feeling within the government and business circles of Saigon that they were to be abandoned by the US. New political groups emerged after the start of the peace talks but they were affected by disagreement. Rivalry between Thieu and his deputy, General Ky, also intensified factionalism within the government.

Vietnamese–US tensions increased significantly in March 1968 as US service troops openly manifested their frustrations of fighting in a hostile environment a war they could not 'win'. The savagery of the Tet battles and the heavy losses further inflamed anti-Vietnamese feelings and the My Lai atrocity in March 1968 revealed the growing tensions between the US troops and the Vietnamese.

The My Lai massacre

One of the best known incidents of the Vietnam War, the My Lai massacre, showed how the Vietnam War had taken a toll on the effectiveness of the US military. On 16 March 1968 men of 'C' Company, 1st Battalion, 11th Infantry Brigade, while out on a search-and-destroy mission in Vietminh-controlled territory, shot in a ditch 300 innocent Vietnamese, mainly women and children. The platoon leader Lieutenant William Calley was eventually convicted of mass murder and sent to prison. Calley only served three years of this prison term and was pardoned by President Nixon. Public pressure convinced President Nixon that

Victims of the My Lai Massacre, 16 March 1968

Calley was a scapegoat for a war that had gone wrong. It would, however, be wrong to assume that Calley represented the vast majority of soldiers in Vietnam; most men served their country with honour.

PARIS PEACE TALKS

Despite the accommodating tone of his speech Johnson approached the negotiations cautiously. He agreed to negotiate with Hanoi but refused to compromise on the fundamental issue of a communist-free and democratic South Vietnam. Within Johnson's administration two factions emerged. The first, led by Secretary of State Rusk, Walt Rostow and Ambassador Bunker together with the military, opposed concessions. It believed that Tet had caused major problems for the north and therefore the USA was in a stronger bargaining position.

On the other hand, Secretary of State for Defence Clifford and Ambassador at Large Averell Harriman, Johnson's personal representative to the peace talks, sought to extricate the US from what they viewed as a hopeless quagmire. They believed that the war was undermining the international prestige of the US and was damaging relationships with US allies. The two factions fought bitterly over such issues as the way in which negotiations should proceed, the scale and purpose of ground operations, and whether to curtail or resume bombing. According to Clark Clifford: 'The pressure became so intense, I felt the government itself would come apart at its seams.'

In early April 1968, Hanoi accepted the offer of face-to-face talks and the two nations finally met in Paris on 13 May. However, the lack of progress was due to Johnson's uncompromising position on the reciprocal de-escalation on the part of the North Vietnamese. Johnson and his military advisers feared that the communists would use the lull in bombing to regroup their troops in the south in preparation for another major offensive. On the other hand, the North Vietnamese had little interest in substantive negotiations while the military balance of forces was unfavourable. They viewed the Paris peace talks as a means of getting the bombing stopped, unsettling the relationship between the South Vietnamese government and the US and intensifying anti-war pressures. Harriman urged Johnson to compromise by offering a complete cessation of bombing in the north and reduced military activities in the south. These proposals were refused by an enraged Johnson and at a press conference on 31 July he threatened that if there was no breakthrough in Paris, he might be compelled to undertake additional military measures.

Breaking the deadlock

In late October 1968, Johnson attempted once more to get the peace talks moving by stopping the bombing of North Vietnam. Encouraged by Johnson's move, Harriman sought to meet Hanoi's continuing objections to reciprocity through the ending of the bombing campaign. The US delegation made it clear that the communists would be expected to stop rocket and mortar attacks on South Vietnamese cities and limit the infiltration of soldiers and supplies across the DMZ. In order to overcome the last obstacle, the refusal by the north to negotiate with the South Vietnamese government, Harriman devised the ingenious formula 'Our side, your side'. This would allow all participants to the conflict to join in the peace talks without formally recognising each other as independent entities. Having established a basis on which to proceed with the peace talks, Harriman was frustrated again by Thieu's reluctance to attend the talks.

Thieu may have been responding to pressures from right-wing politicians in Saigon who saw the talks as a sell-out. More likely, his intransigence was encouraged by the Republicans through the activities of Henry Kissinger and Madame Anna Chennault. Using Madame Chennault as a go-between, Richard Nixon, the Republican presidential candidate for the 1968 elections, and his advisers convinced Thieu that South Vietnam might fare better at the Paris peace talks with a Republican administration as opposed to working with Johnson who was desperate for a peace settlement. Thieu's refusal to participate despite intense pressure from Johnson led to widespread discontent among the American population.

Ultimately it seems doubtful whether South Vietnamese delaying tactics – for example, the refusal of the South Vietnamese to sit at a round table for the Paris peace talks – sabotaged the opportunity for a peaceful settlement. At the end of the day, the North Vietnamese flexibility was related more to getting the bombing stopped than it was to any serious commitment to ending the struggle. There is nothing to indicate that Hanoi would have settled for anything less than complete withdrawal of US forces and a coalition government in South Vietnam. On the other hand, Johnson also stuck to his original goals for South Vietnam, and made it clear to Thieu that he would never accept a coalition government nor a total withdrawal of US troops. The year 1968 ended as it began, with a stalemate on the battlefield and deadlocked peace talks. Despite claims of victory both sides

Table 9.1 Army losses in South Vietnam, 1961–9

Year	Killed in Action		Wounded	
	US	South Vietnam	US	South Vietnam
1960	0	2223	0	2788
1961	11	4004	2	5449
1962	31	4457	41	7195
1963	78	5665	218	11,488
1964	147	7457	522	17,017
1965	1369	11,242	3308	23,118
1966	5008	11,953	16,526	20,975
1967	9377	12,716	32,370	29,448
1968	14,589	27,915	46,797	70,696
1969	9414	21,833	32,940	65,276

Source: **George Herring**, *America's Longest War: The United States and Vietnam, 1950–75* (2002), p.267

were seriously weakened. Table 9.1 reveals the US death toll rising year on year between 1961 and 1969.

After the Tet Offensive, the US administration realised that it could no longer continue the war because of the high costs, not only human but also economic, which if they continued to grow would seriously undermine the social and political reforms such as the Civil Rights Bill (1964), the Elementary and Secondary Education Act and Higher Education Act (1965), introduction of Medicare (1965) and the Voting Rights Act (1965) set in place by Johnson between 1964 and 1965.

CONCLUSION

After the Gulf of Tonkin Incident in August 1964, the Johnson administration escalated the war through intensive bombing campaigns and the rapid expansion of US ground troops, in effect Americanising what was in reality a struggle between the South and North Vietnamese over the reunification of Vietnam. Unable to counter the strength of the North Vietnamese and following the humiliation of the Tet Offensive, on 31 March 1968 Johnson began the process of peace talks with the leaders of North Vietnam. At the same time, he announced he would not be seeking renomination for the presidency.

In November 1968, Republican Richard Nixon was elected president. His campaign slogans 'Peace with Honour' and 'Bring the Troops Home' reflected what many in the USA wanted: an end to the fighting and loss of US lives in a war that for many appeared to be unwinnable.

CHAPTER 10

Nixon, Vietnamisation and 'Peace with Honor', 1969–73

AN OVERVIEW

In November 1968, Richard Nixon was elected as president of the US with a commitment to end the war in Vietnam and achieve 'Peace with Honor'. Throughout the campaign period, Nixon had condemned the Johnson administration for the way in which it had managed the war and accused it of failing to take the necessary measures to reduce the power and influence of the National Liberation Front (NLF) in the south and the communists in the north.

The situation in South Vietnam had continued to deteriorate after the Tet Offensive as the North Vietnamese-backed insurgents sought to undermine Thieu's government. In the US, there was a growing opposition among the public towards the war culminating in major anti-war demonstrations in the period 1969–72. In this period, Congress was also exploring ways of reducing the president's ability to continue to wage a war that many felt was unwinnable and that was bringing US credibility into question with its allies and the international community.

In 1969, Nixon was determined to crush the NLF insurgency and expanded the war in an attempt to stop supplies and equipment getting through from North Vietnam to insurgents in the south. In February 1969, Nixon appeared to be expanding the war when he ordered the secret bombing of Cambodia. In 1970, he supported the Army of the Republic of Vietnam (ARVN) invasion of Laos, which highlighted the weaknesses of the South Vietnamese troops. At the same time, he announced his policy of Vietnamisation, the gradual withdrawal of US troops from Vietnam, and an enlargement and modernisation of the ARVN force.

In May 1971, Nixon and his National Security Adviser, Henry Kissinger, embarked on a different strategy – diplomatic negotiations with the Soviet Union, China and the North Vietnamese. Initially most of the talks were carried out in secret, primarily because Kissinger did not want Thieu and the South Vietnamese government to feel that their allies were about to abandon them. However, in February 1972 at the China Summit and in May at the Moscow Summit, Nixon and Kissinger sought to influence the Chinese and the Soviets to put pressure on the North Vietnamese to restart the peace negotiations in Paris. In October 1972, the Peace Accords were signed by the North Vietnamese, the South Vietnamese and the Americans despite Thieu's opposition. In April 1975, following a brief military operation, the north and south were finally reunified as the Democratic Republic of Vietnam, first declared in August 1945.

BIOGRAPHIES

Richard Nixon (1913–94) In November 1968, Nixon won the presidential election. His strong anti-communist stance possibly helped him to win the trust of the Americans at a time when the war in Vietnam appeared to be causing deep cleavages within their society. In 1972, together with Kissinger he developed a détente with the Soviet Union and China. But he was severely criticised for extending the war in Indochina and then taking so long to end the war in Vietnam. In 1974, he was forced to resign because of the Watergate scandal.

Henry Kissinger (born 1923) In 1969, he was appointed National Security Adviser to President Richard Nixon. In this role, he was given considerable power. His role in developing détente with the Soviet Union and the opening to China and peace in Vietnam led to his being seen as an effective diplomat. In 1973, he became Secretary of State. The collapse of Vietnam in 1975 and moral doubts about his secret diplomatic activities undermined respect for him.

INTRODUCTION

President Nixon implied in his campaign speeches that he had a 'secret plan' to end the war in Vietnam. His approach was more pragmatic than that of any of the previous presidents. In January 1969, he commissioned a thorough study of the situation in Vietnam. Various agencies contributed to National Security Study Memorandum 1, including the Departments of State and Defence, the Joint Chiefs of Staff, the CIA, the US Ambassador in Saigon and the US military command in Vietnam. All agreed that the South Vietnamese army alone could not contain the threat from the north, nor could the US continue to increase the number of troops in Vietnam without seriously undermining commitments in other parts of the world, including West Germany. In other words, there appeared to be no strategy that would either give the US a military victory or allow the US to withdraw and leave the South Vietnamese in a position to defend themselves.

After his constant criticism of Johnson for not fighting hard enough Nixon now realised that he could not escalate the war and that he had to seek a negotiated settlement. Determined to leave Nguyen Van Thieu at the head of a friendly government in South Vietnam, Nixon now sought ways to preserve South Vietnam while at the same time reducing the military commitments. The three strategies that Nixon and his National Security Adviser Kissinger took in order to secure peace in South Vietnam were:

- Vietnamisation
- the escalation of aerial bombing and the extension of the war into Cambodia and Laos

- diplomatic initiatives including détente with the Soviet Union and China in an attempt to isolate North Vietnam from its major allies.

THE NIXON DOCTRINE AND VIETNAMISATION

In June 1969, the announcement of the **Nixon Doctrine** revealed a shift in US military policy from one of US intervention to one in which nations were responsible for their own defence. The doctrine stated:

> *The nations of Asia can and must increasingly shoulder the responsibility for achieving peace and progress in the area with whatever cooperation we can provide. Asian countries must seek their own destiny for if domination by the aggressor can destroy the freedom of a nation, too much dependence on a protector can eventually erode its dignity. But it is not just a matter of dignity, for dependence on foreign aid destroys the incentive to mobilise domestic resources – human, financial and material – in which the absence of which no government is capable of dealing effectively with its problems and adversaries.*

The Nixon Doctrine implied an intention to withdraw from Vietnam with dignity and to give some meaning to a war that had seen huge sacrifices.

Vietnamisation was to provide Nixon with a way of removing US troops from South Vietnam while at the same time ensuring peace with honour and US international credibility. On 3 November, in his 'Silent Majority' speech Nixon outlined his Vietnamisation policy, which included the slow, phased withdrawal of US combat troops from Vietnam and their replacement by well-equipped and trained ARVN troops. The policy was intended to reduce the number of US casualties, while at the same time allowing the ARVN to take command of the war against the NLF insurgents.

Making Vietnamisation work was a formidable task for the US military experts. Many believed that without US support the ARVN would be unable to repel attacks by the NLF and the PAVN troops. But Nixon's policy ensured that the ARVN became one of the most well-equipped armies in the world by 1973. Military schools with a capacity for 100,000 students were introduced for new recruits and officers. To improve morale among the South Vietnamese armed forces the promotion system was modernised, pay scales were raised, leave improved, veterans' benefits expanded, and systematic efforts made to improve conditions in the military camps and the housing of dependants.

The US replaced the old M-1 rifles which dated from the Second World War with more than one million M-16 Armalites. The rifle had a selector switch for full or semi-automatic fire. It was lighter in weight than the old M-1 and more reliable. The ARVN was also supplied with 12,000 M-60 machine-guns, 40,000 M-79 grenade launchers and 2000 heavy mortars and howitzers. The latest tanks, military vehicles, planes and helicopters were also supplied to allow the army a greater flexibility in the way it fought.

South Vietnam increased the size of the armed forces to over one million by 1970. However, the impressive size of the ARVN was often compromised by the traditional problems of desertion and 'ghosting'; officers kept the names of deserters and dead soldiers on the rosters and claimed the pay.

After 1969, the Accelerated Pacification Campaign was extended to improve security in the villages. Village elections were restored, and responsibility for roads, schools, hospitals and the local militia was passed to the village councils. By 1970, the tactics of the ARVN combined with the new strategies of the US combat troops led by General Creighton Abrams had on the surface led to a reduction in the activities of the insurgents in South Vietnam. Abrams had abandoned the policies of search and destroy in favour of combat missions designed to cut off the insurgents from civilian support in the rural areas. He also introduced the Civilian Operations and Revolutionary Development Support (CORDS), which provided economic support for road construction and training for self-defence forces. The People's Self Defence Front grew to over three million participants by 1972. Some US officials argued that the pacification came from US operations such as the **Phoenix Programme**. This programme focused on neutralising the activities of the NLF as they worked openly in the villages gathering taxes, supplies and recruits. In the period 1968–72, over 34,000 Vietcong operatives were captured and thousands more neutralised. But this improvement in the security of the countryside was deceptive. There were major criticisms of the programme. The number of converts from the NLF was grossly inflated by the Vietnamese and US officials. There were also more than 26,000 assassinations of those involved in the programme.

The success of the Vietnamisation programme for the Nixon administration in the period 1969–71 is demonstrated by:

- the fall in the number of US casualties (see Figure 10.1)
- the withdrawal of military personnel (see Table 10.1).

Vietnamisation was not the only strategy adopted by the Nixon administration to pressure the North Vietnamese to end the war; it also used widespread bombing.

ESCALATION OF THE US BOMBING CAMPAIGN

In January 1969, Nixon and his National Security Adviser Kissinger reopened the Paris peace talks with the North

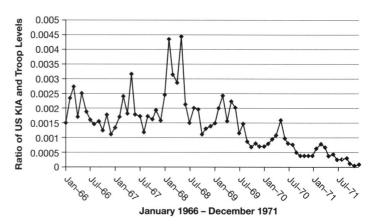

January 1966 – December 1971

Ratio of Monthly US-KIA to Troop Levels during the Vietnam War

Table 10.1 US military strength in South Vietnam, 1969–72

Year	Army	Navy	Marines	Air force	Coast guard	Total
Jan 1969	359,500	36,400	81,400	58,400	400	**536,100**
June 1969	360,500	35,800	81,500	60,500	400	**538,700**
Jan 1970	331,100	30,200	55,100	58,400	400	**475,200**
June 1970	298,600	25,700	39,900	50,500	200	**414,900**
Jan 1971	249,600	16,700	25,100	43,100	100	**334,600**
June 1971	190,500	10,700	500	37,400	100	**239,200**
Jan 1972	119,700	7600	600	28,800	100	**156,800**
June 1972	31,800	2200	1400	11,500	100	**47,000**

Vietnamese. As a first step towards peace Nixon proposed the mutual withdrawal of US and People's Army of Vietnam (PAVN) troops from South Vietnam and the restoration of the Demilitarised Zone (DMZ) at the 17th Parallel. In March 1969, Nixon began the secret bombing, 'Operation Menu', of NLF/PAVN sanctuaries in Cambodia. Nixon's motivation for the bombing was to indicate that he would take measures that Johnson had avoided, thus pressurising the north into negotiating peace on his terms. In April 1969, Nixon and Kissinger approached the Soviet Union with a set of proposals, based on the linking of strategic arms talks and issues on the Middle East to the amount of pressure the Soviets could place on North Vietnam. However, the Soviets refused to agree to a summit with Nixon because of its objections to the linkage of issues. The fundamental reason for their refusal was the fact that the Soviets recognised that they had limited influence over the north Vietnamese at this time.

In July 1969, Nixon sent a secret message to Ho Chi Minh reiterating his desire for a 'just peace' but adding an ultimatum: unless some progress towards a settlement was made by 1 November he would have no choice but to resort to 'measures of great consequence and force'. Nixon and Kissinger now looked to an alternative strategy to pressurise the North Vietnamese, 'Operation Duck Hook', a massive air offensive that included attacks on targets deep in North Vietnam, including the bombing of Hanoi and the mining of Haiphong harbour. However, the National Security Council was apprehensive of the success of this operation because:

- air attacks would not seriously affect the north's ability to carry on the war
- there were few industrial targets to strike
- the Soviet Union and China would help the north clear the mines from Haiphong port
- it would be viewed as an expansion of the war with high civilian casualties
- it would increase public protest and demonstrations in the USA.

This was a risky policy for the US. The Soviet Union had stated on a number of occasions that the mining of the port of Haiphong would not be tolerated. However, Kissinger and Nixon were hoping that such a threat would create uncertainty in the minds of the North Vietnamese.

Because of the combined opposition of the National Security Council and the Secretaries of State and Defence, and growing public discontent with the war, Nixon abandoned this plan. In his 'Silent Majority' speech Nixon called for public support:

> *I have initiated a plan of action which will allow me to end the war in a way that we could win the peace. The more support I can have from the US people, the sooner the pledge can be redeemed; for the more we are divided at home, the less likely the enemy is to negotiate at Paris.*

However, Nixon and Kissinger had already made the decision to secretly bomb the North Vietnamese sanctuaries in Cambodia and this action extended the war.

EXTENSION OF THE WAR TO CAMBODIA

The NLF and PAVN troops had sanctuaries on the borders with Cambodia which had posed a problem for the US military campaign from the start of the Vietnam War. As a signal to both North Vietnam and the Soviet Union, Nixon showed that he was prepared to take measures that Johnson had avoided to get the North Vietnamese to negotiate a peace treaty. In February 1969, he ordered intensive bombing attacks against the sanctuaries in Cambodia. Over the next fifteen months, 3630 B-52 raids were conducted against these sanctuaries in Cambodia dropping more than 100,000 tonnes of bombs. The raids, conducted in secret, were intended to put pressure on the North Vietnamese to begin peace negotiations and to buy time to put in place the Vietnamisation programme.

In March 1970, Cambodia's neutralist ruler Prince Sihanouk was overthrown by pro-US General Lon Nol whose first action was to order the North Vietnamese out of Cambodia. However, the North Vietnamese now supported the communist Khmer Rouge insurgents in Cambodia and together they mounted a new campaign against the troops of Lon Nol. The Nixon administration, alarmed by the threat to Lon Nol, now agreed to support US–ARVN military intervention in Cambodia to defeat the communist forces. On 29 April 1970, ARVN units together with US air support attacked the strategic Parrot's Beak section of Cambodia, a strip of land 53 kilometres from Saigon, and destroyed the NLF/PAVN headquarters, the Central Office for South Vietnam (COSVN), on the Cambodian border. This operation was followed by further attacks in the Fishhook region, an area 88 kilometres north-west of Saigon where the North Vietnamese were preparing their forces for the next offensive.

Military operations in Cambodia and Laos, 1970–1

Together, 30,000 US and 50,000 ARVN troops inflicted a major defeat on the communists, even though the US troops had to exit Cambodia by 30 June because of limitations imposed on US military operations by Congress in December 1969.

In Cambodia, US actions contributed to one of the greatest tragedies in Indochina. The US invasion forced the North Vietnamese to move further into Cambodia and provided the Khmer Rouge insurgents fighting Lon Nol with large-scale support leading to a bloody civil war.

Congress and the Cambodian conflict

The Cambodian invasion also provoked a major challenge to presidential power from Congress because of the lack of prior consultation by Nixon and his advisers. In December 1969, the US Congress first sought to impose control of Nixon's power to commit troops to south-east Asia when an amendment to the defence appropriations bill prohibited the president from introducing a ground force in Laos and Thailand. Many senators were outraged at the secrecy that surrounded Nixon's actions in Cambodia, and others were angered by the broadening of the war. In June 1970, the Senate voted overwhelmingly to terminate the Gulf of Tonkin Resolution of 1964 (see page 125), thereby stripping the president of his control over the war and the armed forces. The problem that now faced Nixon was how to achieve 'peace with honour'. Congressional restrictions on the future use of US troops meant he had to find other strategies to force the North Vietnamese to negotiate. Hanoi delegates boycotted the official peace talks in Paris and refused to restart the secret talks until US troops had been removed from Cambodia.

Reactions to the invasion of Cambodia

By widening the war into Cambodia, Nixon was convinced that force would push the North Vietnamese into making a decision about negotiations. In a televised speech on 30 April 1970, Nixon justified the Cambodian offensive as a response to the aggression of the North Vietnamese and to protect US forces. He assured the American population that COSVN, the NLF/PAVN headquarters, had been destroyed and large amounts of weapons and supplies had been uncovered and destroyed.

The extension of the war to Cambodia reignited an anti-war movement that had quietened down since autumn 1969. Aware that Nixon's peace initiatives were not producing results, the first major demonstrations against his policies began in 1969. In late spring, a number of young activists who included Sam Brown and David Hawk organised the Moratorium, a suspension of normal activities by going to church services and discussions instead of work or college. The first Moratorium on 15 October saw the participation of at least one million US citizens. They conducted vigils, attended religious services or discussion groups, showed films or joined candlelight processions singing John Lennon's song 'Give Peace a Chance'. The second Moratorium held between 13 and 15 November sponsored a Mass for Peace and a 36-hour March against Death, one of the period's most moving actions.

However, the autumn demonstrations did not bring about a change in Nixon's policies. Late 1969 was the high point of the anti-war demonstrations because as the troop withdrawals continued into 1970 and the number of casualties began to fall, the peace movement began to fragment. Many activists continued to protest but most of the largest demonstrations after this period were reactions to specific events. The invasion of Cambodia triggered major demonstrations on 4 May 1970 that culminated in the shooting of students. Four students at Kent State University and two at Jackson State College were killed in angry confrontations with the National Guard. On 9 May, 100,000 demonstrators gathered in Washington to protest against the Kent State Massacre and call for the immediate withdrawal of all US troops from Indochina. Around 350 colleges and universities were closed because of strikes and as many as 500 schools were closed down to avert further violence. As a response to the dramatic outbursts following the invasions of Cambodia, Nixon approved one of the most blatant attacks on individual freedom and privacy, the Huston Plan. This authorised the intelligence agencies to use surveillance methods and even burglaries to spy on Americans. Like Johnson, Nixon was convinced that the left, including communists, were behind the mass protests and rallies.

A student kneels over one of the victims of the Kent State Massacre, 4 May 1970

THE WAR EXTENDS TO LAOS

Instead of rethinking policies that brought no results, Nixon continued with the removal of US troops from South Vietnam in order to appease his critics. On the other hand, he continued to mount heavy air attacks against Cambodia and Laos using the pretext that the North Vietnamese were firing against reconnaissance planes.

In February 1971, Nixon again expanded the war by approving a major operation by the ARVN into Laos, 'Operation Lam Son 719'. The success of the Cambodian offensive had forced the NLF/PAVN to become more reliant on the Laos section of the Ho Chi Minh Trail. Thieu warned the US government of a communist build-up on the Laos border and requested support for a pre-emptive attack. The Laotian offensive from 8 February to 24 March 1971 was to be carried out by the ARVN with US air support.

Unfortunately, the 21,000 ARVN troops faced a well equipped NLF/PAVN force of some 36,000 troops supported by the newest Russian-built T-34 and T-54/55 tanks. After six weeks of bloody fighting during which the ARVN performed extremely well, they were forced to retreat into South Vietnam but in the end only half the ARVN force returned and 108 US helicopters were lost. Nixon and Kissinger claimed a great victory for the ARVN despite the fact that it was poorly commanded by General Lam. The ARVN had killed 15,000 enemy troops and destroyed most of the major supply network in Laos. However, as Abrams concluded, South Vietnam could not 'sustain large scale cross border operations without external support'. The main outcome of 'Lam Son 719' was to reassure the NLF that it could deal with the ARVN even with US air support.

The invasion of Laos and the anti-war movement

Following the withdrawal of troops from Laos, a series of events further challenged the Nixon administration's management of the war. On 29 March 1971, the much publicised trial and conviction of Lieutenant William Calley once again brought to the public attention the horrors of the Vietnam War. Calley was tried for the murder of 500 unarmed Vietnamese civilians at My Lai. The trial split the nation between those who defended the killing as an act of war, those who saw the event as a massacre and those who believed Calley was a scapegoat while other higher ranking officers avoided responsibility. When Calley was sentenced to life imprisonment, a further debate was triggered about who was responsible for this war crime, Calley and his detachment or the government who sent them to fight in the first place.

The Vietnam Veterans Against War (VVAW), newly formed at Howard Johnson's Motor Lodge in Detroit, conducted their own investigations into US war crimes. On 19–23 April, the VVAW went to Washington and, standing in front of the Capitol, recited their own war crimes before ceremoniously throwing away their medals. After this they descended on Washington with the intention of shutting down the government, and proceeded to conduct lie-ins on bridges, major roads and at the entrances to government buildings. More than 12,000 protestors were arrested; many did not violate any law. The principal criterion by which arrests were made appeared to be evidence of youthfulness such as long hair, rather than an unlawful act. The courts ruled that the massive number of arrests of innocent bystanders was illegal.

THE PUBLICATION OF THE PENTAGON PAPERS

The publication of the Pentagon Papers on 13 June 1971 by the *New York Times* further undermined the Nixon administration in the eyes of the nation. These were commissioned by Robert McNamara in early 1968. He ordered a small staff in the Department of Defence to undertake a secret study of US decision-making about Vietnam since the end of the Second World War. Classified as top secret, only fifteen copies of the study were made. Daniel Ellsberg, an employee of the RAND Corporation who had two copies of the study, leaked the documents to the *New York Times*. The study revealed to the American public that Kennedy and Johnson had consistently misled them about their intentions in Vietnam. Kissinger and Nixon were both unnerved by these revelations and were obviously concerned that their own actions with regard to the secret bombings of Cambodia might be disclosed. President Nixon attempted to stop the publication of the Pentagon Papers but the Supreme Court ruled against him.

Neither Nixon's withdrawal policy nor his vigorous attacks against the opposition could stem the war weariness and general demoralisation felt by the American public in summer 1971. The discontent that affected the American public had an impact on the morale of the US combat troops. Vietnamisation was welcomed by the US troops because the chances of getting killed were reduced and becoming a casualty in a war that many back home perceived was over was hardly a motivation to fight. According to **Gabriel Kolko** in *Anatomy of a War: Vietnam, The United States, and the Modern Historical Experience* (1985), after 1969, troop morale began visibly to break down and became a highly publicised organisational problem involving discipline and, ultimately, the very capacity of the US forces to function. The purpose of the war was now less clear and alienation among the troops increased.

THE CRISIS OF THE US ARMY, 1969–73

Drug abuse among US troops in Vietnam was becoming more common because of the availability of high-quality drugs brought into South Vietnam from Laos and the complicity in this of the CIA and senior figures in the South Vietnamese government. The drug epidemic that emerged after 1969 was to some extent related to the sheer boredom among enlisted men, as long days on bases replaced search-and-destroy missions. In mid-1971, the Pentagon tried to argue that only 5 per cent of US soldiers were drug users. In 1973, it conceded that 35 per cent of all enlisted troops who had been in South Vietnam had tried heroin and 20 per cent were addicted at some time during their tour.

Nowhere was the breakdown of morale and discipline more apparent than in the incidences of **fragging**, the use of fragmentation grenades to assassinate officers. As with the problem of drug-taking the number of incidents was much higher after 1969. The official figure for the number of fragging incidents in the period 1969–73 is 788, with 86 deaths. However, it is estimated that the actual number was around 1012, far higher than incidents in the Second World War. One of the major causes of fragging was the ambitious officer attempting to force his men to take unnecessary risks when confronted by the enemy. Units where the officer was responsible to his men and not his superiors tended to have higher morale and solidarity and minimum losses.

Another cause of the breakdown of discipline in the armed forces was that, of the 2,150,000 men sent to Vietnam, a high percentage were poor white and black people. They were also more likely to become infantry riflemen, the 'grunts' who were most often sent into combat. They were often led by officers who served for six months in Vietnam and, from the military point of view, lacked both the experience and the motivation to make good leaders. A major weakness for the US armed forces was the constant turnover of experienced leaders and the long periods of waiting for action. The relatively extravagant effort to sustain morale while in the field with excellent food, medical care and the provision of rest and recuperation breaks in exotic resorts in Thailand, it is argued, softened the soldiers. In comparison, they were fighting against Vietnamese men and women who had few luxuries and limited amounts of food, and who were determined, hardened fighters.

DIPLOMATIC INITIATIVES TO END THE WAR

Realising that a military solution to end the war was not possible now, Nixon turned towards a diplomatic solution. In May 1971, Kissinger began secret talks once again with representatives of the North Vietnamese and presented a comprehensive peace offer that included:

- a date for the total withdrawal of US troops
- a cease-fire in place throughout Indochina under international supervision
- the guarantee of independence, neutrality and territorial integrity for Laos and Cambodia
- the immediate release by both sides of all prisoners of war and innocent civilians

- the political future of South Vietnam to be left to the South Vietnamese
- the completion of a withdrawal timetable.

In exchange for the release of US prisoners of war, Kissinger pledged to withdraw all troops within seven months of an agreement being signed. The US also dropped the concept of mutual withdrawal in return for the end of NVA infiltration into South Vietnam. The north refused this offer and in a counter-offer agreed to release the POWs simultaneously with the withdrawal of US troops, as long as the USA dropped its support for Thieu in the forthcoming presidential elections in South Vietnam. Kissinger refused this offer but was impressed by the way the two sides appeared to be moving closer together. Throughout the summer and autumn the secret talks progressed but collapsed in November 1971 primarily because of the two sides' failure to agree on:

- the timing of the withdrawal and the return of the US and North Vietnamese POWs
- the removal of President Thieu from South Vietnam
- the establishment of a Tripartite Commission for South Vietnam after the cease-fire, made up of representatives of the South Vietnamese government, the National Liberation Front and neutralists.

CHANGING STRATEGIES AND THE SEARCH FOR PEACE

For Nixon and Kissinger after the bombing and ground campaigns of 1969–71 and negotiations with the North Vietnamese the realisation that a peace with honour that would guarantee a reasonable chance that the division of Vietnam along the 17th Parallel would provide a secure border between the Democratic Republic of Vietnam and the Republic of Vietnam had become unrealistic. The Laotian and Cambodian campaigns, together with the withdrawal of US troops, had revealed that the ARVN was militarily weaker on the ground. So the USA changed its strategies towards attaining peace with honour from one of military force to diplomacy. In the period 1971–3, a triangular relationship between the Americans, the Soviets and China emerged.

The Sino–Soviet conflict following the Ussuri River border clashes in March 1969 worsened the division between the two communist superpowers. Kissinger exploited the conflict in order to exert pressure on the Soviets and China for greater responsiveness in the superpower détente process and to find a negotiated settlement for Vietnam. **Evelyn Goh**, in *Nixon, Kissinger and the 'Soviet Card' in the US Opening to China, 1971–74* (2005), shows how Kissinger was able to use China's security fears about possible war with the Soviet Union to re-establish harmonious relations with China. In July 1971, a secret trip to China offered Kissinger the first opportunity to use the Chinese as an effective mediator in the ongoing peace talks with the North Vietnamese. In a conversation with Premier Zhou Enlai, Kissinger stated: 'There should be some agreement at negotiations between the Vietnamese parties; if the agreement breaks down then it is quite possible that the people of Vietnam will fight it out.' Kissinger was seeking a transition period between the withdrawal of US troops from South Vietnam and a political resolution on the unification of Vietnam.

However, his attempts to win support from the Chinese leadership to pressure the North Vietnamese into accepting the peace plan were not successful. When told of Kissinger's comments, Mao stated there would be no change in the position of the PRC. In addition, Zhou was sent to North Vietnam to reassure the North Vietnamese of China's continued support for their war. The real intention of Kissinger's visit was to increase pressure on the Soviets by making them think the USA was about to enter into a Sino–US alliance. Kissinger's secret meeting was revealed on national television on 15 July at the same time that Nixon announced he would be going to China for a summit in March 1972.

The outcome of Kissinger's diplomatic initiative with the Chinese was better than he had anticipated. On 10 August 1971, the Soviets issued a formal invitation for a Moscow summit in May 1972. On 3 September 1971, the Soviets signed the Berlin Four-Power Agreement, under discussion since March 1969. Unfortunately there was no move on the Vietnam issue. In fact, Kissinger's triangular diplomacy had not translated into an obvious US advantage for the simple reason that the Chinese and the Soviet Union now sought to increase their influence with North Vietnam by offering enhanced aid packages. On the other hand, they did try to exert pressure on the North Vietnamese towards a diplomatic settlement.

In February 1972, Nixon's visit to China resulted in a few agreements as outlined in the Shanghai Communiqué, dealing mainly with Taiwan, released at the end of the visit. On the issue of Vietnam both sides publicly agreed to disagree. Zhou reiterated to Nixon the PRC's support for the north because of US support of the Thieu government in the south. Both sides agreed that the Soviets were responsible for the continuation of the war in Vietnam because of the quantities of military aid they supplied to the north. On the issue of the peace plans, Nixon tried to persuade the Chinese to exert pressure on the North Vietnamese to return to the

President Richard Nixon meeting Chairman Mao Zedong in Beijing, 21 February 1972

negotiations in Paris, but Zhou could promise nothing. When the North Vietnamese launched the Easter Offensive on 30 March 1972 they did so with the support of both China and the Soviet Union.

THE EASTER OFFENSIVE

On 30 March 1972, the NLF crossed the DMZ and launched a massive conventional invasion of South Vietnam. In the Easter Offensive, General Giap hoped to win a decisive victory and end the war. In the first stages, the NLF launched attacks on three fronts, across the DMZ, in the central highlands and across the Cambodian border north-west of Saigon. The reasons for the attack were as follows.

- The offensive was timed to discredit Nixon's Vietnamisation policy.
- The NLF believed that, following the withdrawal of the US troops, ARVN troops were now weakened and could be defeated.
- More importantly, the NLF believed that North Vietnam was to be abandoned by its allies, the Soviet Union and the People's Republic of China. Certainly Kissinger's linkage policies were beginning to show some success with Nixon visiting China in February 1972.
- It was timed to coincide with the start of the US presidential elections.
- The North Vietnamese wanted a victory in order to pursue the peace negotiations from a position of strength.

The PAVN forces quickly established a foothold in the two northern provinces of South Vietnam. The Battle for An Loc on 2–13 April resulted in the NLF/PAVN forces fighting in the city. The ARVN held out with the help of US air strikes but An Loc was subjected to a siege until mid-June, when fresh reinforcements broke through the NLF/PAVN defences. On 1 May the PAVN took control of the provincial capital of Quang Tri and were advancing on Hué. Despite being vastly outnumbered, the ARVN forces managed to hold Hué with massive amounts of US air support and by the second week in July had managed to retake Quang Tri. In the central highlands, the NLF overran all the ARVN defensive points. A counter-offensive was launched by the ARVN in early July and it was quickly able to re-establish its control of the highlands.

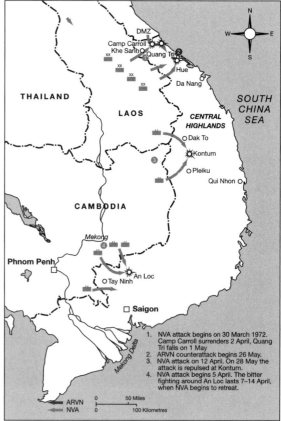

The Communist Easter Offensive, March – May 1972

Kissinger talks with the Soviet Union, 21 April 1972

During the Easter Offensive, Kissinger continued to have secret talks with the Soviets in an attempt to get them to put pressure on Hanoi. On 21 April, he informed Brezhnev that the USA's two principal objectives were to:

- bring about an honourable withdrawal of all its forces
- put a time-frame between US withdrawal and the political process, which would then start.

As he had hinted to the Chinese, Kissinger was implying that the US now recognised that South Vietnam could not be saved from the north. What he wanted from the Soviets and Chinese was a decent interval of time between the removal of US troops and advisers and the eventual overthrow of the south by the north. This interpretation of Kissinger's motives for the meetings with Soviet and Chinese leaders in 1972 is very persuasively argued by **Jussi Hanhimaki** in *Selling the 'Decent Interval': Kissinger, Triangular Diplomacy, and the End of the Vietnam War, 1971–73* (2003). However, the North Vietnamese, confident they were on the verge of a great victory, continued to reject the peace terms offered by the US.

Bombing campaign Linebacker 1

On 8 May 1972, US General Abrams warned that Hué and Kontum would soon fall and the whole war might be lost. In an attempt to block supplies for the PAVN forces clearly involved in the offensive, Abrams asked Nixon to intensify the bombing above the DMZ. Secretary of Defence Laird, Secretary of State Rogers and Kissinger did not want the war extended because they feared months of steady negotiations with the North Vietnamese would be lost and the forthcoming summit in Moscow on May 24 might be cancelled.

Stunned by the Easter Offensive launched by Hanoi on 30 March 1972, Nixon set out to make clear he was 'determined to end the war by whatever steps were necessary'. On 8 May, 'Operation Linebacker 1' was launched. This was a massive bombing campaign involving 210 B-52s, representing one half of the US Strategic Air Command bomber fleet. Unlike 'Operation Rolling Thunder' (see pages 131–2), 'Linebacker 1' bombed a wide range of strategic targets in North Vietnam, including Hanoi and Haiphong, and mined the harbour of Haiphong – the strategy of 'Operation Duck Hook' that Nixon was forced to abandon in 1969 (see page 159). By this time, a number of Washington officials had reassured Nixon that the Russians had too much at stake to abandon the summit. Nixon, however, was more concerned about defending the credibility of the office of the president than about giving into any pressure from the Russians.

In late May, both China and the Soviet Union had come to realise that nothing should be allowed to jeopardise the major diplomatic alignment then taking place in world politics. While both governments sent formal protests about the damage the bombing caused to their ships neither sought to sever relations with the US. Both China and the Soviet Union urged Hanoi to reach an agreement with the US. Both sides continued to help the north with mine-clearance vessels provided by the Chinese to clear the mines from Haiphong harbour and with other supplies necessary to give the North Vietnamese the military edge over the ARVN, but both wanted an end to the war.

'Operation Linebacker' 1 badly damaged the North Vietnamese in terms of manpower and equipment. The military tactics employed in a conventional battle like the Easter Offensive required vast amounts of fuel and ammunition but 'Linebacker 1' had devastated what was left of the north's economy and paralysed the transportation system. In the past, the Soviet Union had

American B-52s in the Linebacker bombing campaign of 1972

supplied equipment, but now there were strings attached. Moscow wanted to let Nixon get his 'Peace with Honor' as an aid to détente and therefore the Russians were no longer willing to encourage further engagements.

In the final analysis, the Easter Offensive revealed that the war had reached stalemate. Both sides had suffered huge losses: the north some 100,000 casualties; the south 30,000 killed, 78,000 wounded and 14,000 missing in action. By spreading its forces over three fronts rather than concentrating on one, the north had gained very little. The Easter Offensive had emphasised the vulnerability of the ARVN forces when faced with a massive assault. Without the support of US air power the ARVN would have been destroyed.

THE MOSCOW SUMMIT AND VIETNAM

When Nixon and Kissinger met with their Soviet counterparts in Moscow on 24 May 1972 they were exposed to a lecture about the cruel policies the USA had inflicted on Vietnam. The final Soviet statement on Vietnam was that the US should accept the North Vietnamese request to remove Thieu in order to get the peace process restarted. In his memoirs *The White House Years* (1979), **Kissinger** asserted that the entire purpose of this Soviet statement was to show their North Vietnamese allies they had not been soft on the 'capitalists'. However, in a meeting between Kissinger and Soviet Foreign Minister Andrei Gromyko, without the presence of either Nixon or Brezhnev, Kissinger once again offered a way to restart negotiations with the North Vietnamese:

> *If North Vietnam were wise it would make an agreement now and not haggle over every detail, because one year after the agreement there would be a new condition, a new reality. If the DRV were creative, it would have great possibilities. All we ask is a degree of time so as to leave Vietnam for Americans in a better perspective. We are prepared to leave so that a communist victory is not excluded, though not guaranteed.*

Kissinger told Gromyko that this message could be communicated to the North Vietnamese.

TOWARDS PEACE

On 15 July 1972, the North Vietnamese moved towards a strategy for peace. Before his arrival in Paris, Le Duc Tho who led the North Vietnamese delegates, had met with the Chinese. Zhou En Lai told the Vietnamese delegation that it must negotiate. On the issue of the Tripartite Commission for the south and the role of Thieu, Zhou said the North Vietnamese had to accept the US proposals; if they continued to block the role of Thieu the negotiations would collapse and the north would have to continue to fight.

The talks began in July and were completed on 12 October 1972. The terms included:

- a cease-fire commencing on 24 January 1973
- the armed forces of the two Vietnams to remain in place
- the withdrawal of US troops and civilian personnel
- the return of POWs by all sides on the same day
- the establishment of free and democratic elections and the right of the South Vietnamese to decide their political future
- the US and all other countries respect the independence, sovereignty, unity and territorial integrity of Vietnam as recognised by the 1954 Geneva Accords.

Aware that Nixon was about to win a landslide victory in the presidential election, the North Vietnamese were convinced that now was the time to finally end the involvement of the US in Vietnam. Nixon and Kissinger moved away from their absolute commitment to Thieu by agreeing to a tripartite election commission based on the Saigon regime, the Provisional Revolutionary Government and the neutralists. These elections would address the eventual unification of Vietnam by peaceful means and a US contribution to post-war reconstruction. The north now dropped its demands for the removal of Thieu.

Reaction of Thieu and the South Vietnamese

The Saigon government was uneasy about the negotiations, feeling it would be left in a vulnerable position once the US had withdrawn. For this reason Thieu refused to sign the agreement. Nixon shared some of Thieu's reservations and, unlike Kissinger, he had never abandoned his quest for 'Peace with Honor'. Certain that he was about to achieve an enormous mandate in the forthcoming election, Nixon was willing to wait until after the election to complete the process; however, Nixon was not prepared to let Thieu hold up the talks indefinitely. A brief delay would be an opportunity for the USA to send hundreds of aircraft and armoured vehicles to South Vietnam to strengthen its military. Believing the US was using Thieu's demands to delay the talks, Hanoi accused the US of abandoning the deal. After three weeks of unsuccessful discussions, the Paris peace talks broke down.

The Christmas bombings

Partly to pressurise the north into making concessions, but mainly to reassure Thieu of continued US commitment, Nixon ordered 'Linebacker 2' on 18 December. B-52s were allowed to bomb Hanoi and the other main cities in the north. This was the heaviest bombing of the war, and the US suffered its highest loss of aircraft, including fifteen B-52 bombers and 92 air personnel. The bombing produced international opposition including from US allies and Nixon's approval rating plummeted to 32 per cent. Nixon, however, believed 'Linebacker 2' would end the war with a dramatic flourish. It would allow him to present the US as the victor and would demonstrate to Hanoi that he was prepared to uphold the peace.

Although on the surface it would appear that Nixon's actions had forced the North Vietnamese back to the negotiations on US terms the final settlement, signed on 27 January 1973, closely resembled the October document. Thieu eventually agreed to sign only after pressure was put on him by both Kissinger and Nixon. However, the fundamental issue of South Vietnam's viability as an independent democratic state was not resolved. Ultimately, the US had found a way out of Vietnam despite not achieving 'Peace with Honor'.

Representatives of the US, North Vietnam, South Vietnam and Viet Cong sign the ceasefire accord in Paris, 27 January 1973

War Powers Act, 1973

The role of Congress in the period is also an important consideration when exploring why Nixon and Kissinger were motivated to use linkage as a way of ending US involvement in South Vietnam. Congress wanted to restore its authority over the presidency because many members, including

Senate majority leader Mike Mansfield, believed that the Vietnam War had led the US into a situation that was damaging for its reputation in both the international and domestic communities. Many argued that the involvement of Johnson and Kennedy in Vietnam had isolated the US from their traditional allies. In 1969, Congress sought to redefine the Vietnam War; it was not a defensive war. The fact that the policy of containment had been defined as a way of protecting the US from the perceived threat of Soviet expansion in 1947 was not applicable in 1969. Early détente had shown that the Soviet Union and the US could work together through diplomatic channels to protect their interests.

Furthermore, the increased defence-related spending by the governments of Johnson and Nixon had led to 30% inflation in domestic goods in the period 1965 to 1970. This together with increased debt and loose control by the Federal Reserve of the value of the dollar led to the first foreign trade deficit in 1971 since the end of the Second World War. Pressure on the dollar continued to grow throughout 1971 and Nixon was forced by Congress to adopt a programme that required less spending on defence. The US administration also withdrew the gold backing of the dollar and ended the Bretton Woods System which had dominated the world capitalist economy since 1945. On 18 December 1971 the dollar was formally devalued. This imposed further limits on the capability of the Nixon administration to sustain the war in Vietnam and this therefore was an important reason for Nixon to end the Vietnam War quickly.

When Nixon extended the war to Cambodia in 1969, he argued it was to defend US troops in South Vietnam. However, Congress was no longer willing to accept this argument and began to exert its influence by restricting the president's power. This was done through the passage of the national commitments legislation which prohibited the US from funding advisers or ground troops in Cambodia. In 1972 and 1973, these restrictions were extended to Laos and South Vietnam.

However, Nixon continued to fund bombing operations and the use of helicopter gunships in Cambodia and Laos. The costs were estimated at US$890 million in military aid and US$503 million in economic aid to Cambodia. In 1973, because of repeated failures to constrain the presidential war-making powers, Congress passed the War Powers Act, despite Nixon's veto. It reasserted congressional authority in making war and gave itself the power to stop presidents engaging the US in war without congressional support. On 3 April 1975, President Ford blamed Congress for its failure to provide adequate military and economic aid to defend South Vietnam against invasion from the north.

US WITHDRAWAL AND IMPLICATIONS FOR SOUTH VIETNAM

With the signing of the Paris Accords, few (if any) of the Vietnamese representatives believed that this was the end of the struggle. Hanoi remained determined to unify the country, while Saigon was determined to maintain itself as an independent state. The withdrawal of the US troops and the return of POWs were the only tangible gains. In the rural areas of South Vietnam, new struggles led by the NLF to consolidate its position began almost immediately. In reaction to these initiatives Thieu used the ARVN to destroy and remove any units of the PAVN/NLF present in South Vietnam. In the first three months of the peace, the ARVN suffered 6000 deaths. The north, on the other hand, wishing to win the sympathy of the USA and South Vietnam, quietly infiltrated troops and equipment into the south in preparation for the big push for unification.

Nixon meanwhile promised to maintain full economic and military aid to the Saigon government, an offer reaffirmed when Thieu visited the US in April 1973. In the run-up to the Paris Accords, Nixon had sanctioned US$1 billion worth of military hardware, leaving Thieu with the fourth largest airforce in the world. In other secret talks Nixon had promised up to US$4.75 billion over five years to aid the north with reconstruction. In Cambodia, the US airforce continued to attack communist insurgents in an attempt to prop up the regime of Lon Nol and to provide some time for the South Vietnamese to establish their military control over the country. However, in June 1973 Congress approved an amendment requiring the immediate cessation of all military operations in and over Indochina. This revealed the deep division between Nixon and Congress, now trying to reassert its authority over foreign affairs. It was felt by many in Congress that Nixon's credibility and integrity had hit rock bottom as the revelations of Watergate increased.

IMPACT OF WATERGATE ON NIXON

When the Watergate scandal broke in January 1973 it became evident that the Democratic Party campaign offices had been bugged in 1972 during the presidential election campaign and the information gained was used to discredit McGovern, Nixon's opponent. Frederick LaRue, one of the key figures in the case, had worked with John Mitchell on Nixon's re-election campaign. In April 1973, Nixon forced two of his principal advisers, Robert Haldeman and John Ehrlichman, to resign. A third adviser, John Dean, refused to leave his office and on 20 April 1973 issued a statement saying he was not going to be a scapegoat for the Watergate case. When ordered to speak to the Senate committee in charge of investigating the Watergate break-in, Dean claimed that Nixon had tape recordings of meetings where the issue of bugging the Democrats was discussed.

Under pressure from the Supreme Court, Nixon supplied the tapes which clearly implicated him in the Watergate affair and the subsequent cover-up. On 9 August 1974, rather than face impeachment, Nixon resigned as president, the first to do so in the history of the USA. In his study, *A Tangled Web: The Making of Foreign Policy in the Nixon Presidency* (1998),

William Bundy states that no matter how formidable Nixon's talents they were tainted by his 'unshakeable bent to deceive'. Deception, based on secrecy, was a way of thinking for Nixon, and he readily used it in his presidency. Nixon not only deceived the American public in the elections of 1972; he had also deceived them about how he intended to end the war in Vietnam.

Nixon's resignation and his policy of 'Peace with Honor' really marked the end of South Vietnam as an independent nation. No future president was prepared to give the type of commitments that Kennedy, Johnson and Nixon had given, nor was Congress prepared to endow a president with the power to take the nation to war without first discussing and voting on such actions. So, after 20 years of nation-building, South Vietnam still lacked a solid foundation on which to build a democratic government.

THE REUNIFICATION OF THE DRV

South Vietnam was finally unified with the north in April 1975. The problems in the south coincided with changes in military strategy in the north. In late 1974, the North Vietnamese began to prepare for a major offensive against the south calculating that it would take up to two years to win the war. Still uncertain about US reactions, the North Vietnamese began their campaign in mid-December 1974 in the central highlands. Very quickly they captured the capital, Phuoc Long, and this inspired confidence in the leaders to push on into the south. Their victories caused demoralisation among the ARVN troops and this was further compounded by Thieu's order to retreat to a defensive line just north of Saigon.

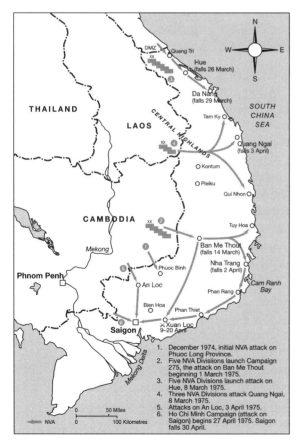

The final campaign and fall of South Vietnam, 1975

Hué fell on 26 March 1975 and Danang four days later. Officials in the US were amazed at the speed with which South Vietnam collapsed but many were resigned to the final outcome. Congress rejected any requests for further support; the US was caught in an economic recession and Congress was disinclined to 'waste' any more dollars in Vietnam.

On 21 April, Thieu resigned and fled from Vietnam. On 30 April, General Minh surrendered South Vietnam to the north. It

People escaping to a helicopter from 22 Gia Long Street in Saigon shortly before the fall of the city to communist forces, 29 April 1975

had taken the NVA 55 days instead of the planned two years to defeat the best equipped armed forces in Indochina. Despite more than one million deaths since the start of the conflict, the north had never lost sight of its original goal – to achieve an independent, unified Vietnam. The North Vietnamese were victorious because of their determination, superior leadership, strong identification with Vietnamese nationalism and social reform. By using the strategy of protracted war they were able to grind down US resolve, and use the political and social divisions that emerged among the American population.

The most famous photograph from the end of the Vietnam War shows people desperately climbing up ladders to the rooftop of the US Embassy where a US helicopter was waiting to take them away. However, as with much about the Vietnam War, the caption is wrong. The building is an apartment building. The people fleeing are Vietnamese, not Americans. The last helicopter left twelve hours later. In its way the photograph is a metaphor for all the misunderstanding that plagued the Vietnam War. Many Americans put their own interpretations on the events as they unfolded without taking time to reflect on why they were in Vietnam in the first place.

CONCLUSION

When Nixon came to power in January 1969, he was determined to end the war in Vietnam. Initially he chose to use military force and an escalation in bombing to break the North Vietnamese resolve and to end the insurgency. When this failed he chose to destroy the NLF/PAVN sanctuaries in Laos and Cambodia thereby extending the war into what were neutral countries. This in turn led to nationwide anti-war demonstrations, which in themselves did not influence policy, but certainly made the US public question why they were involved in Vietnam a country many in the US had never heard of before 1965.

Nixon's policy of Vietnamisation was meant to reduce the opposition at home to the war, while at the same time reinforcing the ARVN troops with the most up-to-date military equipment. However, the Laotian and Cambodian campaigns led to the realisation by Nixon and Kissinger that the ARVN troops were no match for the PAVN troops and so other strategies had to be explored.

The final steps to peace were the result of diplomatic activities by Kissinger, who met secretly in 1970 and 1971 with the governments of the Soviet Union and China and representatives of the North Vietnamese. Nixon and Kissinger realised the only way to achieve peace with honour was to abandon Thieu and the South Vietnamese government.

Kissinger and Nixon had accepted that South Vietnam could not be saved. The gradual withdrawal of the US from Vietnam and the opening to China and détente with the Soviet Union did provide some sense of direction of foreign policy. However, the fact that Kissinger and Nixon had given in to so many North Vietnamese demands left many in the US administration with a feeling of betrayal and lost credibility. According to **Jussi Hanhimaki** (2003), Kissinger and Nixon shared the conviction that Vietnam was an 'irritant' which needed to be removed by any means necessary in order to play the great game, involving greater international competition as all three superpowers sought to expand their influence in the non-aligned countries of the Middle East, Africa and Latin America.

A2 ASSESSMENT

EDEXCEL'S UNIT 4

Unit 4 is an essay-based examination or individual study. The Unit 4 examination requires you to answer one question from a choice of two. You should aim to build your answer on the selection and deployment of accurate and relevant historical information. Examiners will be looking for a sustained argument that shows an explicit understanding of the issues appropriate to the question and clear judgement(s) made.

Unit 4 questions present you with two kinds of challenge. Some questions invite you to present an analysis of the causes or perhaps the causes and consequences of a historical event or episode. These questions may appear in a variety of forms:

- single focus cause; there is one event, episode or issue to be explained
- double focus cause; there are two distinct causes identified in the question and both must be addressed
- indirect cause; offers a claim about causes which you are invited to assess not only by examining the cause in the question but also other causes.

Other questions may require you to make and justify a historical judgement about, for example, the significance of a key event or individual. These may require a single judgement.

Remember to do the following.

- Think about the issues that are relevant to the question.
- If you wish to expand your argument by focusing on recent historical research or debates, give the historian's name.
- Ensure you address the stated factor(s) in the question and/or other factors.
- Make sure you develop a clear line of argument.
- Focus on the question and make sure you answer it directly. If it has a causal focus, ensure you comment on the relative importance of causes.
- If asked to make a judgement about a particular individual, event or consequence, ensure that you are able to substantiate your judgement with accurate and relevant historical information.
- Do not be tempted to write all you know on the topic, and do not write a narrative account by giving the examiner a blow-by-blow account of what happened.

You must follow two rules.

- **Plan your answer.** This involves working out your argument, how you will develop it and how you will make use of your knowledge.
- **Allocate your time.** Remember it is important that you allow up to fifteen minutes of examination time to plan your answer. It is anticipated that your answer will be between 1000 and 1300 words long.

Here are two answers written by candidates who received very good marks because they were direct in their response to the question, giving supported analysis throughout and offering valid, sustained and appropriately critical judgements, which show an explicit understanding of all the appropriate issues.

EXAMPLE PAPER: 6524 PAPER 17B

Containing communism? The USA in Asia, 1950–73

Question 1: To what extent was the USA's decision to withdraw from Vietnam in 1973 the result of military defeat?

(Edexcel, 2004)

In 1973 President Nixon oversaw the American withdrawal from Vietnam and a war which had claimed the lives of 58,000 US soldiers and torn apart the fabric of US society. Clearly the decision to end this war was taken because continuing it seemed impossible. But I do not think that military failure was solely responsible for the outcome of the war in Vietnam, although it did play an important role.

The US failure to win the war in Vietnam and subsequent withdrawal can be seen as fundamentally a result of military defeat. The Vietnamese opposition, both the southern Vietcong and the Northern NVA, were completely different enemy from any America had faced before, and they succeeded in inflicting a defeat on a world superpower. Totally at ease in their own country, they fought a guerrilla war which the US never really succeeded in responding to, their booby traps for example were said to be responsible for 11 per cent of the US deaths and 12 per cent of the US injuries in Vietnam. American troops, despite their intention of fighting a war of attrition and wearing the enemy down through 'search and destroy' missions and chemical destruction of their country, never succeeded in reaching the crossover point where more Vietnamese were killed than survived. Neither the USA nor its South Vietnamese allies succeeded in defeating the communists despite their military superiority, and so they were forced to withdraw in 1973 partly because of a military defeat.

The Americans were also defeated and forced to withdraw, however, because of failure to understand the Vietnamese context and the nature of their opposition. Ho Chi Minh was leading a nation which had been fighting against foreign invaders for decades, and in which every part of Vietnamese society was dedicated to the war effort. His communist principles were almost coincidental, what mattered was that he was a nationalist, and his beliefs were relevant to the peasant society he led. In a country where only 5 per cent of the population worked in industry, Nixon's 'mad bomber' threats to carpet bomb industrial bases made little difference. The US forces, on the other hand, suffered from desperately low morale and discipline, enormous problems of drug addiction and desertion, and the South Vietnamese allies to whom they were trying to hand over were even worse. In 1973, therefore, the Americans were forced to withdraw partly because of a long-term inability to deal with the reality of the situation in Vietnam.

The Americans also had to withdraw from Vietnam in 1973 because the regime they had been fighting to support was fundamentally unviable. From Diem's crusades against the Buddhists in 1963 to Thieu's refusal to accept a coalition government a decade later, the Saigon government was not so much an American ally as a dependency. It was as alien to South Vietnam's Buddhists peasant population as the French colonists had been. Yet ironically the more it lost popular support, the more important it became to America as a beacon of freedom and democracy. Supporting it, however, was costing the USA its moral position on the global stage as well as its domestic political stability, and draining the US economy: US$2 billion a month in 1968. Nixon's decision to withdraw from Vietnam in 1973 was therefore partly a result of the reality which American presidents had been ignoring for two decades. Nation building in South Vietnam had failed and it was more than ever 'an army without a country'.

Nixon was also forced to oversee the American withdrawal from Vietnam in recognition that the war was tearing US society apart. The 'Home Front' had collapsed. This can be divided into two sections: Congress and public opinion. In 1972, Nixon had managed to get re-elected but had lost Congress to the Democrats who began to cut off his finances for the war, forcing him to seek a quick solution. Congress also began to assert itself over what Arthur Schleisinger called an increasingly 'imperial' presidency, passing for example the War Powers Act in 1973, which limited the president's ability to go to war without Congressional support. Nixon's advisers were also turning increasingly against the war and so political realities in 1973 forced his withdrawal from Vietnam.

Wider public opinion also pushed America to withdraw from Vietnam in 1973. By 1973 America was a deeply divided society. There were enormous marches and protests against the war, even involving Vietnam War Veterans, and Nixon's attempts to placate the public through token withdrawals and his Vietnamisation programme had little effect. Vietnam was the first TV war and the press portrayal of it was overwhelmingly negative. In 1968, for example, the Tet Offensive was portrayed as a catastrophe even though the USA had won. American society was not entirely anti-war, however; in 1969, Nixon's 'Silent Majority' speech saw his approval ratings rise to 68 per cent and, in 1970, construction workers who attacked anti-war protestors complaining about the murder of four students in demonstrations at Kent State University were cheered. These deep divisions, however, were seriously damaging to US political stability and encouraged a sense of frustration and siege mentality in Nixon himself. In 1973, therefore, the US leaders decided to withdraw from Vietnam partly because of the terrible domestic turmoil caused by the war.

On the world stage, the Vietnam War was also impacting badly on the USA. The 'credibility gap' in domestic politics was matched by international doubts about the legitimacy of the war and the USA's moral position. Although America had originally entered Vietnam to uphold freedom and fight communism and so a withdrawal would signify a loss of prestige, the moral authority of a country which supported a regime like that in Saigon and was responsible for massacres like My Lai was increasingly called into question. By 1973, therefore, in the light of improving relations with Russia and China and increasing international approval the USA decided to withdraw from Vietnam.

Finally, 1973 saw the culmination of diplomatic manoeuvring concerning Vietnam and so marked the right time for the USA to withdraw. Talks had been continuing on an off for years, and an agreement had almost been reached in 1972 before Nixon's fears of being seen to surrender before an election caused him to reject it. In 1973, however, his policy of linkage, linking concessions to Russia and China in return for their pressure on Hanoi for concessions, finally had an affect at the same time as Thieu was finally persuaded to compromise. In a way therefore, the USA's 1973 withdrawal from Vietnam can be seen as the result of a diplomatic breakthrough which had taken years to achieve.

Revisionists [**N.B. here it would be better to name historians**] have suggested that the USA could have won the war in Vietnam if the civilian leaders had given more resources and freedom to the military. This viewpoint suggests that the US withdrawal in 1973 was primarily the result of a military defeat. I do not think that this is true. The Americans did fail to defeat the communists, but this is largely due to their failure to learn the lessons of France and relate their strategy to the Vietnamese context. By supporting an untenable regime in the south and failing to compare the lack of popularity with the nature of Ho Chi Minh's country and army, they turned what was primarily a civil war into an extension of the Cold War. Pressures from outside Vietnam, internationally but more importantly domestically, also added to the hesitancy that paralysed US leaders and prevented them from winning a decisive victory or a withdrawal in the 1960s. By 1973, the US war effort had burned itself out and diplomatic manoeuvring had created an exit path. But it was primarily a realisation of its ideological and strategic failure in Vietnam which caused the US to withdraw in 1973, with military factors only coming second along with the collapse of the home front. As journalist Henry Brandon commented, the Vietnam War 'was to have a sobering effect on the US belief that anything was possible'.

Examiner's comments
A clear, sustained analysis of the question set. The evidence is explored and clear judgements are made.

> Question 2: 'The decision of the USA to defend South Korea against invasion arose largely from the desire to protect US interests in Japan, rather than in Korea itself.' How far do you agree with this judgement?
>
> (Edexcel, 2005)

There are historians [**N.B. it would be useful to name historians**] who would argue that the decisions of the USA to defend South Korea against invasion arose largely from the desire to protect US interests in Japan, rather than in Korea itself. The geographical position of Korea and America's idea of a sphere of influence in the Pacific can support this view. However, other historians would disagree with this view, arguing that America had alternative reasons such as the desire to defend democracy and the effect of the Cold War.

After Japan surrendered in 1945 America perceived itself as the dominant force in the Pacific, and considered the Pacific to be in its sphere of influence. This can be used to support the view that US intervention was due to a desire to protect US interests in Japan. The security of Japan became a major priority for President Truman. The Soviet dominance in Eastern Europe can be seen as a further reason for America's desire to protect her interests in Japan. Truman was angry at how the Soviet Union had swept across Eastern Europe, creating a large European sphere of influence for itself. This hardened President Truman's resolve to defend US interests in US-occupied Japan and his desire to maintain a strong US influence in the Pacific.

After the fall of China to communism in October 1949, the USA had to find an alternative market for Japanese goods or risk Japan descending into communism. By defending South Korea the USA could provide Japan with an economic partner with which to trade products and ensure economic and political stability in Japan. The decision to defend Japan led to increased military expenditure which provided a 'divine gift' for Japan as US$3 billion worth of products, including jeeps, transport trucks and construction materials, were ordered. Toyota truck production leapt from 300 to 1500 a month in 1950. In order to further rehabilitate Japan the San Francisco Treaty was signed in 1951 that resumed normal relations between Japan and the USA, a vital economic and military ally. Defending South Korea helped to provide for the economic rehabilitation that Japan needed to prevent it falling to communism.

The geographical position of Korea can be interpreted as a significant factor causing US intervention in Korea in order to protect Japan; Korea and Japan are separated by less than 160 kilometres of sea. Truman feared that South Korea would be a good strategic place for communist forces to launch an invasion on Japan. Truman could not allow communist forces to be in such close proximity to Japan as it threatened US interests. A communist South Korea would also upset the balance of power in the Pacific, swinging power away from America and towards the communist bloc. Therefore, the geographical importance of Korea can be seen as a significant factor causing America to intervene in Korea.

However, other historians would argue that America had other more important reasons for defending South Korea. US collaboration with the UN can be seen as a reason for intervening as a device to defend democracy. Following the invasion of South Korea by the north on 25 June 1950, America went to the UN. Two resolutions were passed condemning North Korean actions and justifying intervention against the aggressor to defend democracy. Therefore it is possible to say that America intervened to uphold the democratic government of South Korea.

The Cold War is another significant reason for US intervention. The North Korean forces were also communist turning the Korean War into an ideological war. America felt threatened by communism; on 1 October 1949 China had become communist and the Soviet Union also tested their first atomic bomb. America had just lost its nuclear superiority and the loss of China to communism was a significant blow. This left America with a desire to gain ground against the communist bloc in the context of the Cold War. America felt that victory over communist forces would restore their position in the world. Therefore the connection of Korea and the Cold War can be seen as a reason for US involvement in Korea.

The impact of Truman must be assessed as a reason for US intervention to defend South Korea. In 1947 Truman introduced the policy of containment and issued the Truman Doctrine. After witnessing the failures of appeasement and isolationism Truman took a new line. He believed that quick direct action was necessary. The Truman Doctrine assumed that America would defend any country against a foreign aggressor, and by the policy of containment America would block the expansion of communism. The Republican hawks accused Truman of being soft on communism and blamed him for the fall of China. Truman was therefore adamant to uphold his policy new policies. North Korea was an aggressor and was trying to impose communism on the south, therefore the USA was willing to step in and contain the threat. Therefore it is possible to say that US intervention was due to Truman and his policies, and not the desire to defend Japan.

The idea that American intervention in Korea was due to a desire to protect its sphere of influence in the Pacific can be easily countered. This is because in 1950 Secretary of State Dean Acheson made a speech outlining US interests in the Pacific, and South Korea was not included. American intervention as a desire to defend democracy can also be countered. The government of Syngman Rhee was by no means a model of democracy and freedom, and the elections by which Syngman Rhee came to power were corrupt.

The Korean connection with the Cold War was the most influential reason for the US decision to defend South Korea against invasion. The opportunity to defeat a communist army caused the Americans to intervene. After the loss of China, America needed to assert its position. Truman needed to show that he was strong and that he could and would implement his new policies of containment and direct action. Therefore it was not a desire to protect its interests in Japan that led to the US decision to defend South Korea, it was the desire to win a small battle in the much larger Cold War that caused the USA to intervene.

Examiner's comments
A clear and sustained explanation supported with relevant and accurate evidence. Substantiated judgements made on the role of the USA. The quality of written communication in parts weakens the argument.

PRACTICE QUESTIONS
The following questions can be used as practice for the Edexcel Unit 4 examination, *Containing communism? The USA in Asia, 1950–73.*

- To what extent did public opinion in the US contribute to the withdrawal of US troops from South Vietnam in 1973?
- How far was the US's military involvement in the conflict in Korea the consequence of a desire to defend democracy?
- To what extent was the US's failure to win the Vietnam War a result of its failure to counter the tactics deployed by the National Liberation Front?
- To what extent was the Vietnam War 'Johnson's War'?

BIBLIOGRAPHY

Books

W. Bundy, *A Tangled Web: Making of Foreign Policy in the Nixon Presidency,* I.B. Tauris, 1998

P. Caputo, *A Rumour of War,* Ballantine, 1977

B. Catchpole, *The Korean War,* Constable and Robinson, 2000

B. Cummings, *The Origins of the Korean War Vol. 1: Liberation and the Emergence of Separate Regimes,* Princeton Uni. Press, 1981

B. Cummings, *The Origins of the Korean War Vol. 2: The Roaring of the Cataract* Princeton Uni. Press, 1990

R. Dallek, *John F. Kennedy: An Unfinished Life,* Penguin, 2003

W.J. Duiker, *Ho Chi Minh: A Life,* Hyperion, 2000

D. Ellsberg, *The Pentagon Papers,* Gravel Edition, Beacon Press, 1971

F. Fitzgerald, *Fire In the Lake: The Vietnamese and the Americans in Vietnam,* First Back Pay, 2002

R. Foot, *A Substitute for Victory: The Politics of Peacemaking at the Korean Armistice Talks,* Cornell Uni. Press, 1990

J.L. Gaddis, *The Long Peace: Inquiries into the History of the Cold War,* Oxford University Press, 1987

J.L. Gaddis, *We Now Know, Rethinking Cold War History,* Oxford, 1997

L. Gelb and R.K. Betts, *The Irony of Vietnam: The System Worked,* Washington, 1978

D. Halberstam, *The Best and the Brightest, Twentieth-Anniversary Edition* Ballantine Books, 2002

M. Hall, *The Vietnam War,* Pearson, 2000

G.C. Herring, *America's Longest War: The United States and Vietnam, 1950–75,* 4th edition, McGraw-Hill, 2002

S. Karnow, *Vietnam: A History,* Penguin Books, 1983

H. Kissinger *The White House Years,* Little Brown, Boston, 1979

F. Logevall, *The Origins of the Vietnam War,* Pearson Education, 2001

R. Leckie, *Conflict: The History of the Korean War* Da Capo Press, 1996

M.P. Leffler & David S. Painter (ed) *Origins of the Cold War, An International History,* Routledge, 1995

P. Lowe, *The Origins of the Korean War,* Longman, 1986

C. Malkasian, *The Korean War 1950–53,* Osprey Publishing, 2001

D. McCullough, *Truman,* Simon and Schuster, 1992

G.McT. Kahin, *Intervention: How America Became Involved in Vietnam,* Anchor, 1987

R.S. McNamara, *In Retrospect: The Tragedy and Lessons of Vietnam,* First Vintage Books, 1996

N.M. Naimark, *The Russians in Germany: A History of the Soviet Zone of Occupation, 1945–49,* Cambridge, Mass, 1995

J. Newman. *Vietnam: Deception, Intrigue and the Struggle for Power,* Warner, 1993

R.D. Schulzinger, *A Time for War: The United States and Vietnam, 1941–75, Oxford Uni. Press 1997*

D. Rees, *Korea the Limited War,* Macmillan, 1964

E. Roman, *Hungary and the Victor Powers, 1945–50,* New York, 1996.

W. Shawcross, *Sideshow: Kissinger, Nixon and the Destruction of Cambodia, Revised Edition,* Cooper Square Press, 1987

W. Stueck, *The Korean War,* Princeton Uni. Press, 1995

W. Stueck, *Rethinking the Korean War: A New Diplomatic and Strategic History,* Princeton Uni. Press, 2002

D. Yergin, *A Shattered Peace, The Origins of the Cold War and the National Security State,* Penguin, 1978

Articles

M. Atwood Lawrence, Transnational Coalition-Building and the Making of the Cold War in Indochina, 1947–49, *Diplomatic History,* Vol. 26, 2002

I. Gaiduk, The Vietnam War and Soviet-American Relations, 1964–73: New Russian Evidence, *Cold War International History Project, Bulletin 6–7, Cold War in Asia,* 1995

J. Gailbraith, Exit Strategy: In 1963, JFK ordered a complete withdrawal from Vietnam, *Boston Review,* 2003

E. Goh, Nixon, Kissinger and the "Soviet Card" in the U.S. Opening to China, 1971–74, *Diplomatic History,* Vol. 29, 2005.

Ang Cheng Guan, The Vietnam War 1962–64: The Vietnamese Communist Perspective, *Journal of Contemporary History,* Vol. 35, 2000

J. Hanhimaki, Selling the 'Decent Interval': Kissinger, Triangular Diplomacy, and the End of the Vietnam War, 1971–73, *Diplomacy and Statecraft,* Vol. 14, March 2003

Yang Kuisong, Changes in Mao Zedong's Attitude toward the Indochina War, 1949–73, *Cold War International History Project, Working Paper 34,* February 2002

M.P. Leffler, The Cold War: What Do 'We Now Know', *The American Historical Review,* Vol. 104, 1999

F. Logevall, A Critique of Containment, *Diplomatic History,* Vol. 28, 2004

D.J. Macdonald, Communist Bloc Expansion in the Early Cold War: Challenging Realism, Refuting Revisionism, *International Security,* Vol. 20, 1995–6

A.A. Offner, "Another Such Victory": President Truman, American Foreign Policy, and the Cold War, *Diplomatic History,* Vol. 23, 1999

G. Roberts, Moscow and the Marshall Plan: Politics, Ideology and the Onset of the Cold War, 1947, *Europe-Asia Studies,* Vol. 46, 1994

H.B. Ryan, A New Look at Churchill's 'Iron Curtain' Speech, *The Historical Journal,* Vol. 22, 1979

R.B. Smith, The Work of the Provisional Government of Vietnam, August-December 1945, *Modern Asian Studies,* Vol. 12, 1978

K. Weathersby, Soviet Aims in Korea and the Origins of the Korean War, 1945–50: New Evidence from Russian Archives, *Cold War International History Project, Working Paper 8,* November 1993

K. Weathersby, "Should We Fear This?" Stalin and the Danger of War with America, *Cold War International History Project, Working Paper 30,* July 2002

Qiang Zhai, Transplanting the Chinese Model: Chinese Military Advisers and the First Vietnam War, 1950–54, *The Journal of `Military History,* Vol. 57, 1993

GLOSSARY

Accelerated Pacification Campaign, 1968. An attempt to bring stability to the countryside in South Vietnam by a range of military and civilian methods. This would enable the South Vietnamese government to claim that it was actively in control of as much territory as possible.

Active positional defence. A strategy of meeting any attack with an immediate counter-measure used by the UN forces in Korea in 1952.

Agrovilles. Fortified villages protected by the South Vietnamese army. Peasants resented being moved, often under force, into these villages.

Allied powers. Britain, the US and the USSR during the Second World War.

Atlantic Charter. A declaration issued by Roosevelt and Churchill in August 1941. It called for independence and democracy to be the guiding principles for those countries liberated at the end of the Second World War.

Attrition. A strategy of wearing down the enemy. It was employed by General Ridgway in Korea using heavy artillery and close air support against the communist forces.

Bay of Pigs invasion, 1961. An attempt by supporters of the ex-Cuban dictator Batista to invade Cuba and remove Castro's communist government from power. The invading force was backed by the CIA under orders from Kennedy. The invasion was a fiasco and it damaged Kennedy's reputation.

Capitalism. Upheld as the guiding values of the West. Capitalism involved the key principles of economic and political freedom. This included: private enterprise (i.e. businesses, factories and land owned by individuals or groups of individuals with the minimum of government interference), liberal democracy (i.e. a political system in which each person has the freedom to vote, freedom to stand for election, freedom of speech, freedom of worship and freedom of the press).

Carvelle Manifesto, 1960. A statement drawn up by a group of prominent anti-communists in South Vietnam, which heavily criticised Diem's regime.

Cold War. The term given to the conflict that existed between the US and the USSR after the Second World War. It was a conflict that involved economic measures, non-cooperation and propaganda but no direct armed fighting between the two sides. Thus, despite a breakdown in relations between the superpowers, 'hot' war was avoided. With the advent of nuclear weapons both sides used a range of less destructive methods of conflict.

Collective security. The idea that nations would no longer need to maintain security by arming independently but by trusting in the united strength of an international organisation dedicated to the resolution of conflict through peaceful means.

Comecon. The Council for Mutual Economic Aid. An organisation controlled by the USSR set up to co-ordinate the communist economies of Eastern Europe.

Cominform. Communist Information Bureau. An organisation controlled by the USSR set up to co-ordinate communist political parties across Europe.

Communism. Upheld as the guiding principle of the Soviet Union. Based on the ideas of Karl Marx and adapted by Lenin, these came to mean in practice: a state-owned economy (i.e. an economy in which all industries and agriculture are owned by the government on behalf of the people), a one-party state (i.e. a political system in which there is only one political party to represent the people). In the Soviet Union all political parties other than the Communist Party were banned. Elections were contested between individuals who had to be members of this party.

Containment. The US policy of actively seeking to prevent the spread of communism.

Council of Foreign Ministers. A body set up to discuss post-war problems and issues left over from the Yalta and Potsdam

Conferences of 1945. The Council was made up of the foreign ministers of Britain, the US, the USSR, France and China.

Counterinsurgency. Military action against guerrilla activity.

Cuban Missile Crisis, 1962. The crisis broke out when evidence was revealed that the Soviet Union was building nuclear missile bases on Cuba. Kennedy responded with firm action. A quarantine zone was placed around the island and Kennedy threatened to use nuclear missiles if the USSR entered the zone. The USSR backed down and agreed to dismantle its bases.

Demilitarised Zone (DMZ). A strip of land, 10 kilometres wide, along the 17th parallel in which no military presence was allowed. It was designed to minimise tension along the border between North and South Vietnam.

Domino theory. The belief that if one country fell to communism, neighbouring states would follow one by one – like dominoes.

Flexible response. The strategy of developing a range of military options rather than relying solely on nuclear weapons. The policy was used by Kennedy's administration.

Fragging. The murder of US officers by their own soldiers using fragmentation bombs, usually in protest at what were seen as needless orders.

Free French. The French armed forces and volunteers who had not fallen into German or Japanese hands in 1940.

French Union. The name applied to the French Empire between 1946 and 1958.

Indochina. The area made up of Vietnam, Laos and Cambodia. The whole of Indochina was ruled by the French between 1884 and 1940.

Interdiction. Operations, such as air bombardment, conducted to destroy, neutralise or delay the enemy's capacity to attack.

Internationalism. The principle of working at a level above individual nation states to resolve issues. This involved countries working together and making joint decisions and taking joint actions. It was a concept that gained in popularity immediately after the Second World War, a war that many politicians felt had been caused in part by nationalism.

Iron Curtain. The name given to the figurative line that divided the communist East from the capitalist West in Europe.

Isolationism. The foreign policy pursued by the USA in the 1920s and 1930s. It involved keeping out of conflicts abroad and refusing to take part in any military alliances.

Joint Chiefs of Staff. The committee consisting of the highest ranking member of each branch of the US military, the Army, Navy, Marine Corps and Air Force. Its role was chiefly to advise the President and Secretary of Defense on military matters.

League of Nations. A world peace-keeping organisation set up in 1919. It had failed to prevent the Second World War but its principles were used as the basis of the United Nations (UN) in 1945.

Limited war. A war limited in its scope and scale by the adoption of traditional rather than nuclear weapons and by pursuing limited goals in order to avoid provoking other countries into the conflict.

Massive deterrence. The strategy of relying on the threat of using nuclear weapons to deter your opponent. This policy was promoted by Dulles, Eisenhower's Secretary of State.

McCarthyism. The wave of anti-communist feeling that spread through the US in the early 1950s. It is sometimes referred to as the Red Scare and was encouraged by sections of the Republican Party, most notably by Joseph McCarthy. The movement aimed to remove communist sympathisers from all sections of American life, including members of Truman's government who were seen as soft on communism.

Modus vivendi. An arrangement between those who agree to differ.

National Liberation Front. Formed in December 1960 to coordinate political opposition to the US-backed government in

South Vietnam. It was a loose coalition of twelve different groups, ranging from communists to Buddhists. Its nationalist aims were ones that many were prepared to fight for by joining the PLAF (see below).

Neutrality. A policy of deliberately refusing to take sides in a dispute between others.

Nixon Doctrine. The policy of Vietnamisation.

Nuclear Test Ban Treaty, 1963. Banned the testing of nuclear weapons above ground and below water. The treaty was signed by the US, the USSR and Britain, but France and China refused.

OPLAN 34A. The US programme of secret commando and diversionary raids into North Vietnam.

Peaceful coexistence. A policy of the Soviet Union towards the West that was developed by Khrushchev. It was a belief that the superpowers should accept each other's existence rather than mutual destruction.

Peoples' Committees. These were set up by the Koreans to administer local government after the defeat of Japan. They were involved in food distribution and land reform, and were often genuinely popular in both the north and south of Korea. Communists were often in a strong position of influence within the committees, and the USSR therefore used them as the basis of government in the Soviet zone. In the US zone the committees were viewed with suspicion and a series of regulations was introduced that effectively reduced their influence. During the Korean War, Peoples' Committees in South Korea were often able to organise resistance to the US forces.

People's Revolutionary Committees. Set up to administer local government in Vietnam in 1945. The Vietminh used them throughout Vietnam to ensure food was distributed. Vietminh control was quickly established over these committees.

Phoenix Programme. The neutralisation of NLF (see below) elements by the army of South Vietnam through the use of intelligence operations.

Politburo. Established by Lenin to direct the Russian Revolution, it became the key governing body of the Soviet Union as all central policy decisions were made there.

Pusan Perimeter. The defensive line around the port of Pusan, which the US army used to make a stand against the North Korean army in July 1950.

Reparations. Payment in money or goods to cover the damage caused during war.

Representative Democratic Council (RDC). An alliance of groups opposed to the idea of trusteeship for Korea. Its aim was to present a united front of political groups in South Korea that could be used by the US as the basis of a provisional government in Korea. The RDC, led by Syngman Rhee, was seen by the Americans as a useful organisation against the spread of communist influence.

Roll back. The policy of pushing back the frontiers of communism and liberating states where communism had been imposed by force. It was a term that gained currency in the 1950s and marked a more assertive US stance than that of Containment, which had dominated US government thinking since 1945. It was actively considered during the Korean War.

Rolling Thunder. The code name for the US bombing of strategic targets in North Vietnam.

SEATO. The South East Asia Treaty Organisation. Formed in 1954, it was a defensive organisation set up to try to prevent the spread of communism in the region. In addition to the US, the treaty was signed by Australia, Britain, France, New Zealand, Pakistan, the Philippines and Thailand.

self-determination. The principle of people deciding their own form of government through democratic means.

San Antonio formula, 1967. President Johnson's proposal that the US would stop bombing North Vietnam if they agreed to engage in peace talks.

The Resistance. A group opposed to the US government's policy in Vietnam. They gained publicity through their campaign to collect draft cards of those who refused to join the army in protest over Vietnam.

United Action. An attempt by Eisenhower's Secretary of State, Dulles, to get support from other countries for US action in Vietnam.

United front policy. A policy employed by the Soviet Union in Korea of encouraging a range of political parties to establish closer links with the communists in North Korea.

UNTCOK. The United Nations Temporary Commission on Korea, set up to oversee the organisation of elections in Korea in 1945. It was hoped that these elections would unify the country under a democratic government.

Vietcong. Originally a term of abuse, meaning 'Vietnamese Communist', used by Americans to describe the opposition in South Vietnam. Opposition to the South Vietnamese government was much more broadly based than the communists alone, the National Liberation Front was made up of twelve different groups. It was a point the US government failed to understand.

Vietminh. A nationalist organisation formed in May 1941, the aim of which was to challenge both Japanese and French rule and work for full Vietnamese independence. The Vietminh (or Vietnam Independence League) covered a range of political viewpoints but the dominant group was the Indochinese Communist Party (ICP) led by Ho Chi Minh.

Vietnamisation. A policy promoted by Nixon in 1969 to hand over the fighting of the communists in Vietnam to the South Vietnamese army. This would allow US troops to be withdrawn.

Yenan group. The group of North Korean communists who were pro-China. They had fought in China for the communists during the civil war before returning to Korea after 1945. They were involved in a power struggle with a pro-Soviet faction. Kim Il Sung was able to defeat both factions and dominate the North Korean communists.

ARVN	Army of the Republic of Vietnam
CCP	Chinese Communist Party
CIA	Central Intelligence Agency
CMAG	Chinese Military Advisory Group
COSVN	Central Office for South Vietnam
CPV	Communist Party Volunteers Army Corps
DMZ	Demilitarised Zone
DPRK	Democratic People's Republic of Korea
DRV	Democratic Republic of Vietnam
FBI	Federal Bureau of Investigation
ICP	Indochinese Communist Party
KPR	Korean People's Republic
MAAG	Military Assistance Advisory Group
MACV	Military Assistance Command, Vietnam
NATO	North Atlantic Treaty Organisation
NCRC	National Council of Reconciliation and Concord
NKCP	North Korean Communist Party
NKPA	North Korean People's Army
NLF	National Liberation Front (South Vietnam)
NSAM	National Security Action Memorandum
NSC	National Security Council
OSS	Office of Strategic Services
PAVN	People's Army of Vietnam (North Vietnam)
PLA	People's Liberation Army (Communist China)
PLAF	People's Liberation Armed Force (Vietcong)
POW	Prisoner/s of War
PRC	People's Republic of China
PRG	Provisional Revolutionary Government
PRP	People's Revolutionary Party
ROK	Republic of Korea
RVN	Republic of Vietnam
SEATO	Southeast Asia Treaty Organisation
UNC	United Nations Command Force
US	United States
USSR	Union of Soviet Socialist Republics
VC	Vietcong
VWP	Vietnam Workers Party (*Lao Dong*)

INDEX